INTERNATIONAL TRIBUNAL FOR THE LAW OF THE SEA
TRIBUNAL INTERNATIONAL DU DROIT DE LA MER

Pleadings, Minutes of Public Sittings and Documents

Mémoires, Procès-verbaux des Audiences Publiques et Documents

2001

VOLUME 7

Abbreviated reference:

ITLOS Pleadings, Minutes and Documents 2001, Vol. 7, "Grand Prince" (Belize v. *France), Prompt Release*

Référence abrégée :

TIDM mémoires, procès-verbaux et documents 2001, vol. 7, « Grand Prince » (Belize c. France), prompte mainlevée

INTERNATIONAL TRIBUNAL FOR THE LAW OF THE SEA

PLEADINGS, MINUTES OF PUBLIC SITTINGS AND DOCUMENTS

THE "GRAND PRINCE" CASE
(Belize *v.* France)
PROMPT RELEASE

TRIBUNAL INTERNATIONAL DU DROIT DE LA MER

MÉMOIRES, PROCÈS-VERBAUX DES AUDIENCES
PUBLIQUES ET DOCUMENTS

AFFAIRE DU « GRAND PRINCE »
(Belize c. France)
PROMPTE MAINLEVÉE

MARTINUS NIJHOFF PUBLISHERS
LEIDEN/BOSTON

International Tribunal for the Law of the Sea
Tribunal international du droit de la mer
Am Internationalen Seegerichtshof 1, 22609 Hamburg, Germany

Published by
Martinus Nijhoff Publishers

Printed on acid-free paper.

ISBN 978 90 04 16248 8

Printed and bound in The Netherlands

THE "GRAND PRINCE" CASE
(BELIZE *v.* FRANCE)
PROMPT RELEASE

AFFAIRE DU « GRAND PRINCE »
(BELIZE c. FRANCE)
PROMPTE MAINLEVÉE

The proceedings relating to *The "Grand Prince" Case* were instituted on 21 March 2001 by an Application for prompt release pursuant to article 292 of the United Nations Convention on the Law of the Sea.

L'instance relative à l'*Affaire du « Grand Prince »* fut introduite le 21 mars 2001 par une demande de prompte mainlevée conformément à l'article 292 de la Convention des Nations Unies sur le droit de la mer.

TABLE OF CONTENTS – TABLE DES MATIÈRES

THE "GRAND PRINCE" CASE
(Belize *v.* France), Prompt Release
AFFAIRE DU « GRAND PRINCE »
(Belize c. France), prompte mainlevée

Designation of Judge *ad hoc* – Désignation d'un juge *ad hoc*

Completion of Documentation – Complément d'information

Responses to questions from the Tribunal – Réponses aux questions du Tribunal

Additional documents submitted before the closure of the written proceedings
Documents additionnels soumis avant la clôture de la procédure écrite

Submitted by Belize

Institution of Proceedings – Introduction de l'instance

APPLICATION SUBMITTED ON BEHALF OF BELIZE

INTERNATIONAL TRIBUNAL FOR THE LAW OF THE SEA

APPLICATION FOR PROMPT RELEASE OF FISHING VESSEL "GRAND PRINCE" UNDER ARTICLE 292 OF THE UNITED NATIONS CONVENTION ON THE LAW OF THE SEA

ON BEHALF OF: THE STATE OF BELIZE, represented by:

Mr. Alberto Penelas Alvarez, Avocat, Lawyers Bar Association of Vigo, Spain, of Pintor Laxeiro 11, 2º A, 36211, Vigo (Spain) , phone number: 34 986 210301 , Fax number: 34 986 294162, E-mail amyavigo@jet.es and with passport number 36.058.322 A

AGAINST : FRANCE

TABLE OF CONTENTS

LIST OF DOCUMENTS

Number 6.- Proces Verbal D´Apprehension of the navigational equipment

Number 7.- Proces Verbal D´Apprehension of the fishing gear

Number 8.- Copy of the act of Proces Verbal D´Interpellation

Number 9.- Copy of the act of Proces Verbal de Saisie of the vessel

Number 10.- Copy of the act of Proces Verbal de Saisie of the fishing material

Number 11.- Copy of the act of Proces Verbal de Saisie of the fishing gear

Number 12.- Copy of the act of Proces Verbal de Saisie of the fish on board

Number 13.- Copy of the Ordennance nº 3/2001 of the Tribunal D´Instance de Saint Paul

Number 14.- Fax to the Maritime Authorities in Reunion justifying the fishing licence in Brazil

Number 15.- Request for release the vessel

Number 16.- Ordennance nº 6/2001 of the Tribunal D´Instance of Saint Paul rejecting the request for release.

Number 17.- Expertise appraisal of the vessel market price , by the naval engineer , Faustino Carceller Villalta , of "Taxo Valoración, S.L"

Number 18.- Expertise appraisal of the vessel market price , by the Marine Surveyor, Captain Antonio Alonso Pérez

PART I

MEMORIAL

Statement of facts

1.- The Grand Prince is a fishing vessel, flying the flag of Belize. It´s owner is PAIK COMMERCIAL CORP, a company registered in Belize at 35A Regent Street PO Box 1777, Belize City, Belize, who bought it on the 27 March 2.000 in the amount of forty five million (45.000.000.-) Pesetas , in virtue of the purchase contract , duly legalised and apostilled on the date of signature, which is enclosed as **document number 2 ,** toguether with it´s tranlation into english language.

The vessel characteristics are:

Flag	Belize
Call Letters	V 3 UJT
IMO number	6701656
Registration number	07972047
Material of the hull	Steel
Gross Tonnage	669
Net Tonnage	267
Number of decks	1
Number of masts	2
Number of bridges	1
Number of funnels	1
cargo capacity	186 MT
Year of built	1.966
Place of built	Portweller Drydocks , Ltd, Canada
Lengh	39,67 Meters
Breath	10,00 Meters
Depth	4,80 Meters
Engine	1 Diesel GM, General Motors

The above is evidenced by documents enclosed as numbers **2 and 3.**

2.- Grand Prince crew is compossed by thirty seven (37) workers, who are listed in **document number 4.**

3.- The vessel was engaged in the fishing of lobster (as an experimental campaigne) and toothfish in the international waters of the southern seas. Its master was Mr. Ramón Francisco Pérez Novo, of Spanish nacionality, who was working on board the ship for the first time.

4.- On 26 December 2.000 at approximately 08:53 hours was boarded by the crew of the French survelliance frigate Nivose in the Exclusive Economic Zone of the Kerguelen Islands in the French Southern and Antartic territories.

5.- According to the Captain of Grand Prince , he had never , before that date, fished within the said area . However, he recognised that , in fact, he entered in the zone on the 26 December 2.000 , and that he was decided to fish. He also recognised, since the first moment, that he had very clear instructions from the shipowner not to enter into the Exclusive Economic Zone of the Kerguelens or other restricted areas. I refer in this respect to page two (first paragraph) of document number 8º ("Procés Verbal D´Interpellation), where the statement of the Captain was recorded.

It must be pointed out that also according to the statments of the Maritime Athorities in Reunion the Grand Prince was fishing out side french waters on the days before she was detained.

6.- The vessel has never been adjudjed nor condemned before any Tribunal of any State for any reason whatsoever, not even forillegal fishing.

7.- From the first moment the said Captain followed the orders and requirements given by the Captain of the frigate, and fullly cooperated with the french authorities , facilitating the inspection on board Grand Prince and showing all the books and documents related to the same.

8.- The Grand Prince had on board approximately 16 / 18 Tons of toothfish and two Hundred (200) Kilos of lobster.

9.- The Captain of the Frigate recorded the apprehension of the Grand Prince , the fish catch, the navigation and communication equipment in the documents of "Proces Verbal DÁpprehension" , enclosed as **documents numbers 5, 6 and 7**

10.- The Grand Prince was rerouted and escorted by the Frigate to Port-des-Galets (Reunión), where it arrived on 9 January , 2.001.

11.- On 11 January 2.001 , the Regional and Departmental Director of Maritime Affairs of Reunion drew up one "Procés Verbal D´Interpellation" and four "Procés Verbal de Saisie" , with the content stated in **documents 8, 9, 10, 11 and 12** , enclosed.

On the four procés - verbaux of seizure it was decided the seizure of all the fish on board thé vessel , (that should be sold by means of a limited tender and the proceeds be credited to the public treasury) , the fishing gear and the vessel.

The following estimations where made by the Maritime Authorities of Reunion:

- Fishing equipments	24.392 Euros
- Fishing gear	5.610 Euros
- Vessel	1.981.837 Euros
- Fish on board	123.848 Euros
TOTAL	2.135.323.- Euros

12.- By Order nº. 3/2001 of 12 January 2.001 , the Court of First Instance of Saint Paul confirmed the seizure of the Grand Prince. Copy of the Order is enclosed as **document number 13**, with it´s translation into english language.

13.- The same Order ruled that <<the release of the vessel seized shall be carried out after the payment to the official Receiver of a bond amounting to a total of 11,400,000.00 FF or 1,737.918.70 Euros ....>>

14.- On the amount of the said bond , the Court took the following into account:

1) the value of the ship appraised by Mr. Chancerel, marine surveyor, at 13,000,000.00 FF

2) the fines incurred by the Master of the vessel (on the bais of 18 Tons of fish on board), estimated in an amount to a maximum of 9,000,000.00 FF,

3) damages caused by the offence, at 400,000.00 FF

This must be put in relation with the amount of the fine and damages impossed by the Correctionnel Court , to which we will refer later : a fine of 200.000.- FF and Damages ; 21.000 FF

15.- In attention to the said valuations, the Court set the Bond as follows:

- to secure the representation of the Captain of the arrested vessel: 1,000,000 FF

- to secure payment of damages caused by the contraventions found ; 400.000 FF

- to secure payment of the fines incurred and the confiscation of the vessel ; 10,000,000.00 FF

The total amount of the bond was thus fixed on 11,400,000.00 FF or 1,737,918,70 Euros

16.- As to the form or nature of the bond the said Court ordered that should be "<in kind, by certify cheque or by bank cheque"

Bank guarantee is not (and , as we will refer , was not) allowable.

17.- The Court also observed that, by virtue of the provisions of articles 73 paragraph 2, and 292 of the Convention, the bond must be `reasonable´, and `that this means , more precisely, that the overall balance to be established between the amount , the form and the nature of this bond must be reasonable´.

18.- As we will refer later, the bond set by the said Court is far from being a "reasonable bond or other security" within the meaning of article 73, paragraph 2, of the Convention, neither on it´s amount nor on it´s form or nature.

19.- Despite the shipowner´s disagreement with the amount and form of the bond set by the Court, and without prejudice of legal actions, several arrangements with the authorities in Reunion were done in order to be able to avoid the detention of the vessel, and in turn the commencement of legal actions by the vessel creditors (crewmembers and workers ashore, suppliers, reparators, ship agents , banks , etc...) , by posting the bond in the form of bank guarantee.

More precisely, the intention of the shipowner was to place the said bank guarantee in the amount fixed by the mentioned Court , get the vessel released , and afterwards put the matter of the unreasonableness of the amount of the Bond to an conciliation or arbitration procedure or before this Tribunal.

20.- In this regard, the shipowner commenced all the banking arrangements in order to prepare the bank guarantee.

21.- The inttended wording of the said bank guarantee was in similar terms to that specified to by this Tribunal under paragraph 95 of the Judgement on the Monte Confurco case.

22.- The Maritime Authorities in Reunion were informed that the vessel , at the moment of the detention, was going to be refflaged and registered in Brasil, were she had allocated a fishing licence.

As **document number 14,** with it´s translation, we enclose the communication which was sent to the Maritime Authorities , at their request, in order to evidence the importance that the prompt release of the ship had, otherwise the vessel could loose the fishing licence.

23.- However , In first place, it was not allowed a bond in the form of bank guarantee but only by payment in cash or by cheque. (we refer in this regard to document number 13)

24.- Furthermore, only eight (8) days after the notification to the Captain of Grand Prince of the said Ordennance where the bond was fixed, the "Tribunal Correctionel of Saint Denis" (Reunion), on the 23 January, 2001, decided to confiscate the ship and, in order to avoid prompt (or late) release upon the posting of the guarantee sanctioned by article 73.2 of the Convention, also decided to execute provisionally the confiscation. A fine was impossed to the Captain in the amount of 200.000 FF, plus
20.000 FF as indemnification for the four french shipowners (the companies : Les Mascararaignes , La Comata, Legarrec and Sapmer) , plus 1 FF for the Regional Fishing Comitte .

25.- Through such "artifice" the said Correctionnel Tribunal managed, at least for the moment, to evade the clear and relevant exigencies for the States parties to the Convention contained in it´s article 73.2º, and very clear remarked and construed by this high Tribunal with occasion of the previous cases ("Saiga", "Camouco" , Monte Confurco").

26.- Neither the shipowner, nor the Captain, have received as yet any formal notification of the said decision, but the fact is that the vessel cannot be released by posting a guarantee, which suposses that the ship will remain under arrest and detained during all the time of duration of legal proceedings.

27.- Despite lack of notification of the decision of the Correctionnel Court , the shipowner, in order to saveguard his rights , announced the appeal of the decision, on the understanding that it is an unlawful decision , being the punishment extremely disporportionate with the nature and extent of the offence.

The appeal will be heard at the Court of Appeal of Saint Denis, but no date for the hearing has been appointed as yet.

28.- As result, the vessel could not be released neither upon posting a reasonable guarantee , nor upon posting the bond initially fixed by the First Instance Tribunal of Saint-Paul.

29.- And the above, Honorable members of the Tribunal, as we will refer in the legal grounds of this application, constitutes a grave infringement by France of the provisions of the Convention and of the Jurisprudence of this Tribunal , on prompt release of vessels.

30.- Just in order to get some kind of evidence of this abnormal situation it was file before the Tribunal D'Instance of Saint Paul a request of release of the ship upon posting of a bank guarantee in the amount fixed by the Tribunal (**document number 15**), which was rejected by Ordonnance nº 6/2001 (**document number 16**) alleguing that , as far as the tribunal correctionnel ordered confiscation and provissional execution , it ha no competence "to order the release of the vessel **in view of a simple bank guarantee"**

What France calls a "simple bank guarantee" is precisely what this Tribunal considerered in previous cases a reasonable nature or form of the bond.

31.- We have expossed above the infringement by France of the provisions stated under article 73 of the Convention, and the Jurisprudence of this Tribunal, by not allowing the posting of a bond in the form of bank guarantee, and, in parallel, by evading the exigency of prompt release through the artifice of deciding the confiscation of the vessel, and it´s provisional execution, with the enough celerity to prevent it´s release by posting of any kind of guarantee.

We will now treat in detail the matter related to the amount of the bond.

We understand that a bond in the amount of 11.400.000,00 FF or it´s equivalent of 1.737.918 Euros , cannot be regarded , from any point of view, to be a "reasonable bond or other security" within the meaning of of article 73, paragraph 2 of the Convention.

In effect, the marine surveyor who made the appraisal of the vessel on behalf of the maritime authorities in Reunion , Mr. Chancerel, seems to have forgotten about the following:

a) that we are talking about a vessel of more than **34 years old**

b) that , as stated in page 7 of the report of the Marine Surveror, Captain Antonio Alonso, enclosed as document 17 , the price of a new built vessel of he characteristics of Grand Prince is approximately 2.560.240 Euros.

c) That Grand Prince was built as a stern trawler , and afterwards was remodelled being converted to a botton-liner by the dismantelation of her trawling windlass and astern ramp. Every expert in fishing vessels knows that this adaptation implies that the vessel lacks the optimal characteristics, such as size, general arrangement and power for her present fishing activity. We refer in this regard to the reports enclosed as documents 17 and 18, were this issue is dealt with in detail

In fact, the international market price for a vessel of the age and characteristics of Grand Prince is in the region of **360.000.- Euros** which is less than a third party of the value indicated by Mr. Chancerel.

In order to evidence that what we are saying is true and accurate, we have enclosed as **documents numbers 17 and 18** the expert opinions of two remarkable experts on the fishing vessel´s market, the Marine Surveyor Captain Mr. Antonio Alonso Pérez and the naval Engineer Mr. Faustino Carceller Villalta.

All this makes sense with the purchase price of the vessel paid by the shipowner (paik Commercial Corp) on the 27/03/00, which, as we have evidenced through the Bill of

Sale duly signed before a Public Notary and apostilled , enclosed as document number 2, was : 45.000.000.- Pesetas (271.084 Euros)

For all these circumstances, it is impossible to accept that the amount of the bond fixed by France is "reasonable".

32.- Furthermore, we must recall that, as stated by this Tribunal in paragraph 86 of the Judgement pronounced in the Monte Confurco case, <<the value of the fish and of the fishing gear seized is also to be taken into account as a factor relevant in the assesment of the reasonableness of the bond>>, which , as far as we understand, supposes that the value (as determined by the french authorities) of the fish (123.848 Euros) and of the fishing gear (24.393 Euros) and fishing materials (5.610 Euros) , should be considered as part of the guarantee, as it was decided in the mentioned previous case .

This means that the sum of those three concepts , 153.851 Euros , should be computed when fixing the amount of the guarantee.

33.- For all the above reasons , we consider that , even contemplating the worst scenario for the shipowner, and trying not to take into account that the vessel did not catch any fish inside the EEZ of Kerguelen any fish , the final and firm decision of the case by the french Courts would be fully guaranteed by a bank guarantee in the amount of **206.142 Euros**

34.- A large number of third parties (crewmembers , workers ashore, suppliers, reparators, ship agents , banks, etc...) are being affected by the unjustified detention of the vessel.

Statement of Law

Jurisdiction

35.- The Tribunal has jurisdiction in virtue of article 292 paragraph 1 of the Convention, and provided that :

a) Belize and France are both parties to the Convention. Belize ratified the Convention on the 13-8-1983, and France on the 11.05.1996.

b) the Grand Prince flied the flag of Belize at the time of the detention subject matter of this application.

c) the parties did not agree to submit the question of the detention to any other court or tribunal within 10 days of the time of detention

d) the submissions stated in this application concern the alleged violations of article 73 paragraph 2 of the Convention.

Authorization

36.- The undersigned has been duly authorised to make the present application on behalf of the State of Belize in virtue of the Letter enclosed as document number 1.

Non compliance with article 73, paragraph 2, of the Convention

37.- <u>As to the exigency of prompt release:</u>

The arrest of the Grand Prince was made by the french authorities alleguing that she was fishing illegaly within the **Exclusive Economic Zone** of Kerguelen Islands, and basing said actuation on article 73 of the United Nations Convention of the Law of the Sea , to which , both Belize and France are parties, which reads as follows:

(1) The coastal State may, in the exercise of its sovereign rights to explore, exploit, conserve and manage the living resources in the exclusive economic zone, take such measures, including boarding, inspection , **arrest and judicial proceedings**, as may be necessary to ensure compliance with the laws and regulations adopted by it **in conformity with this convention .**

(2) Arrested vessels and their crews shall be promptly released upon de posting of a reasonable bond or other security.

It is evident that when the Convention allows the States to take measures to protect the resources of the EEZ, including arrest and judicial proceedings, sets very clearly the following limits that must be observed by the States:

a) the measures must be adopted in conformity with the Convention;

b) the vessels (and crews) must be promptluy release

In this regard , the Tribunal, with occasion of previous cases ("Saiga" , "Monte Confurco" and "Camouco") , made very clear what is the interpretation that must be given to the mentioned article :

"Article 73 identifies two interests , the interest of the Coastal State to take appropiate measures as may be necessary to ensure compliance with the laws and regulations adopted by it on the one hand and the interest of the flag State in securing prompt release of this vessels and their crews from detention on the other. <u>It strikes a fair balance between two interests . It provides for release of the vessel and its crew upon</u>

the posting of a bond or other security, thus protecting the interests of the flag State and other persons affected by the detention of the vessel and its crew. The release from detention can be subject **only** to a `reasonable´ bond." (point 70 - pag 25- Judgement related to The Monte Confurco Case.

It is equally evident that States cannot use anykind of subterfugies or tricks to evade such crucial requirements.

France , in this particular case, fixed initially a bond for release of the vessel, and only a few days later decided to confiscate the vessel (and it´s equipment and fish) , as well as to execute provisionally the decision, which in practical terms supposed that the vessel could not be released even by posting the bond fixed by France.

We are concious , that this way of proceeding has been carefully designed , so that - apparently- the State complies with the requisite of fixing a bond for prompt release, but in reality the release becomes impracticable because whilst the arrested party is either making the arrangements to prepare the bond or questionning the reasonableness (amount, nature or form) of the same, the confiscation is decided and executed provisionally.

And with all respects, this is nothing else but a "trick", which in most Statal legislations is regulated as "Fraud of Law". Fraud of Law consists of using a provision of Law just with the objective of evading the compliance with a legal requirement.

If this type of actuations were permitted , then article 73 of the Convention would be "dead letters" , and every State could arrest vessels for infringements in the EEZ and upon arrival to Port (or even before) put the matter to a Court and decide inmediatly the confiscation and it´s provisional execution, irrespectively of any remedies of appeal (as did France in the present case; confiscation was decided by the Court by the way) .

We are confident that this Tribunal will restore the legality in this respect.

38.- As to the nature of the bond

Irrespectively of what has been explained in paragraph 36, France did not comply neither with the requisite of "reasonableness of the bond" as to tit´s form or nature.

Let me recall what this Tribunal decided in previous matters with regard to this aspect:

In the "Saiga" case it was decided for the first time that the form of the bond shall be "a letter of credit or bank guarantee" (paragraph 85 of the Judgement)

With occasion of the cases Camouco and Monte Confurco the Tribunal went againt over this issue, and insisted on the same exigency as follows:

"The Tribunal notes that, in the 'Camouco' case , it decided that the bond should be in the form of a bank guarantee (judgement of 7 February 2000, paragraph 74). No difficulty was encountered in the implementation of this judgement. Consequently, the claim of the respondent that cash or certified cheque are the only possible forms for the bond does not seem reasonable to the Tribunal." (paragraph 93 of the judgement of 18 December 2.000, in the Monte Confurco case)

In our particular case, France has again limited the nature of the bond by requesting a "certified cheque or a bank cheque" (which does not differ to much from a payment in cash) , not allowing a bank guarantee.

Consequently, the bond cannot be considered "reasonable" as to it's nature or form, and we are confident that the Tribunal will determine that it shall be in the form of a bank guaratee.

39.- As to the form of the bond

Following the criteria of the Tribunal in the previous cases referred above , we understand that the form and wording of the bank Guarantee shall be as follows:

"The bank guarantee it is issued in consideration of France releasing the Grand Prince , in relation to the incidents dealt with in the Order of 12 January 2.001 of the Court of First Instance of Saint-Paul and that the issuer undertakes and guarantees to pay to France such sums, up to 206.149 Euros , as may be determined by a final and firm judgement or decision of the appropiate domestic forum in France or by agreement of the parties. Payment under the guarantee would be due promptly after receipt by the issuer of a written demand by the competent authority of France accompained by a certified copy of the final and firm judgement or decision or agreement."

40.- As to the amount of the bond

Article 73.2 of the Convention requires that the amount of the bond must be reasonable.

The Tribunal , with occasion of the previous cases ("Saiga", "Camouco" and "Monte Confurco") specified a number of relevant factors to be taken into consideration in an asessment of the reasonableness of bonds, which include; (a) the gravitity of the allegued offences; (b) the penalties imposed or imposable under the laws of the detaining State; (c) the value of the detained vessel and the cargo seized (e) the quantity of fish carried on board.

As to the value of the vessel, we have evidenced that:

- it was bought in the price of 45.000.000.- Pesetas equal to 271.000 Euros (document number 2º)

- it's market price is in the region of 360.000 Euros (documents numbers 17 and 18)

- the appraisal made by the French surveyor is near the cost of a new built ship of similar characteristics of Grand Prince. (documents numbers 19 and 20)

There are other several circumstances that should be take into account in this particular case, such as ;

-the short quantity of fish carried on board (18 Tns)
-that although the Captain had the intention to fish within the EEZ of the Kerguelen, fact that we do not deny, he had clear instructions from the shipowner not fish in the said area.
- that this vessel was about to proceed to Brazil where she had good possibilities to fish under a Brazil fishing licence.
- the attitude of full cooperation by the Captain , crew and shipowner of Grand Prince with the french authorities.
- that the correctionnel court of Saint Denis , which decision has been appealed, has impossed a fine to the Captain in the amount of 200.000 FF.

The result, is that even contemplating the worst scenario for the shipowner, the final and firm decision of a domestic Court would be fully guaranteed by a bank guarantee in the amount of **206.149 Euros**

SUMMARY OF ARGUMENTS

41.- Grand Prince was detained on the 26 December 2.000 by the french authorities accused to fish within the EEZ of the Kerguelen Islands. (page 4 paragraph 4)

42.- At the time of the detention the vessel flied Belize flag , being both, France and Belize, parties to the Convention. (page 3 - paragraph 1)

43.- The Captain declared that although the vessel did not catch any fish in the area, he was in fact dispossed to fish, despite the clear instructions given to him by the shipowner not to enter in the zone. (page 4 - paragraph 5)

44.- The vessel had on board approximatelly 2 Tns of lobster 18 Tns of toothfish (page 4 - paragraph 8)

44.- The vessel was about to proceed to Brazil, were he had been allocated with a fishing licence.(page 7 - paragraph 22)

45.- By order nº 3/2001 of 12 January 2.001, the Court of first instance of Saint Paul confimed the seizure of the vessel, the fishing gear and materials, and the fish on board, fixing a bond for release of the vessel in the amont of 1,737,918 .70 Euros, to be posted in the form of certify cheque or bank cheque. The form of bank guarantee was not allowed. (pages 5 and 6 - paragraphs 12 to 18, both inclusive)

46.- The said bond cannot be considered "reasonable" neither as to it´s form , (as it not allows a bank guarantee) nor in repect of it's amount, as it exceeds three times de current market price of the vessel. (page 8- paragraph 31, 32 and 33, pages 13, 14 and 15 , paragraphs 38, 39 and 40)

47.- Irrespectively of the unreasonableness of the bond, it happened that a few days after the said Order was notified , the Tribunal Correctionnel of Saint Denis , on the 23 January 2.001, decided to confiscate the vessel and that the said decision was provisionally executed. (pages 7 and 8- paragraphs 24 to 30, both inclusive, and pages 12 and 13 - paragraph 37)

48.- As result thereof the vessel could not be released by posting any kind of bond (reasonable or not) , and that she will remain detained whilst the proceedings of appeal of the said decision are in course and a final and firm decision is pronounced.(page 8 - paragraph 28)

49.- Through said subterfuge or "fraud of law" France, in addition to having fixed a unreasonable bond, has evaded the crucial and clear requirement of prompt release sanctioned under article 73.1 of the Convention. (page 8 - paragraph 29 and and pages 12 and 13 - paragraph 37)

50.- In the meantime, the infringment by France of article 73.1 is affecting very seriously , apart from the shipowner, the rights of third parties with interests on the vessel , such as the company workers (37 members of the crew and 6 ashore) , suppliers, ship agents , reparators banks , etc... (page 10 - paragraph 34)

On the basis of the foregoing facts and statements of law, and after having been carefully studied and considered by the flag State the circumstances of this matter, I make the folllowing;

50.- **SUBMISSIONS**

1.- To declare that the Tribunal has jurisdiction under article 292 of the United Nations Convention on the Law of the Sea to hear the present application .

2.- To declare the present application admissible.

3.- To declare that France failed to comply with article 73, paragraph 2, of the Convention, as the guarantee fixed for release of Grand Prince is not reasonable as to it´s amount, nature or form.

4.- To declare that France failed to comply with article 73, paragraph 2, of the Convention by having evaded the requiment of prompt release under this article by not allowing the release of the vessel upon the posting of a reasonable, or any kind, of guarantee alleguing that the vessel is confiscated and that the decision of confiscation has been provissionally executed.

5.- To decide that France shall promptly release the Grand Prince upon the posting of a bond or other security to be determined by the Tribunal

6.- To determine that the bond or other security shall consist of an amount of two hundred and six thousand one hundred forty nine (206.149) Euros or it´s equivalent if French Francs.

7.- To detemine that the monetary equivalent to (a) 18 tones of fish on board the Grand Prince held by the french authorities, and valued on 123.848 Euros (b) the fishing gear , valued on 24.393 Euros (c) the fishing materials valued on 5.610 Euros , totalising 153.851 Euros , shall be considered as security to be held or, as the case may be, returned by France to this party.

8- To determine that the bond shall be in the form of a bank guarantee .

9.- To determine that the wording of the bank guarantee shall , among other things, state the following:

A.- In case France returns to the shipowner the concepts referred to under point 7 (of the present submissions):

"The bank guarantee it is issued in consideration of France releasing the Grand Prince , in relation to the incidents dealt with in the Order of 12 January 2.001 of the Court of First Instance of Saint-Paul and that the issuer undertakes and guarantees to pay to France such sums, up to 206.149 Euros , as may be determined by a final and firm judgement or decision of the appropiate domestic forum in France or by agreement of the parties. Payment under the guarantee would be due promptly after receipt by the issuer of a written demand by the competent authority of France accompained by a certified copy of the final and firm judgement or decision or agreement."

B.- In case France does not return to the shipowner the concepts referred to under point 7 (of the present submissions):

"The bank guarantee it is issued in consideration of France releasing the Grand Prince , in relation to the incidents dealt with in the Order of 12 January 2.001 of the Court of First Instance of Saint-Paul and that the issuer undertakes and guarantees to pay to France such sums, up to 52.298 Euros , as may be determined by a final and firm judgement or decision of the appropiate domestic forum in France or by agreement of the parties. Payment under the guarantee would be due promptly after receipt by the issuer of a written demand by the competent authority of France accompained by a certified copy of the final and firm judgement or decision or agreement."

10.- To determine that the bank guarantee shall be invoked only if the monetary equivalent of the security held by France is not sufficient to pay the sums as may be determined by a final and firm judgement or decision of the appropiate domestic forum in France.

21st March , 2.001

Agent´s Signature:

Alberto Penelas Alvarez

INTERNATIONAL MERCHANT MARINE REGISTRY OF BELIZE • IMMARBE •

This Designated Office certifies that this is a true copy of its original. This Designated Office does not take responsibilities for its content.

BRUNO B. VARELA GARCIA DE PAREDES
DEPUTY REGISTRAR

/Deputy Registrar
Designated Office, Madrid

PART II

DOCUMENTS IN SUPPORT OF PLEADINGS

21st March , 2.001

Agent´s Signature:

Alberto Penelas Alvarez

INTERNATIONAL MERCHANT MARINE REGISTRY OF

This Designated Office certifies that this is a true copy of its original. This Designated Office does not take responsibilities for its content.

BRUNO B. VARELA GARCIA DE PAREDES
DEPUTY REGISTRAR

/Deputy Registrar
Designated Office, Madrid

Annex 1
Authorization issued to Mr Penelas Alvarez by the Attorney General of Belize dated 15 March 2001 (reproduced *infra* under the title Documents – Authorizations)

Annex 1-1
Letter from the Attorney General of Belize to the Registrar dated 15-March 2001 transmitting the authorization (not reproduced)

Annex 2
Bill of Sale (in Spanish) (not reproduced), with:
– Bill of Sale and Acceptance of Sale (in Spanish and English)

CONTRATO DE COMPRA Y VENTA
BILL OF SALE AND ACCEPTANCE OF SALE

Detalles de la NAVE (posteriormente denominada "la NAVE").
Particulars of the VESSEL (hereinafter called "the VESSEL").

Número de Patente 07972047 / Navigation License No.	Nombre de la NAVE "GRAND PRICE" / Name of the Vessel	
Puerto de Registro BELIZE / Port of Registry		Clase de Nave PESCA / Type of Vessel
Caballos de Fuerza, si hay 1.500 / H.P. of Engines, if any		Eslora 39,67 / Length
Registrado. / Recorded.	Tonelaje / Tonnage	Manga 10,00 / Breadth
Libro / Book	Bruto 669 / Gross	Puntal 4,80 / Depth
Página / Page	Neto Registrado 267 / Net Registered	y como se describe más detalladamente en el Certificado / and as described in more detail in the Certificate of the
Folio / Entry	Bajo Cubierta / Under deck	Técnico y Libro de Registro. / Surveyor and the Register Book

CONTRATO DE VENTA
Bill of Sale

Nosotros REARDON COMMERCIAL CORP. (posteriormente denominados "los VENDEDORES") con domicilio
We (hereinafter called "the VENDORS") having our principal place

en BELIZE
of business at

hemos recibido la suma de CUARENTA Y CINCO MILLONES DE PESETAS (45.000.000 PTS)
in consideration of the sum of

Pagados a nosotros por PAIK COMMERCIAL CORP.
paid to us by

de BELIZE (posteriormente denominados "Los COMPRADORES) y que por medio de la
of (hereinafter called "the PURCHASERS") the receipt whereof is

presente acusamos recibo, y por lo tanto, transferimos a "los COMPRADORES" nuestro título completo, propiedad e
hereby acknowledged, therefore, we do transfer our whole title, owership and interests in

intereses en "LA NAVE" así como en sus botes, aparejos y otras pertenencias de "la NAVE". Nosotros, "los VENDEDORES",
the VESSEL above particulary described, including the boats, tackles and other appurtenances to the PURCHASES. VESSEL to the PURCHASERS.

a nombre nuestro y de nuestros sucesores, convenimos con "los COMPRADORES" y sus designados en que tenemos el poder
FURTHER WE, the VENDORS for ourselves and our successors covenant with the PURCHASERS and its assignees that we have power

para transferir "la NAVE" y título antes mencionado y en la manera antes descrita. Aseguramos que "la NAVE" está libre de
to transfer the said VESSEL and title there to in manner aforesaid

Gravámenes, Deudas y Demandas Marítimas.
and that the same is free from lines, debts, maritime claims or any incumbrances.

En testimonio de lo cual, hemos otorgado este Contrato de Venta el día 27/03/00
In witness whereof, we have hereto affixed our common seal this day of

de Mil Novecientos
One thousand nine hundred and

El Sello Corporativo de los VENDEDORES fue fijado a este documento en presencia de:
The Common Seal of the VENDORS was affixed hereunto in the presence of:

Annex 2 (continued)
– Notarial Certificate of the Bill of Sale (in Spanish and English)

TIMBRE DEL ESTADO

NOTARIA DE D. EDUARDO MENDEZ ... NIHIL PRIUS FIDE ... VILATON - PONTEVEDRA

PTA

3B7867378

Notarización del Contrato de Venta
Notarial Certificate of The Bill of Sale

Yo........EDUARDO MENDEZ APENELA.................................... Notario Público, debidamente autorizado, facultado
I NOTARY PUBLIC duly authorized, admitted and

y juramentado, con residencia y ejerciendo en .....PONTEVEDRA..
sworn practicing at

por este medio Certifico que:
do hereby certify that:

1. las firmas de "..................
the signatures"

JOSE COSTA PRIETO.................. "y" .... JOSE NOGUEIRA GARCIA........................ en representación del VENDEDOR son sus firmas auténticas.
"and" on behalf of the VENDORS are their respective authentic signatures.

2. Suficientes pruebas me han sido presentadas de que :
Sufficient proof has been produced to me that:

(a) Los Vendedores inmediatamente antes del otorgamiento del Contrato de Venta eran los propietario de la NAVE a que ésta se refiere y tiene el derecho para vender y traspasar "la NAVE".
The Vendors were immediately prior to the execution of the said Bill of Sale the owners of "the VESSEL" therein referred to and had the rigtht to sell and transfer the said "VESSEL".

(b) Los de arriba firmantes tenían el poder para otorgar dicho CONTRATO DE VENTA en representación de LOS VENDEDORES en la forma antes mencionada,
The above mentioned signatories had power to executive the Bill of Sale on behalf of the Vendors in manner aforesaid

AUTENTICACION
AUTHENTICATION

EN TESTIMONIO de los cual he suscrito mi nombre y fijado mi sello
IN TESTIMONY where of I have here unto suscribed my name and affixed my seal of office

en este día ....
this day of

de.................................. de mil novecientos
of One Thousand nine

....
hundred and

Notario Público
Notary Public

Annex 2 (continued)
– Acceptance of Sale (in Spanish and English)
– Notarial Certificate of Acceptance of Sale (in Spanish and English)

ACEPTACION DE COMPRA
ACCEPTANCE OF SALE

El Suscrito JOSE MANUEL MAGDALENO FERNANDEZ a nombre y representación de
The Undersigned on behalf of and representing

La Corporación llamada PAIK COMMERCIAL CORP. en el anterior Contrato de Venta y
The The Corporation named in the Bill of Sale overleaf

en mi carácter de APODERADO de la mencionada sociedad,
and in my position as of the said Corporation

por este medio y para todos los efectos legales ACEPTO LA COMPRA Y EL TRASPASO DE "la NAVE" a la citada sociedad por
HEREBY ACCEPT for all legal purposes the sale and transfer effected by the said Bill of Sale to the said Corporation by.

de la nave "GRAND PRINCE" a la que se refiere el Contrato de Venta
of the Vessel referred to in the above Bill of Sale.

Fechado el ______ día de ______, 19____
Dated the day of , 19

Notarización de la Aceptación de Compra
Notarial Certificate of Acceptance of Sale

Yo EDUARDO MENDEZ APENELA debidamente autorizado, facultado
I duly authorized, admitted and

y juramentado, con residencia y ejerciendo en PONTEVEDRA POR ESTE MEDIO CERTIFICO QUE
sworn, residing and practising at DO HEREBY CERTIFY THAT the

la firma ...... que aparece al pie de la ACEPTACION DE COMPRA es la
signature which appears at the foot of above written ACCEPTANCE

firma auténtica del antes mencionado JOSE MANUEL MAGDALENO FERNANDEZ
is the authentic signature of the above named

quien ha presentado pruebas suficientes de su poder para poder realizar dicha Aceptación de Compra en nombre
who has produced sufficient proof of his power to execute the said Acceptance of sale of behalf of

y representación de la sociedad PAIK COMMERCIAL CORP. antes mencionada.
the Corporation above named

EN TESTIMONIO de lo cual he suscrito aquí mi nombre y
IN TESTIMONY where of I have here unto suscribed my name

fijado mi sello de Oficio hoy ...... de ......
and affixed my Seal of Office this of

de Mil Novecientos ......
One Thousand nine hundred and

Annex 2 (continued)
English translation of Bill of Sale

3B7867373

NUMBER ONE THOUSAND NINE HUNDRED AND FOURTEEN

IN PONTEVEDRA, at my residence on March twenty-seventh of the year Two Thousand and One. --

I, **EDUARDO MENDEZ APENELA**, Notary and member of the distinguished Association of Notaries of A Coruña do hereby certify that the following parties have appeared before me---

MR. JOSE NOGUEIRA GARCIA, of legal age, married, domiciled in Ardán Casas in the municipality of Marín, and bearer of National Identity Card number 35.277.482.------

MR. JOSE COSTA PRIETO, of legal age, married, domiciled at Nuestra Señora de la Sainza Street, number 10-2° Izq., in Orense and bearer of National Identity Card number 34.583.164-L.--

MR. JOSE MANUEL MAGDALENO FERNANDEZ, of legal age, married, domiciled in Goyán in the municipality of Tomiño and bearer of National Identity Card number 35.551.170-R--

A) The first two parties intervene on behalf and in representation of the company "**REARDON COMMERCIAL CORP.**", of Belize nationality, with main offices in 35 A regent Street, Belize City, founded on 14 May 1999 before the Registered Agent Morgan & Morgan Trust Corporation (Belize), registered under number 10680.---

   Pursuant to the Power of Attorney granted on 22 September 1999 before Plinio Valdés, Eleventh Notary Public of the Circuit of Panama, in which among other acts, authorises them to "...sell....or to dispose of in any other way, property or real estate belonging to the Company whether it be corporeal or incorporeal". This is derived from said Power of Attorney, which I have at sight, in witness whereof, I certify that nothing of what has been omitted changes in any way the text that has been inserted, and the appearing parties have guaranteed that their authority remains in force, and that no changes have been made in the legal capacity of the Company which they represent.---

B) And the latter intervenes on behalf and in representation of the company "**PAIX COMMERCIAL CORP"** of indefinite duration, domiciled in 35 A Regent Street, Belize City, founded on 1 January 2000 before the Registered Agent Morgan & Morgan Trust Corporation (Belize), registered under number 12968.------------------

   Pursuant to the Power of Attorney, granted on 24 March 2000 before Boris Sucre Martín, Notary Public Number Eight of the Circuit of Panama, in which among other acts, authorises them to "...sell....or to dispose of in any other way, property or real estate belonging to the Company whether it be corporeal or incorporeal". This is derived from said Power of Attorney, which I have at sight, in witness whereof, I certify that nothing of what has been omitted changes in any way the text that has been inserted, and the appearing parties have guaranteed that their authority remains in force, and that no changes have been made in the legal capacity of the Company which they represent.

In this sense:

1. They exhibit a document written in the Spanish and English, consisting of two pages; the appearing parties proceed to sign this instrument, in my presence, specifying that:
   a.- They are familiar with the contents of said document.
   b.- And, of their own free will and voluntarily they wish that the applicable effects take place, in accordance with what has been established by foreign law.

2. I, the Notary, proceed to legitimise the signatures affixed by the appearing parties to this instrument.
3. And a photocopy of which I attach to this original.

I have read the aforementioned to the appearing parties and fully aware of the content, they ratify the instrument and sign with me, the Notary, and in witness whereof, I certify that they have identified themselves by means of the above-mentioned National Identity Cards and the rest of the contents drawn up in this act, consisting of two pages of series 3G,numbers 1044407 and this page. The signatures and endorsements of the appearing parties are included herein.- Signed: E. Méndez, endorsed and seal affixed. ----------------

PROCESS- Served by me, the Notary, to verify that on the same day as the authorisation of the foregoing act, I proceed to attach this photocopy of the instrument of "Notarisation of the Bill of Sale" to legitimise the signatures of the appearing parties, and corresponding to the bill of sale and acceptance of sale which has been attached to the present instrument.--

I, the Notary, DO HEREBY BEAR WITNESS TO all of which is included on two pages of series 3G, numbers 1044408 and this page.- Signed: E. Méndez endorsed and seal affixed--

ATTACHED DOCUMENTS

Annex 2 (continued)
English translation of Acceptance of Sale

ACCEPTANCE OF SALE

THIS AGREES WITH THE ORIGINAL NUMBER EXPRESSED IN THIS GENERAL PROTOCOL. AT THE REQUEST OF THE COMPANY PAIK COMMERCIAL CORP, I ISSUE THIS COPY IN FIVE PAGES OF SERIES 3B NUMBER SEVEN MILLION EIGHT HUNDRED AND SIXTY-SEVEN THOUSAND THREE HUNDRED AND SEVENTY-THREE, THE FOLLOWING IN CORRELATIVE ORDER, SEVEN MILLION EIGHT HUNDRED AND SIXTY-SEVEN THOUSAND THREE HUNDRED AND SEVENTY-SEVEN, THE FOLLOWING IN CORRELATIVE ORDER AND THIS PAGE IN PONTEVEDRA, ON THE SAME DAY AS THE AUTHORISATION. IN WITNESS WHEREOF.

Apostille (OR legitimisation)
Convention de la Haye du 5 Octobre 1961
(Royal decree 2433/1978 of October 2nd)

1. Country : Spain
   This public document
2. Has been signed by EDUARDO MENDEZ APENELA
3. Acting in the capacity of Notary
4. Bears the seal of the Notary

Certified

5. In Moaña
6. On 17 January 2001
7. By José Luis Espinosa de Soto, Proctor of the Distinguished Association of Notaries of La Coruña.
8. Number 6091
9. Seal/Stamp
10. Signature:

Annex 3
Provisional Patent of Navigation of the *Grand Prince*

RECEIVED 02/04/2001

INTERNATIONAL MERCHANT MARINE REGISTRY OF BELIZE
"IMMARBE"
REGISTRATION OF MERCHANT SHIPS ACT. 1989
PROVISIONAL PATENT OF NAVIGATION

NAME OF VESSEL
"GRAND PRINCE"

CALL LETTERS	IMO NUMBER	REGISTRATION Nº
V 3 U J 7	6701656	07972047

NAME AND ADDRESS OF OWNERS
PAIK COMMERCIAL CORP. – 35A Regent Street P.O. BOX 1777 – Belize City, Belize

DESCRIPTION OF VESSEL

TYPE OF VESSEL	MATERIAL OF THE HULL	GROSS TONNAGE	NET TONNAGE	UNDER DECK
FISHING	STEEL	669	267	-----

No. DECKS	No. MASTS	No. BRIDGES	No. FUNNELS	NAME OF BUILDERS	YEAR BUILT
1	2	1	1	PORTWELLER DRYDOCKS LTD.,CANADA	1966

LENGTH	BREADTH	DEPTH	TYPE OF ENGINES	NAME OF ENGINES MAKERS	SPEED
39,67 meters	10,00 meters	4,80 meters	1 DIESEL GM	GENERAL MOTORS	12,5 knots

PREVIOUS NAME: "GRAND PRINCE" PREVIOUS NATIONALITY: CANADIAN

TYPE OF RADIO EQUIPMENT: RADIOTELEPHONE

ENTITY RESPONSIBLE FOR RADIO ACCOUNTS: RADIO HOLLAND B.V.

COMPLETE ADDRESS OF ENTITY RESPONSIBLE FOR RADIO ACCOUNTS: POSTBUS 5068 – 3008 AB ROTTERDAM (HOLLAND)

RESIDENT AGENT: MORGAN & MORGAN TRUST CORP. (BELIZE) LTD.

DATE OF ISSUANCE	DATE OF EXPIRATION
OCTOBER 16TH, 2000	DECEMBER 29TH, 2000

The Registrar of the International Merchant Registry of Belize, by the powers vested thereupon by Registration of Merchant Ships Act, 1989 and amendments thereto, hereby authorizes and extends the present Provisional Patent of Navigation.

SEE FISHING CONDITIONS
ON REVERSE SIDE OF PATENT

BRUNO B. VARELA GARCIA DE PAREDES
DEPUTY REGISTRAR
Registrar

C O P Y CONTROL Nº 02 - 000492

VESSEL SHALL NOT ENGAGE IN ILLEGAL FISHING AND SHALL COMPLY WITH ALL FISHING REQUERIMENTS AND REGULATIONS APPLICABLE TO THE SPECIFIC FISHING AREA. FAILURE TO COMPLY WILL RESULT IN A PENALTY UP TO US$50,000.00 DEPENDING ON THE SERIOUSNESS OF THE OFFENCE AND RELAPSING COULD LEAD TO THE EX – OFFICIO CANCELLATION OF STATUS.

Annex 4
Crew list

CREW LIST VESSEL " GRAND PRINCE "

	CARGO	NAME-SURNAME	NATIONALITY
1	CAPTAIN	RAMÓN FCO. PÉREZ NOVO	SPANISH
2	1st OFFICIAL	ANTONIO SEVILLA LUSTRES	SPANISH
3	CHIEF ENGEENIR	PERFECTO PINTOS FONTENLA	SPANISH
4	1st ENGEENIR	ISAAC NOGUEIRA BUCETA	SPANISH
5	2nd ENGEENIR	JORGE GÓNZÁLEZ PIÑEIRO	SPANISH
6	1st COOK	CARLOS COYA PIÑEIRO	SPANISH
7	2nd COOD	HERIBERTO LUIS ÁLVAREZ QUICEL	CHILEAN
8	OVERSEER	JOAQUÍN M MARTÍNEZ SAYANS	SPANISH
9	2nd OVERSEER	MARCELINO SCHONFEELDT MILLACU	CHILEAN
10	OVERSEER	JUAN JOSÉ AGUÍN SABOR	SPANISH
11	2nd OVERSEER	JUAN CARLOS MONTOTO AREAN	SPANISH
12	SEAMEN	CARLOS LOVEIRA COSTAS	SPANISH
13	SEAMEN	PABLO ALEJANDRO SILVA HERRERA	CHILEAN
14	SEAMEN	MARCEL A. CANALES FARIAS	CHILEAN
15	SEAMEN	MIGUEL E. SANCHEZ ROGEL	CHILEAN
16	SEAMEN	CARLOS A. GUZMAN MUÑOZ	CHILEAN
17	SEAMEN	CRISTIAN EMILIO TORRES SAN MARTÍN	CHILEAN
18	SEAMEN	JUAN ENRIQUE ALVAREZ DÍAZ	CHILEAN
19	SEAMEN	BALBINO S. CHÁVEZ HERNÁNDEZ	CHILEAN
20	SEAMEN	EMILIO ALEX BARRÍA GONZÁLEZ	CHILEAN
21	SEAMEN	JUAN CLAUDIO VILLARROEL TENER	CHILEAN
22	SEAMEN	JORGE P. ARADENA DÍAZ	CHILEAN
23	SEAMEN	JULIO A. UBEDA HERNÁNDEZ	CHILEAN
24	SEAMEN	SIXTO A. ALMONACID ALMONACID	CHILEAN
25	SEAMEN	MANUEL R. OYARZO CÁRDENAS	CHILEAN
26	SEAMEN	CLAUDIO HARDY RUÍZ HEINZ	CHILEAN
27	SEAMEN	CRISTIAN A. CAICOMPAI SANTANA	CHILEAN
28	SEAMEN	HERNAN HENRY URIBE ZANZANA	CHILEAN
29	SEAMEN	IVÁN RODRIGO BELIZAR ZUMELZO	CHILEAN
30	SEAMEN	ANDRÉS FREDY GUALA OJEDA	CHILEAN
31	SEAMEN	CLAUDIO IVAN GUALA OJEDA	CHILEAN
32	SEAMEN	MARCELO A. DÍAZ VARGAS	CHILEAN
33	SEAMEN	MARCO A. SILVA HERRERA	CHILEAN
34	SEAMEN	NEFTALÍ SEGUNDO LAVADOS VERA	CHILEAN
35	SEAMEN	MARCOS AUGUSTO PINOCHET M.	CHILEAN
36	SEAMEN	MARIO A. FARÍAS CARGAGENA	CHILEAN
37	SEAMEN	ERWIN FERNANDO BARRÍA BÁEZ	CHILEAN

Annex 5

Procès-verbal d'appréhension n° 05/00 (fish catch) (in French)

DOC. 5º PROCES VERBAL D'APPREHENSION OF THE VESSEL

MARINE NATIONALE

FORCE D'ACTION NAVALE

COMMANDEMENT MARITIME DE NOUVELLE CALEDONIE

FREGATE NIVOSE

PROCES VERBAL D'APPREHENSION

N° 05 / 00 NIVOSE

- L'an deux mille, le mardi 26 décembre 2000,
- Nous, soussigné Gilles DEPELLEY, capitaine de corvette, commandant en second de la frégate de surveillance «NIVOSE», en action de police des pêches,

Vu :
- La loi du 1er mars 1888 modifiée, relative à l'exercice de la pêche dans les eaux sous souveraineté ou juridiction française s'étendant au large des côtes des territoires d'outre mer;
- La loi 66-400 du 18 juin 1966 sur l'exercice de la pêche maritime et de l'exploitation des produits de la mer dans les Terres Australes et Antarctiques Françaises,
- La loi n° 83-582 du 5 juillet 1983 modifiée, relative au régime de la saisie et complétant la liste des agents habilités à constater les infractions dans le domaine des pêches maritimes,
- le décret n° 84-846 du 12 septembre 1984 fixant les modalités d'application de la loi 83-582 susvisée;

Nous trouvant à bord du «GRAND PRINCE» , à la position GPS: 47° 24,7 SUD, 073° 24,9 EST, agissant pour faire suite à l'infraction de pêche sans autorisation dans la ZEE de KERGUELEN à la position GPS 47°47' SUD, 073°44' EST, en route au 250 à 01 (un) nœuds, le mardi 26 décembre 2000 à 08h53 Echo, infraction constatée par le PV N°04/ NIVOSE en date du mardi 26 décembre 2000, établi à l'encontre de M. RAMON FRANCISCO PEREZ NOVO, né le 05/10/57 à RIBEIRA, capitaine du navire "GRAND PRINCE".

Déclarons procéder à l'appréhension sur le Navire "GRAND PRINCE", port d'attache BELIZE, des objets énumérés ci-dessous :

Produits de la pêche

- 15 (quinze) tonnes de légine congelée (-18°C (moins dix-huit degrés Celsius) dans la soute frigorifique située au fond du bateau, soute à – 27°C (moins vingt sept degrés Celsius)),
- 2,5 (deux et demies) tonnes de légine fraîche située dans deux des trois tunnels

et, en la présence constante du capitaine, apposons les scellés sur les objets appréhendés.

Nous lui notifions l'appréhension et le déclarons gardien des objets appréhendés.
Une traduction en espagnol a été effectuée par le patron des pêches Antonio SEVILLA LUSTRES, membre de l'équipage du navire "GRAND PRINCE".

Fait à bord du "GRAND PRINCE", le mardi 26 décembre 2000 à 2000 heures (E).

Le commandant
Le capitaine de frégate Marc LANNE,
commandant la frégate NIVOSE

L'auteur du délit

TRADUCTOR:

Le capitaine de corvette Gilles DEPELLEY,
commandant en second de la frégate NIVOSE

[ ] Transmis au directeur départemental des affaires maritimes de La Réunion le

Annex 6
Procès-verbal d'appréhension n° 07/00 **(navigation and communication equipment) (in French)**

DOC. 6º PROCES VERBAL D'APPREHENSION OF THE NAVIGATIONAL EQUIPMENT

MARINE NATIONALE

FORCE D'ACTION NAVALE

COMMANDEMENT MARITIME
DE NOUVELLE CALEDONIE

FREGATE NIVOSE

PROCES VERBAL D'APPREHENSION

N° 07 / 00 NIVOSE

- L'an deux mille, le mardi 26 décembre 2000,
- Nous, soussigné Gilles DEPELLEY, capitaine de corvette, commandant en second de la frégate de surveillance «NIVOSE», en action de police des pêches,

Vu :
- La loi du 1er mars 1888 modifiée, relative à l'exercice de la pêche dans les eaux sous souveraineté ou juridiction française s'étendant au large des côtes des territoires d'outre mer;
- La loi 66-400 du 18 juin 1966 sur l'exercice de la pêche maritime et de l'exploitation des produits de la mer dans les Terres Australes et Antarctiques Françaises,
- La loi n° 83-582 du 5 juillet 1983 modifiée, relative au régime de la saisie et complétant la liste des agents habilités à constater les infractions dans le domaine des pêches maritimes,
- le décret n° 84-846 du 12 septembre 1984 fixant les modalités d'application de la loi 83-582 susvisée;

Nous trouvant à bord du «GRAND PRINCE» , à la position GPS: 47° 24,7 SUD, 073° 24,9 EST, agissant pour faire suite à l'infraction de pêche sans autorisation dans la ZEE de KERGUELEN à la position GPS 47°47' SUD, 073°44' EST, en route au 250 à 01 (un) nœuds, le mardi 26 décembre 2000 à 08h53 Echo, infraction constatée par le PV N°04/ NIVOSE en date du mardi 26 décembre 2000, établi à l'encontre de M. RAMON FRANCISCO PEREZ NOVO, né le 05/10/57 à RIBEIRA, capitaine du navire "GRAND PRINCE".

Déclarons procéder à l'appréhension des objets énumérés ci-dessous:

Navire : "GRAND PRINCE", port d'attache BELIZE.

Matériel de navigation et de transmission

- Un émetteur-récepteur MF/HF ICOM IC-M 710,
- Deux GPS FURUNO,
- Un RADIO METEO FURUNO,
- Un sondeur CVS 8831 KODEN,
- Un sondeur FURUNO,
- Un RADAR FURUNO RDP106,
- Un téléviseur,
- Un NAVTEX NCR 300 A,

1/2

- Un FAX téléphone INMARSAT FURUNO FELCOM 81,
- Deux ordinateurs (en passerelle) (disque dur HRE) avec modem + imprimante,
- Un LORAN GPS 6700 APELCO,
- Un RADAR SIMRAD.

Documents de bord

- ~~Un journal~~ Deux journaux de navigation commun au journal de bord,
- Une liste d'équipage,
- Trente cinq passeports,
- 1 feuille d'impression du journal de pêche (PC Passerelle)
- modes d'emploi des appareils situés en passerelle,
- cinq cartes de visite de shipshandlers,
- six cahiers à spirale contenant des informations diverses et schémas,
- un relevé de deux positions de balise,
- La patente de navigation,
- Une licence radio,
- Une pochette contenant divers certificats (certificats de jauge, de radiotéléphoniste de sécurité),
- Trois classeurs d'archives,
- Liste de numéros de téléphones imprimés depuis la passerelle,
- Une carte nmr 4711 (sur laquelle la position du GRAND PRINCE à 11h04 LAT 47°46'S, LONG 073°44' E) a été reportée et signée par le capitaine,
- Une liste des déclaration des appareils de communication et électroniques détenus par le personnel du bord,
- Une liste de tabac et alcools détenus à bord.

et, en la présence constante du capitaine, apposons les scellés sur les objets appréhendés.
Nous lui notifions l'appréhension et le déclarons gardien des objets appréhendés.
Une traduction en espagnol a été effectuée par le patron des pêches Antonio SEVILLA LUSTRES, membre de l'équipage du navire "GRAND PRINCE".

Fait à bord du "GRAND PRINCE", le mardi 26 décembre 2000 à 2000 heures (E).

Le commandant
Le capitaine de frégate Marc LANNE,
commandant la frégate NIVOSE

L'auteur du délit

TRADUCTOR.

Le capitaine de corvette Gilles DEPELLEY,
commandant en second de la frégate NIVOSE

[ ] Transmis au directeur départemental des affaires maritimes de La Réunion le

Annex 7

Procès-verbal d'appréhension n° 06/00 (fishing gear) (in French)

DOC. 7º PROCES VERBAL D'APPREHENSION OF THE FISHING GEAR

MARINE NATIONALE

FORCE D'ACTION NAVALE

COMMANDEMENT MARITIME DE NOUVELLE CALEDONIE

FREGATE NIVOSE

PROCES VERBAL D'APPREHENSION

N° 06 / 00 NIVOSE

- L'an deux mille, le mardi 26 décembre 2000,
- Nous, soussigné Gilles DEPELLEY, capitaine de corvette, commandant en second de la frégate de surveillance «NIVOSE», en action de police des pêches,

Vu :
- La loi du 1er mars 1888 modifiée, relative à l'exercice de la pêche dans les eaux sous souveraineté ou juridiction française s'étendant au large des côtes des territoires d'outre mer;
- La loi 66-400 du 18 juin 1966 sur l'exercice de la pêche maritime et de l'exploitation des produits de la mer dans les Terres Australes et Antarctiques Françaises,
- La loi n° 83-582 du 5 juillet 1983 modifiée, relative au régime de la saisie et complétant la liste des agents habilités à constater les infractions dans le domaine des pêches maritimes,
- le décret n° 84-846 du 12 septembre 1984 fixant les modalités d'application de la loi 83-582 susvisée;

Nous trouvant à bord du «GRAND PRINCE» , à la position GPS: 47°24,7 SUD, 073°24,9 EST, agissant pour faire suite à l'infraction de pêche sans autorisation dans la ZEE de KERGUELEN à la position GPS 47°47' SUD, 073°44' EST, en route au 250 à 01 (un) nœuds, le mardi 26 décembre 2000 à 08h53 Echo, infraction constatée par le PV N°04/ NIVOSE en date du mardi 26 décembre 2000, établi à l'encontre de M. RAMON FRANCISCO PEREZ NOVO, né le 05/10/57 à RIBEIRA, capitaine du navire "GRAND PRINCE".

Déclarons procéder à l'appréhension sur le Navire "GRAND PRINCE", port d'attache BELIZE, des objets énumérés ci-dessous :

Engins de pêche :

- 5 bouées oranges numérotées de 2 à 5 et une bouée portant inscription "C" équipées de mâtereaux et boîtiers à batterie,
- 24 (vingt quatre) bouées roses portant l'inscription "POLYFORM N 6001 ALESUND MADE IN NORWAY" sur la partie bleue,
- 5 bouées oranges avec mât et avec dispositif lumineux numérotées 2, 3, 4, 6 et une sans numéro sur lesquelles est inscrit "75 DYNOPLAST AS ALESUND MADE IN NORWAY",
- 10 ancres de fond,
- 180 cagettes d'appâts gréés sur hameçons dans lignes de palangre.
- 40 (quarante) tonnes d'appâts congelés

Matériel électronique et électrique de pêche :

- Deux détecteurs de Balises KODEN-KS5131,
- Logements pour 12 lampes de bouées dont 9 sont en place,
- 7 batteries pour bouées gonio (5 de marque MOLL, 2 de marque TUDOR),
- 7 antennes fouet sur 1 chargeur de 10, antennes sur lesquelles est inscrit un numéro au marqueur, sur lesquelles est gravé un autre numéro et sur certaines figure l'inscription "GRAUTA R.ESP.11R (B)",
- 9 lampes sur un support et un carton de lampes pour bouées.

et, en la présence constante du capitaine, apposons les scellés sur les objets appréhendés.

Nous lui notifions l'appréhension et le déclarons gardien des objets appréhendés.
Une traduction en espagnol a été effectuée par le patron des pêches Antonio SEVILLA LUSTRES, membre de l'équipage du navire "GRAND PRINCE".
Fait à bord du "GRAND PRINCE", le mardi 26 décembre 2000 à 2000 heures (E).

Le commandant
Le capitaine de frégate Marc LANNE,
commandant la frégate NIVOSE

L'auteur du délit

TRADUCTOR.-

Le capitaine de corvette Gilles DEPELLEY,
commandant en second de la frégate NIVOSE

[ ] Transmis au directeur départemental des affaires maritimes de La Réunion le

Annex 8
Procès-verbal d'interpellation of 11 January 2001 (master) (in French)

PARQUET DU TRIBUNAL DE GRANDE INSTANCE DE SAINT- DENIS

PROCÈS-VERBAL D'INTERPELLATION

Le 11 janvier 2001

Devant Nous, Christian LAUQUE, Substitut de Monsieur le Procureur de la République prés le Tribunal de Grande Instance de SAINT DENIS
en présence de Mlle VAR Sophie interprète en espagnol.
(serment préalablement prêté)
est déférée la personne qui, sur interpellation, nous fournit les renseignements d'identité suivants

NOM	: **PEREZ NOVO**
PRÉNOM	: **Ramon Francisco**
NE LE	: **05 octobre 1957 à RIBEIRA**
DOMICILE	: **RIBEIRA (Espagne) rua DA CABALLEIRA 10 Ribeira**
PROFESSION	: **Capitaine de Navire**
SITUATION FAMILIALE	: **Marié**
NATIONALITÉ	: **Espagnole**
CONDAMNATIONS	: **se dit jamais condamné**

Vu les proces-verbaux n° 09/2001 P.C.G "La Jonquille" de la Gndarmerie maritime.

Nous lui donnons connaissance des faits qui lui sont reprochés :

I) d' avoir courant décembre 2000 et notamment à compter du 24 décembre 2000, depuis temps non prescrit, dans la zone économique exclusive des côtes du territoire de la République, en l'espèce au large des Iles Kerguelen, dans les Terres Australes et Antartiques françaises, étant capitaine du navire " Le grand Prince", battant pavillon étranger (BELIZE), omis de signaler son entrée dans la zone économique exclusive et de déclarer le tonnage de poisson détenu à bord.

Fait prévus et réprimés à l' article 1 de la loi du 01/03/1888 modifié par la loi du 05 juillet 1996, les articles 1, 2, 4, 9, 11 de la du 18 juin 1966 modifiée par la loi du 18 novembre 1997 et les articles 2 et 4 de la loi 83-582 du 05 juillet 1983.

II) d' avoir courant décembre 2000, notamment du 24 au 26 décembre 2000, depuis temps non prescrit, dans la zone économique exclusive des côtes du territoire de la République, en l'espèce au large des Iles KERGUELEN dans les Terres Australes et Antartiques françaises, étant capitaine du navire "Le grand Prince" battant pavillon étranger (Belize), pratiqué la pêche sans avoir obtenu d'autorisation préalable des Autorités compétentes.

Fait prévus et réprimés à l' article 1 de la loi du 01/03/1888 modifié par la loi du 05 juillet 1996, les articles 1, 2, 4, 9, 11 de la du 18 juin 1966 modifiée par la loi du 18 novembre 1997 et les articles 2 et 4 de la loi 83-582 du 05 juillet 1983.

Le comparant déclare:

Je reconnais les infractions mises à mon compte. En revanche mon action de pêche illégale à débuté à compter du 26 décembre 2000 et non le 24 décembre comme retenu dans la prévention. Comme le journal de navigation se clôturait à la date du 23 décembre 2000, nous n'avons pas eu le temps de renseigner le nouveau journal de navigation qui était enfermé dans une armoire. Je n'avais reçu de quiconque aucune instruction précise pour entamer une action de pêche en zone interdite.

Nous avertissons l'intéressé qu'il a droit de choisir un avocat ou de demander qu'il lui en soit désigné un d'office.

Il nous répond :

X je souhaite être assisté d'un avocat de mon choix : Maître ANTOINE du Barreau de Saint-Denis

Nous mentionnons que :

X Maître ANTOINE a pu communiquer librement avec le comparant

COMPARUTION PAR PROCES-VERBAL

Vu les articles 388, 393, et suivants du CPP,
Nous avisons l'intéressé que par procès-verbal de ce jour, il sera cité à comparaître des chefs de qualification sus-visés à l'audience du Tribunal correctionnel qui se tiendra le:

MARDI 23 JANVIER 2001 à 08 heures.

Nous informons l'interessé que nous le traduisons immédiatement M./Mme le Magistrat délégué pour que soit pris à son encontre une mesure de contrôle judiciaire.

LA PRÉSENTE NOTIFICATION VALANT CITATION A PERSONNE

Après lecture , le prévenu signe avec Nous

LE PRÉVENU **LE SUBSTITUT**

Ch.LAUQUE

Reçu copie intégra le LE PRÉVENU

Annex 9
Procès-verbal de saisie n° 13/AM/2001 **(vessel) (in French)**

REPUBLIQUE FRANCAISE
PREFECTURE DE LA REUNION

Direction Régional et départementale
Des Affaires Maritimes

Le DIRECTEUR

N°13/AM/2001 **PROCES VERBAL DE SAISIE**

Vu la loi du 1er mars 1888 modifiée relative à l'exercice de la pêche dans les eaux sous souveraineté ou juridiction française s'étendant au large des territoires d'outre mer ;

Vu la loi n°66-400 du 18 juin 1966 modifiée sur l'exercice de la pêche maritime et l'exploitation des produits de la mer dans les Terres Australes et Antarctiques Françaises ;

Vu la loi n°83-582 du 5 juillet 1983 modifiée relative au régime de la saisie et complétant la liste des agents habilités à constater les infractions dans le domaine des pêches maritimes ;

Vu le décret N°84-846 du 12 septembre 1984 fixant les modalités d'application de la loi précitée ;

Vu le procès verbal d'infraction N° 4/00 du 26 décembre 2000 dressé à l'encontre de Monsieur Ramon Francisco PEREZ NOVO né le 5 octobre 1957 à RIBEIRA (Espagne), capitaine du navire «GRAND PRINCE » battant pavillon du BELIZE au moment des faits, cet Etat ayant radié le « GRAND PRINCE » de ses registres à la suite de cette infraction, ayant pour armateur PAIK COMMERCIAL CORPORATION à BELIZE, par le capitaine de frégate Marc LANNE, commandant la frégate NIVOSE.

-pour action de pêche illicite dans les eaux des Terres Australes et Antarctiques françaises .

-pour non déclaration de son entrée en zone économique sous juridiction française,

CONSIDERANT que les infractions sont caractérisées par les faits suivants :

1/ Constatation de la présence du navire «GRAND PRINCE » en action de pêche à l'intérieur de la zone économique française par 47° 49'Sud et 073° 45' Est(95 milles au nord nord/est de Kerguelen le 26 décembre 2000 à 8 H 58.

2/ Constatation de l'absence de déclaration d'entrée en ZEE de Kerguelen.

3/ Constatation de la présence à l'eau d'une palangre, sectionnée par le bord lors du survol par l'hélicoptère, et à 500 mètres du navire de matériel de pêche identique à celui du GRAND PRINCE.

4/ Présence dans l'usine de 200 cagettes d'appâts préparés accrochés sur des hameçons à une ligne

5/ Constatation de la présence de 16 légines fraiches à proximité du poste de remontée de palangre, de 10 légines en cours de lavage dans un bac, de 3 légines fraiches dans un autre bac

6/ Constatation d'un usage très récent de l'usine récent de l'usine qui n'a pas été nettoyée

7/ Constatation de la présence de 54 cartons de poisson à des températures comprises entre – 1 degré et – 12 degrés dans les tunnels de congélation

8/ Constatation de la présence d'environ 18 tonnes de légine à bord

Vu le procès verbal d'appréhension du navire N° 7/00 du 26 décembre 2000, établi à l'issue du procès --verbal d'infraction précité par le capitaine de frégate Marc LANNE à l'encontre du capitaine Ramon Francisco PEREZ NOVO, du navire « GRAND PRINCE».

DECIDE

Par le présent procès-verbal de procéder à la saisie du navire GRAND PRINCE et de tous ses appareils et matériels de navigation et de communication ainsi que les documents de bord. L'ensemble est évalué à 13 millions de francs (1 981 837 euros).

DECIDE que le navire sera placé à quai au port des galets . Le navire pourra être déplacé sur ordre du commandant du Port des Galets

Désigne solidairement le capitaine Ramon Francisco PEREZ NOVO et l'armateur du GRAND PRINCE gardiens de la saisie jusqu'à ce qu'ordre soit donné de décharger.

INFORME M Ramon Francisco PEREZ NOVO et l'armateur que main levée de la saisie concernant le navire «GRAND PRINCE» pourra être prononcée par le juge d'instance de Saint-Paul contre versement de la caution dont celui-ci aura fixé le montant en vertu de l'article L 142 du code de procédure pénale .

Evalue les frais de cette procédure à 5 000 francs (762 Euros) qui seront à la charge du contrevenant.

INFORME le gardien de la saisie que quiconque aura détruit, détourné ou tenté de détruire ou détourner les engins, matériels, équipements, instruments, navires, embarcations ou produits de la pêche saisis et confiés à sa garde, sera puni d'une peine d'emprisonnement de deux mois à deux ans et d'une amende de 3 600 Francs (548,82 Euros) à 2 500 000 Francs (381 122,54 Euros) ou l'une de ces deux peines seulement, et que ces mêmes peines seront applicables à quiconque aura fait obstacle à la saisie ou à appréhension des engins, matériels, instruments, équipements, navires ou embarcations utilisés pour ces pêches en infraction aux dispositions législatives ou réglementaires ainsi que les produits de ces pêche ou des sommes provenant de leur vente (article 9 de la loi 83-582 du 5 juillet 1983).

Interprète Melle BAILLIF Alexandra

9:45 HORAS - 11/01/01 A Saint Denis le 11 JAN. 2001

L'administrateur en chef, Directeur régional et départemental des affaires maritimes de la Réunion

E. de CHAVANES

Annex 10
Procès-verbal de saisie n° 11/AM/2001 **(fishing material) (in French)**

REPUBLIQUE FRANCAISE
PREFECTURE DE LA REUNION

Direction Régional et départementale
Des Affaires Maritimes

Le DIRECTEUR

N°11/AM/2001 **PROCES VERBAL DE SAISIE**

Vu la loi du 1er mars 1888 modifiée relative à l'exercice de la pêche dans les eaux sous souveraineté ou juridiction française s'étendant au large des territoires d'outre mer ;

Vu la loi n°66-400 du 18 juin 1966 modifiée sur l'exercice de la pêche maritime et l'exploitation des produits de la mer dans les Terres Australes et Antarctiques Françaises ;

Vu la loi n°83-582 du 5 juillet 1983 modifiée relative au régime de la saisie et complétant la liste des agents habilités à constater les infractions dans le domaine des pêches maritimes ;

Vu le décret N°84-846 du 12 septembre 1984 fixant les modalités d'application de la loi précitée ;

Vu le procès verbal d'infraction N° 4/00 du 26 décembre 2000 dressé à l'encontre de Monsieur Ramon Francisco PEREZ NOVO né le 5 octobre 1957 à RIBEIRA (Espagne), capitaine du navire [illegible]INCE » battant pavillon du BELIZE au moment des faits, cet Etat ayant radié le « GRAND PRINCE » de ses registres à la suite de cette infraction, ayant pour armateur PAIK COMMERCIAL CORPORATION à BELIZE, par le capitaine de frégate Marc LANNE, commandant la frégate NIVOSE.

-pour action de pêche illicite dans les eaux des Terres Australes et Antarctiques françaises .

-pour non déclaration de son entrée en zone économique sous juridiction française,

CONSIDERANT que les infractions sont caractérisées par les faits suivants :

1/ Constatation de la présence du navire «GRAND PRINCE » en action de pêche à l'intérieur de la zone économique française par 47° 49'Sud et 073° 45' Est(95 milles au nord nord/est de Kerguelen le 26 décembre 2000 à 8 H 58.

2/ Constatation de l'absence de déclaration d'entrée en ZEE de Kerguelen.

3/ Constatation de la présence à l'eau d'une palangre, sectionnée par le bord lors du survol par l'hélicoptère, et à 500 mètres du navire de matériel de pêche identique à celui du GRAND PRINCE.

4/ Présence dans l'usine de 200 cagottes d'appâts préparés accrochés sur des hameçons à une ligne

5/ Constatation de la présence de 16 légines fraiches à proximité du poste de remontée de palangre, de 10 légines en cours de lavage dans un bac, de 3 légines fraiches dans un autre bac

6/ Constatation d'un usage très récent de l'usine récent de l'usine qui n'a pas été nettoyée

7/ Constatation de la présence de 54 cartons de poisson à des températures comprises entre – 1 degré et – 12 degrés dans les tunnels de congélation

8/ Constatation de la présence d'environ 18 tonnes de légine à bord

Vu le procès verbal d'appréhension des engins et matériel de pêche N° 6/00 du 26 décembre 2000, établi à l'issue du procès –verbal d'infraction précité par le capitaine de frégate Marc LANNE à l'encontre du capitaine Ramon Francisco PEREZ NOVO, du navire « GRAND PRINCE»

DECIDE

Par le présent procès-verbal de procéder à la saisie de la tot[illegible]s de [illegible](hors appâts, ceux ci faisant l'objet d'un traitement séparé) d'une valeur estimée [illegible] (5 610 euros).

Désigne solidairement le capitaine Ramon Francisco PEREZ NOVO et l'armateur du GRAND PRINCE gardiens de la saisie jusqu'à ce que le juge du fond en ordonne la destination.

INFORME le gardien de la saisie que quiconque aura détruit, détourné ou tenté de détruire ou détourner les engins, matériels, équipements, instruments, navires, embarcations ou produits de la pêche saisis et confiés à sa garde, sera puni d'une peine d'emprisonnement de deux mois à deux ans et d'une amende de 3 600 Francs (548,82 Euros) à 2 500 000 Francs (381 122,54 Euros) ou l'une de ces deux peines seulement, et que ces mêmes peines seront applicables à quiconque aura fait obstacle à la saisie ou à appréhension des engins, matériels, instruments, équipements, navires ou embarcations utilisés pour ces pêches en infraction aux dispositions législatives ou réglementaires ainsi que les produits de ces pêche ou des sommes provenant de leur vente (article 9 de la loi 83-582 du 5 juillet 1983).

Interprète
Melle BAILLIF

Signé le CAPITAINE
8:50 HORAS / 11/01/01

Fait et clos à SAINT- DENIS
Le 11 JAN. 2001

L'administrateur en chef,
Directeur régional et départemental
des affaires maritimes de la Réunion

E. de CHAVANES

Annex 11
Procès-verbal de saisie n° 12/AM/2001 **(fishing gear) (in French)**

PREFECTURE DE LA REUNION

CABNADA

Direction Régional et départementale
Des Affaires Maritimes

DOC. 11º COPY OF THE ACT OF PROCES VERBAL DE SAISIE OF THE FISHING GEAR

Le DIRECTEUR

N°12/AM/2001

PROCES VERBAL DE SAISIE

Vu la loi du 1er mars 1888 modifiée relative à l'exercice de la pêche dans les eaux sous souveraineté ou juridiction française s'étendant au large des territoires d'outre mer ;

Vu la loi n°66-400 du 18 juin 1966 modifiée sur l'exercice de la pêche maritime et l'exploitation des produits de la mer dans les Terres Australes et Antarctiques Françaises ;

Vu la loi n°83-582 du 5 juillet 1983 modifiée relative au régime de la saisie et complétant la liste des agents habilités à constater les infractions dans le domaine des pêches maritimes ;

Vu le décret N°84-846 du 12 septembre 1984 fixant les modalités d'application de la loi précitée ;

Vu le procès verbal d'infraction N° 4/00 du 26 décembre 2000 dressé à l'encontre de Monsieur Ramon Francisco PEREZ NOVO né le 5 octobre 1957 à RIBEIRA (Espagne), capitaine du navire « GRAND PRINCE » battant pavillon du BELIZE au moment des faits, cet Etat ayant radié le « GRAND PRINCE » de ses registres à la suite de cette infraction, ayant pour armateur PAIK COMMERCIAL CORPORATION à BELIZE, par le capitaine de frégate Marc LANNE, commandant la frégate NIVOSE.

-pour action de pêche illicite dans les eaux des Terres Australes et Antarctiques françaises .

-pour non déclaration de son entrée en zone économique sous juridiction française,

CONSIDERANT que les infractions sont caractérisées par les faits suivants :

1/ Constatation de la présence du navire «GRAND PRINCE » en action de pêche à l'intérieur de la zone économique française par 47° 49'Sud et 073° 45' Est(95 milles au nord nord/est de Kerguelen le 26 décembre 2000 à 8 H 58.

2/ Constatation de l'absence de déclaration d'entrée en ZEE de Kerguelen.

3/ Constatation de la présence à l'eau d'une palangre, sectionnée par le bord lors du survol par l'hélicoptère, et à 500 mètres du navire de matériel de pêche identique à celui du GRAND PRINCE.

4/ Présence dans l'usine de 200 cagettes d'appâts préparés accrochés sur des hameçons à une ligne

5/ Constatation de la présence de 16 légines fraiches à proximité du poste de remontée de palangre, de 10 légines en cours de lavage dans un bac, de 3 légines fraiches dans un autre bac

6/ Constatation d'un usage très récent de l'usine récent de l'usine qui n'a pas été nettoyée

7/ Constatation de la présence de 54 cartons de poisson à des températures comprises entre – 1 degré et – 12 degrés dans les tunnels de congélation

8/ Constatation de la présence d'environ 18 tonnes de légine à bord

Vu le procès verbal d'appréhension des engins de pêche, du produit de la pêche, du matériel de navigation et de transmission, des documents de bord N° 06/00 du 26 décembre 2000, établi à l'issue du procès –verbal d'infraction précité par le capitaine de frégate Marc LANNE à l'encontre du capitaine Ramon Francisco PEREZ NOVO, du navire « GRAND PRINCE».

DECIDE

Par le présent procès-verbal de procéder à la saisie de la totalité des appâts détenus à bord (environ 40 tonnes), considérés comme du matériel de pêche. Evalue ceci en valeur normale du marché à 160 000 francs (1 049 531 euros).

Décide que le poisson sera vendu par appel d'offre et que le produit de la vente sera consigné au Trésor Public jusqu'à ce que le juge du fond en ordonne la destination.

Désigne solidairement le capitaine Ramon Francisco PEREZ NOVO et l'armateur du GRAND PRINCE gardiens de la saisie jusqu'à ce qu'ordre soit donné de décharger.

Evalue les frais de cette procédure à 50 000 francs (7 622 Euros) qui seront à la charge du contrevenant.

INFORME le gardien de la saisie que quiconque aura détruit, détourné ou tenté de détruire ou détourner les engins, matériels, équipements, instruments, navires, embarcations ou produits de la pêche saisis et confiés à sa garde, sera puni d'une peine d'emprisonnement de deux mois à deux ans et d'une amende de 3 600 Francs (548,82 Euros) à 2 500 000 Francs (381 122,54 Euros) ou l'une de ces deux peines seulement, et que ces mêmes peines seront applicables à quiconque aura fait obstacle à la saisie ou à appréhension des engins, matériels, instruments, équipements, navires ou embarcations utilisés pour ces pêches en infraction aux dispositions législatives ou réglementaires ainsi que les produits de ces pêche ou des sommes provenant de leur vente (article 9 de la loi 83-582 du 5 juillet 1983).

8:50 HORAS / 11/01/01

L'Interprète
Mlle BAILLIF

Fait et clos à SAINT-DENIS
Le 11 JAN. 2001

L'administrateur en chef,
Directeur régional et départemental
des affaires maritimes de la Réunion

E. de CHAVANES

Annex 12

Procès-verbal de saisie nº 10/AM/2001 **(fish on board) (in French)**

REPUBLIQUE FRANCAISE
PREFECTURE DE LA REUNION

Direction Régional et départementale
Des Affaires Maritimes

Le DIRECTEUR

N°10/AM/2001 **PROCES VERBAL DE SAISIE**

Vu la loi du 1er mars 1888 modifiée relative à l'exercice de la pêche dans les eaux sous souveraineté ou juridiction française s'étendant au large des territoires d'outre mer ;

Vu la loi n°66-400 du 18 juin 1966 modifiée sur l'exercice de la pêche maritime et l'exploitation des produits de la mer dans les Terres Australes et Antarctiques Françaises ;

Vu la loi n°83-582 du 5 juillet 1983 modifiée relative au régime de la saisie et complétant la liste des agents habilités à constater les infractions dans le domaine des pêches maritimes ;

Vu le décret N°84-846 du 12 septembre 1984 fixant les modalités d'application de la loi précitée ;

Vu le procès verbal d'infraction N° 4/00 du 26 décembre 2000 dressé à l'encontre de Monsieur Ramon Francisco PEREZ NOVO né le 5 octobre 1957 à RIBEIRA (Espagne), capitaine du navire «GRAND PRINCE » battant pavillon du BELIZE au moment des faits, cet Etat ayant radié le «GRAND PRINCE » de ses registres à la suite de cette infraction, ayant pour armateur PAIK COMMERCIAL CORPORATION à BELIZE, par le capitaine de frégate Marc LANNE, commandant la frégate NIVOSE.

-pour action de pêche illicite dans les eaux des Terres Australes et Antarctiques françaises.

-pour non déclaration de son entrée en zone économique sous juridiction française,

CONSIDERANT que les infractions sont caractérisées par les faits suivants :

1/ Constatation de la présence du navire «GRAND PRINCE » en action de pêche à l'intérieur de la zone économique française par 47° 49'Sud et 073° 45' Est(95 milles au nord nord/est de Kerguelen le 26 décembre 2000 à 8 H 58.

2/ Constatation de l'absence de déclaration d'entrée en ZEE de Kerguelen.

3/ Constatation de la présence à l'eau d'une palangre, sectionnée par le bord lors du survol par l'hélicoptère, et à 500 mètres du navire de matériel de pêche identique à celui du GRAND PRINCE.

4/ Présence dans l'usine de 200 cagettes d'appâts préparés accrochés sur des hameçons à une ligne

5/ Constatation de la présence de 16 légines fraiches à proximité du poste de remontée de palangre, de 10 légines en cours de lavage dans un bac, de 3 légines fraiches dans un autre bac

6/ Constatation d'un usage très récent de l'usine récent de l'usine qui n'a pas été nettoyée

7/ Constatation de la présence de 54 cartons de poisson à des températures comprises entre – 1 degré et – 12 degrés dans les tunnels de congélation

8/ Constatation de la présence d'environ 18 tonnes de légine à bord

Vu le procès verbal d'appréhension du produit de la pêche N° 5/00 du 26 décembre 2000, établi à l'issue du procès –verbal d'infraction précité par le capitaine de frégate Marc LANNE à l'encontre du capitaine Ramon Francisco PEREZ NOVO, du navire « GRAND PRINCE».

DECIDE

Par le présent procès-verbal de procéder à la saisie de la totalité [illegible] bord.
Evalue ceci en valeur normale du marché à 810 000 francs [illegible] le cour actuel de la légine se situant à 45 francs du kilo (6,86 euros).
Décide que le poisson sera vendu par appel d'offre et que le produit de la vente sera consigné au Trésor Public jusqu'à ce que le juge du fond en ordonne la destination.

Désigne solidairement le capitaine Ramon Francisco PERÈZ NOVO et l'armateur du GRAND PRINCE gardiens de la saisie jusqu'à ce qu'ordre soit donné de décharger.

Evalue les frais de cette procédure à 90 000 francs (13 720 Euros) qui seront à la charge du contrevenant.

INFORME le gardien de la saisie que quiconque aura détruit, détourné ou tenté de détruire ou détourner les engins, matériels, équipements, instruments, navires, embarcations ou produits de la pêche saisis et confiés à sa garde, sera puni d'une peine d'emprisonnement de deux mois à deux ans et d'une amende de 3 600 Francs (548,82 Euros) à 2 500 000 Francs (381 122,54 Euros) ou l'une de ces deux peines seulement, et que ces mêmes peines seront applicables à quiconque aura fait obstacle à la saisie ou à appréhension des engins, matériels, instruments, équipements, navires ou embarcations utilisés pour ces pêches en infraction aux dispositions législatives ou réglementaires ainsi que les produits de ces pêche ou des sommes provenant de leur vente (article 9 de la loi 83-582 du 5 juillet 1983).

Interprète
[illegible] BAILLIF
[signature]

Signé le CAPITAINE
8:50 HORAS/11/01/01
[signature]

Fait et clos à SAINT- DENIS
Le 11 JAN. 2001

L'administrateur en chef,
Directeur régional et départemental
des affaires maritimes de la Réunion

[signature]

E. de CHAVANES

Annex 13
Ordonnance n° 3/2001 of 12 January 2001 of the Tribunal d'instance at Saint-Paul (in French)
– English translation (not reproduced)

TRIBUNAL D'INSTANCE
DE
SAINT-PAUL

B.P. 61 97862 SAINT-PAUL

ORDONNANCE n°3/2001

L'an deux mil un, et le douze janvier à quatorze heures,

Nous, Frank ROBAIL, juge au tribunal de Saint-Paul ;

Assisté de Joëlle GRONDIN, FF de greffier ;

Vu la requête de Monsieur le Directeur Régional et Départemental des Affaires Maritimes de la Réunion, en date du 11 anvier 2001,

Vu l'article 3 de la loi n°83-582 du 5 juillet 1983 modifiée, relative au régime de la saisie ;

Vu la convention des Nations Unies sur le droit de la mer en date du 10 décembre 1982 ;

Vu le procès-verbal d'infractions n°4/00 dressé 26 décembre 2000, à l'encontre de monsieur Ramon Francisco PEREZ NOVO, capitaine du navire (navire de pêche dénommé "GRAND PRINCE") ; pour action de pêche illicite dans les eaux de la zone économique exclusive des iles Kerguelen ;

Vu le procès-verbal de saisie n°13/AM/2001 en date du 11 janvier 2001 ;

Attendu que le Directeur régional et départemental des Affaires Maritimes de la Réunion sollicite la confirmation de la saisie du navire dont le capitaine et l'armateur ont été constitués gardiens ;

Attendu que cette autorité, après avoir évalué, dans le procès-verbal de saisie susvisé, le produit de la pêche illégale à environ 18 tonnes de légine, demande à notre juridiction d'autoriser la main-levée de cette saisie sous la condition du paiement préalable d'une caution de 17 millions de francs augmentée des frais de justice entre les mains de la Caisse des Dépôts et Consignations, cette somme devant garantir notamment le paiement de la pénalité prévue par la loi n°66-400 du 18 juin 1968 modifiée, et encourue en cas de pêche illicite dans les Terres Australes et Antarctiques Françaises ;

Attendu que la procédure de saisie du navire apparaît régulière, en la forme comme au fond, que la requête en confirmation de cette saisie nous est présentée dans le respect des délais légaux ; qu'il convient dès lors de la valider ;

Attendu que le navire est entré dans la zone économique exclusive des T.A.A.F. sans autorisation préalable, et sans signaler sa présence ni déclarer le tonnage de poisson détenu à bord auprès du chef de district de l'archipel le plus proche, et ce en contravention avec les dispositions de l'article 2 de la loi 66-400 du 13 juin 1966 modifiée par la loi du 18 novembre 1997 ; qu'il a été constaté à bord la présence d'environ 18 tonnes de légine ; que le fait que le navire ait été surpris dans la zone économique exclusive sans avoir signalé sa présence ni déclaré la quantité de poisson détenu, fait présumer que la totalité des prises a été illégalement pêchée dans la zone économique exclusive ;

Attendu qu'au vu de ces éléments, la main-levée de la saisie ne pourra se faire que sous la condition du paiement préalable d'une caution fixée en application des dispositions de l'article 4 de la loi du 18 juin 1966 modifiée (par la loi du 18 novembre 1997), et de l'article 142 du Code de procédure pénale.

Attendu que s'agissant du montant de cette caution, il résulte des dispositions des articles 73 § 2 et 292 de la convention des Nations Unies sur le droit de la mer qu' il doit être " raisonnable", ce critère signifiant plus précisément que l'équilibre global à établir entre le montant, la forme et la nature de cette caution doit être raisonnable ;

Attendu que l'évaluation de ce caractère raisonnable ressort de la gravité des infractions reprochées au propriétaire du navire immobilisé, des sanctions pouvant être imposées par les lois de l'Etat immobilisateur, la valeur du navire immobilisé ;

Attendu que par surcroît, ce cautionnement doit garantir à la fois :

1 - la représentation de la personne à l'encontre de qui le procès-verbal d'infraction a été dressé,

2 - et le paiement des amendes encourues ;

Attendu que le navire de pêche en cause a été évalué par monsieur CHANCEREL, expert maritime, à 13.000.000,00 FF ; que les amendes encourues par le capitaine du navire doivent être évaluées, sur la base de 18 tonnes de poisson illégalement pêchés et des dispositions de la loi du 18 juin 1966 modifié, à un montant maximal de 9.000.000,00 FF (sur la base d'une amende de 1.000.000,00 FF augmentée de 500.000,00 FF par tonne pêchée au delà de deux tonnes) ; qu'enfin les victimes se voient attribuer généralement des indemnités de moins de 400.000,00 FF ;

Attendu que par suite il échet de fixer comme suit le cautionnement demandé :

- pour garantir la représentation du capitaine de navire appréhendé : 1.000.000,00 FF,

- pour garantir le paiement des dommages causés par les infractions relevées : 400.000,00 FF,

- pour garantir le paiement des amendes encourues et la confiscation du navire : 10.000.000,00 FF

de sorte qu'au total la caution sera fixée à la somme de 11.400.000,00 FF. 1 737 918 Euros

Attendu que si les modalités de paiement de cette caution sont également une composante du caractère raisonnable de celle-ci qu'impose la convention internationale sus-visée, il apparaît raisonnable, compte tenu de l'équilibre global sus-défini, d'imposer un paiement, soit en espèces, soit par chèque certifié, soit par chèque de banque ;

PAR CES MOTIFS

Nous, Frank ROBAIL, juge au tribunal d'instance de Saint-Paul, statuant sur requête,

CONFIRMONS la saisie du navire en date du 08 janvier 2001 ;

DISONS que la main-levée de cette saisie se fera sous paiement, entre les mains de la Caisse des Dépôts et Consignations, d'une caution d'un montant total de 11.400.000,00 FF (onze millions quatre cent mille francs) soit 1.737.918,70 EUR (un million sept cent trente sept mille neuf cent dix huit euros et soixante dix cents) soit en espèces, soit en chèque certifié soit en chèque bancaire.

EN FOI DE QUOI LA PRESENTE ORDONNANCE A ETE SIGNEE PAR LE PRESIDENT ET LE GREFFIER.

LE GREFFIER **LE PRESIDENT**

TRIBUNAL D'INSTANCE DE SAINT-PAUL – LA RÉUNION –

Annex 14
Letter from Mr Penelas Alvarez to the *Direction des affaires maritimes de la Réunion* dated 7 February 2001, with fax transmission report (in Spanish) (not reproduced)
– English translation

TRANSLATION OF DOCUMENT NUMBER 14 (PAGE 1) - "FAX TO THE MARITIME AUTHORITIES IN REUNION JUSTIFYING THE FISHING LICENCE"

TO.- DIRECTION DES AFFAIRES MARITIMES DE LA REUNION
ATT.- VICENT ESCLAPEZ FAX 262 217057
FROM ALBERYTO PENELAS
REF.- F/V FRAND PRINCE
TOTAL PAGES 2 (THIS ONE INC)

DEAR VICENT

FOLLOWING MY FAX OF THIS MORNING, AND AS PER THE REQUEST OF ERIK, I ENCLOSE FOR YOUR NOTICE CERTIFICATION OF THE BRAZIL ENTITY WHICH HANDLED THE PROJECT , REFFLAGING AND LICENCE OF GRAND PRINCE IN BRAZIL.

AS I MENTIONED , WE HAVE OBTAINED AN EXTENTION OF APPROX. ONE MONTH IN ORDER NOT TO LOOSE ALL THE OPERATION.

REMAINING PENDENT OF YOUR NEWS, I SEND YOU REGARDS.

ALBERTO PENELAS

I CERTIFY THAT WHAT PRECEDES IS THE TRUE AND FAITHFUL TRANSLATION FROM SPANISH TO ENGLISH LANGUAGE OF DOCUMENT NUMBER 14 (PAGE 1) - "FAX TO THE MARITIME AUTHORITIES IN REUNION JUSTIFYING THE FISHING LICENCE"

21 MARCH 2001

ALBERTO PENELAS ALVAREZ
AGENT

Annex 14 -1
Certification from *Pesqueira da Paraiba Ltda* concerning fishing licence to be received from Brazil (in Spanish) (not reproduced) – English translation

TRANSLATION OF DOCUMENT NUMBER 14 (PAGE 2) - "FAX TO THE MARITIME AUTHORITIES IN REUNION JUSTIFYING THE FISHING LICENCE"

PESQUEIRA DA PARAIBA LTDA

CABEDELO , 22 DECEMBER 2000

TO WHICH CORRESPONDS

WE HEREBY LEAVE NOTICE THAT IN THE MONTH OF OCTOBER OF 2000 THIS COMPANY COMMENCED ALL THE NECESSARY ARRANGEMENTS FOR THE NACIONALIZATION AND REFFLAGING OF THE FISHING VESSEL GRAND PRINCE

THE FISHING DEPARTMENT OF THE MINISTRY OF AGRICULTURE AND PROVISIONING OF BRAZIL , HAS ALREADY GRANTED US A FISHING LICENCE FOR THE MENTIONED VESSEL ONCE IT HAD BEEN NACIONALISED.

WE EXPECT TO RECEIVE THE OFFICAL COMMUNICATION FROM THE MINISTRY IN A FEW DAYS

ONCE RECEIVED IT WILL BE DIRECTED INMEDIATLY VIA FAX FOR THE EFFECTS WHICH CORRESPOND.

WE REMAIN AT TOTAL DISPOSAL FOR ANY ADDICIONAL INFORMATION

REGARDS
FOR PESQUEIRA DA PARAIBA
ALDO F. GLAVERIE

I CERTIFY THAT WHAT PRECEDES IS THE TRUE AND FAITHFUL TRANSLATION FROM SPANISH TO ENGLISH LANGUAGE OF DOCUMENT NUMBER 14 (PAGE 2) - "FAX TO THE MARITIME AUTHORITIES IN REUNION JUSTIFYING THE FISHING LICENCE"

21 MARCH 2001

ALBERTO PENELAS ALVAREZ
AGENT

Annex 15
Request for the release of the vessel addressed by the owner of the *Grand Prince* to the *Tribunal d'instance* of Saint-Paul dated 19 February 2001 (in French)

REQUETE

A Monsieur le Président
du
TRIBUNAL D'INSTANCE DE SAINT-PAUL

La Société PAIK COMMERCIAL CORP propriétaire du navire de pêche "Grand Prince" domiciliés en cette qualité audit siège.

Ayant pour avocat, Maître Alain ANTOINE, Avocat au Barreau de Saint-Denis, demeurant 266 rue du Maréchal Leclerc - BP 122 - 97463 SAINT-DENIS Cedex, lequel se constitue et occupera sur la présente et ses suites.

A L'HONNEUR DE VOUS EXPOSER :

Que la société requérante est propriétaire du navire Grand Prince;

Que suivant ordonnance rendue N° 3/ 2001 du 12 janvier 2001, la juridiction de Céans a confirmé la saisie du navire pratiquée suivant P.V. de saisie N° 13/AM/2001 et dit que la main-levée de cette saisie pourrait se faire sous paiement entre les mains de la Caisse de Dépôt et Consignation de la somme de 11.400.000,00Francs.

Que le Tribunal Correctionnel de Saint-Denis, suivant jugement rendu le 23 janvier 2001, a prononcé à titre de peine principale, assortie de l'exécution provisoire, la confiscation du navire

Attendu que la société requérante requiert qu'il vous plaise bien vouloir dire que malgré le jugement sus-visé, et en application des dispositions de l'article 73 § 2 de la convention des Nations Unies sur le Droit de la Mer, la main-levée de la confiscation du Navire Grand-Prince se fera dès présentation **d'une garantie bancaire,** en garantie du paiement de la somme de 11.400,000,00F ou tout autre montant résultant soit d'un jugement définitif soit d'un accord, à concurrence de 11.400.000,00F

Et se sera justice.

Fait à Saint-Denis le 19/02/01

ORDONNANCE

Nous,

Vu la requête qui précède et par les motifs y exposés,

Disons que malgré le jugement rendu par le Tribunal Correctionnel de Saint-Denis le 23/01/2001, en application des dispositions de l'article 73 § 2 de la convention des Nations Unies sur le Droit de la Mer, la main-levée de la confiscation du Navire Grand-Prince se fera dès présentation **d'une garantie bancaire**, en garantie du paiement de la somme de 11.400.000,00F ou tout autre montant résultant soit d'un jugement définitif soit d'un accord, à concurrence de 11.400.000,00F

Fait en notre Cabinet à SAINT-PAUL
le ....

Le Greffier | Le Président

Annex 16
Ordonnance nº 6/2001 of 22 February 2001 of the *Tribunal d'instance* at Saint Paul (in French)

TRIBUNAL D'INSTANCE DE ST PAUL
BP 61 Quai Brest

97862 SAINT PAUL CEDEX
☎ :45.33.50

DOC. 16º ORDENNANCE Nº 6/2001 OF THE TRIBUNAL D'INSTANCE OF SAINT PAUL REJECTING THE REQUEST FOR RELEASE THE SHIP

R.G. 14-01-06
Stè PAIK COMMERCIAL CORP
Navire de pêche "Grand Prince

ORDONNANCE N°6/2001

Nous Frank ROBAIL, juge chargé du tribunal d'instance de Saint-Paul,

Attendu que le tribunal correctionnel a ordonné confiscation du navire en litige avec exécution provisoire ; que par suite, le juge de ce siège n'est plus compétent pour ordonner la remise dudit navire à son propriétaire ou capitaine au vu d'une simple garantie bancaire ;

P A R C E S M O T I F S

REJETONS la demande de la société PAIK COMMERCIAL CORP.

Fait à Saint-Paul, le 22 février 2001,

Le président,

F. ROBAIL

Annex 17
Valuation of the *Grand Prince* from Mr Carceller Vilalta of *TAXO Valoración, S.L.* (in Spanish) (not reproduced), with annexes:
– general arrangement drawing

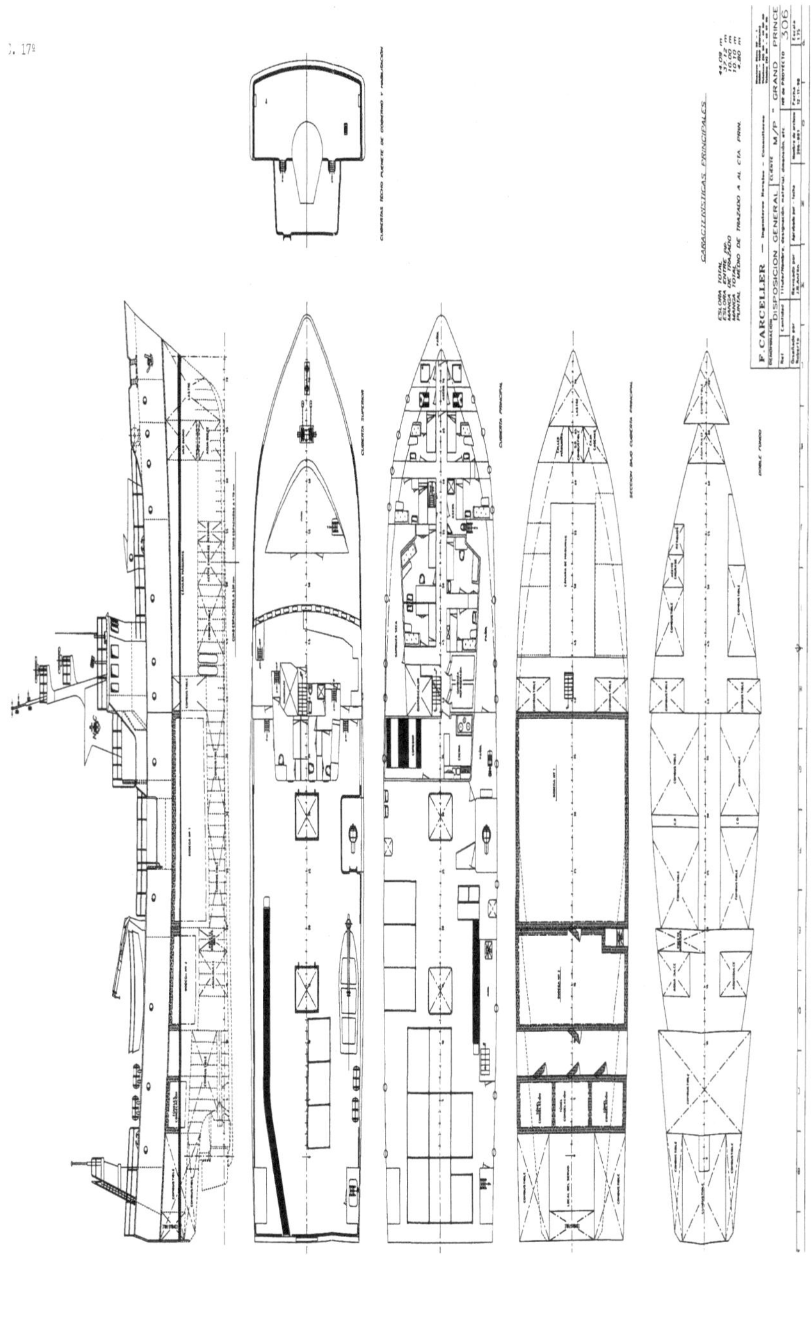

Annex 17 (continued)
– Provisional Patent of Navigation (reproduced as Annex 3 of the Application)

Annex 17 (continued)
– R.I.N.A.: Certificate of Class

REGISTRO ITALIANO NAVALE

RI 76707
RINA Register No.

CERTIFICATE OF CLASS

6701656
IMO number

N. 9902433

Dist. No. / letters V3UJ7

Name GRAND PRINCE

Category MOTORSHIP

Owner NOYCAN S.L. - MOANA - VIGO

Shipyard - Place of build PORT WELLER DRY DOCKS LTD.

Port of registry - No. BELIZE Flag BELIZE

Date of build	01.1967			Date of commissioning	01.1967
Length (moulded)	37.34 m				
Breadth (moulded)	10.01 m	Gross tonnage	534.75 tons	No. of main engines	1
Depth (moulded)	4.81 m	Net tonnage	—	Total power	1103 KW

THIS IS TO CERTIFY that the above ship has been surveyed in accordance with the RINA Rules and, on the basis of the survey report submitted, has been assigned the class (*)

100 - A - 1.1 - Nav IL ; Pes

based on the maximum draught of 3,516 m from the underside of the keel

with special notations —

for a period of class of (years : months) 5 : 0 running from 01.1999

This certificate will be invalidated whenever the requirements of the Rules are not complied with.

Issued at Genova on 23.06.1999

The Director General

This certificate is only valid provided it also contains the pages with the expiry dates of periodical surveys and the endorsements.
(*) Trade and service are described at page 2.

Form CLASSE2-Cer-EE-7/92

RI 76707 Ship's name **GRAND PRINCE** Certificate No. **9902433** Page 2 of 5

Former ship's names

Type of survey	Due date	Frequency	Range(months)	
SPECIAL	01.2004			
HULL ORDINARY	01.2000	Annual (01.2000 - 01.2001 - 01.2002 - 01.2003)	-3	+3
MACHINERY ORDINARY	01.2000	Annual (01.2000 - 01.2001 - 01.2002 - 01.2003)	-3	+3
DRYDOCKING	07.2001	2 years and 6 months from last survey		+6
TAILSHAFT	01.2004	5 years from last survey		+6
In lieu of the 2nd or 3rd Ordinary survey, an Intermediate survey is to be carried out.				

Trade

Fishing operations.

Service

Unrestricted

THE VESSEL'S CLASS WILL BE AUTOMATICALLY SUSPENDED IF THE SPECIAL SURVEY OR THE INTERMEDIATE SURVEY OR THE ORDINARY (ANNUAL) SURVEYS ARE NOT CARRIED OUT WITHIN THE END OF THEIR RESPECTIVE RANGE DATES.

The Certificate of class is issued on the basis of the requirements and conditions as specified in the RINA Rules of which the interested party has acquired full knowledge, accepting them unconditionally, with particular regard to the following clauses: RINA carries out its duties through officers or other persons it considers possess all the requirements of suitability and competence for the tasks which have been assigned to them. In its capacity as expert, RINA only expresses opinions and evaluations of compliance with its own rule requirements and does not, in any case whatsoever, (even if its opinions are requested on matters not expressly covered by Rules) assume the liabilities pertaining to the designers, shipowners, builders, test inspectors, shipyards or any person or organization responsible by law or contractually for providing guarantees for all of whom the respective liabilities remain unchanged even in the case of consultative actions by RINA. For what concerns the tasks taken on and carried out directly, other than those delegated in the following, RINA is answerable in law terms. Within the context of the tasks delegated to RINA by the Italian Administration, liability can only be recognized in the case of fraud or gross negligence by the officers or the persons encharged. In no case shall the liability, regardless of the amount of damage reported, exceed a value equal to 5 times the total of the fees received by RINA as consideration of the services rendered from which the damage reported derives.

Form CLASSE2-Cer-EE-7/92

RI 75707 Ship's name **GRAND PRINCE** Certificate No. 9902433 Page 3 of 5

ENDORSEMENTS

	Signature and seal
Place and date of survey VIGO 02 - 11 - 99 Efectuadas visitas: Anuales de Casco y Máquinas. El buque continua en su Clase. Port VIGO date 02-11-99	REGISTRO ITALIANO NAVALE R. Rivera Rodriguez file: 99 | MD | 406 | NA
Place and date of survey Port date	Signature and seal file
Place and date of survey Port date	Signature and seal file
Place and date of survey Port date	Signature and seal file
Place and date of survey Port date	Signature and seal file

xm CLASSE2-Cer-EE-7/92

RI. 76707 Ship's name GRAND PRINCE Certificate No. 9902433 Page 5 of 5

ENDORSEMENTS

Place and date of survey ____________________ Signature and seal

Port ____________ date ____________ file

Place and date of survey ____________________ Signature and seal

Port ____________ date ____________ file

Place and date of survey ____________________ Signature and seal

Port ____________ date ____________ file

Place and date of survey ____________________ Signature and seal

Port ____________ date ____________ file

Place and date of survey ____________________ Signature and seal

Port ____________ date ____________ file

Form CLASSE2-Cer-EE-7/92

Annex 17 (continued)
– R.I.N.A.: Statement of Class (Spanish and English)

REGISTRO ITALIANO NAVALE

DECLARACION DE CLASE
STATEMENT OF CLASS

N. 1/99

REGISTRO ITALIANO NAVALE
R. Rivera Rodriguez

Nombre del buque y numero RINA / *Name of ship and RINA number*	GRAND PRINCE - RI 76707
Ex nombres / *Former names*	-----------
Bandera / *Flag*	BELIZE
Numero IMO / *IMO number*	-------
Categoria / *Category*	MOTONAVE
Material del casco / *Material of the hull*	ACERO
Armador / *Owner*	NOYCAN S.L.
Astillero - Lugar de construccion / *Shipyard - place of build*	PORT WELLER DRYDOCKS LTD. (CANADA)
Letras de llamada / *Distinctive number or letters*	V 3 U J 7
Fecha de construccion / *Date of build*	1.966
Puerto y numero de matricula / *Port and number of registry*	BELIZE 07972047
Arqueo bruto / *Gross tonnage*	534,75
Arqueo neto / *Net tonnage*	218,18

SE CERTIFICA que el buque ha sido sometido a Visita de Primera Clasificacion, con / sin(+) vigilancia a la construccion, en acuerdo a las Reglas vigentes del RINA y, sobre la base de la constataciones debidas, ha sido propuesto a la Direccion General de otorgar la clase (*):
THIS IS TO CERTIFY that the above ship has been subjected to a First classification survey, with / without (+) supervision during construction, in compliance with the applicable RINA Rules and, based on the survey outcome, it is recommended to the Head Office that the ship be assigned the class (*):

100 - A - 1.1 - NAV.IL ; Pes.

vinculada al franco bordo establecido en el catificado relativo (+) XXXXXXXXXXXXXXXXXXXXX
based on the freeboard indicated in the Load Line Certificate (+)

vinculada al calado maximo de 3,516 m sobre la linea de quilla (+)
based on the maximum draught of ____ m from the underside of the keel (+)

con notas especiales --------
with special notations

Esta Declaracion consiste de 4 paginas / *This statement consists of 4 pages*

(*) Servicio y navigacion son definidos a la pagina 2 / *Trade and service are described at page 2*

(+) Tachar como necesario / *Delete as appropriate*

Form CLASSE5-Dic-BG-10/92

RI 76707 Nombre del buque / *Ship's name* GRAND PRINCE Declaracion N. / *Statement No.* 226/98 Pagina / *Page* 2 de / *of* 4

Servicio / *Trade* PESCA

Navigacion / *Service* ILIMITADA

Esta Declaracion tiene vigencia hasta el / *This statement is valid until*	JUNIO 1.999		
Emetida en / *Issued at*	VIGO	el / *on*	07 ENERO 1.999

La emision de esta Declaracion es sujeta a las mismas reglas y condiciones aplicable para la emision del Certificado de clase.
This statement is issued subject to the same conditions and restrictions which regulate the issue of the Certificate of class.

REGISTRO ITALIANO NAVALE

REGISTRO ITALIANO NAVALE
R. Rivera Rodriguez

Form CLASSE5-Dic-6G-10/92

RI 76707 Nombre del buque *Ship's name* GRAND PRINCE Declaracion N. *Statement No.* 226/98 Pagina *Page* 3 de *of* 4

NOTAS / *REMARKS*

Form CLASSES-Dic-BG-10/92

16707 Nombre del buque / Ship's name GRAND PRINCE

Declaracion N. / Statement No. 226/98 Pagina / Page 4 de / of 4

VISADOS / ENDORSEMENTS

La Declaration de clase, es otorgada en base a las normas y condiciones especificadas en los Reglamentos del RINA, de las que el interesado ha tomado conocimiento aceptandolas incondicionalmente, con especial referencia a las clausulas siguientes : El Registro Italiano Naval, realiza sus actividades por medio de funcionarios o otras personas que son consideradas dotadas de todos los requisitos de idoneidad y competencia para las tareas que se les confian. En su calidad de perito el RINA expresa exclusivamente opiniones y evaluaciones en conformidad a sus propias normas reglamentarias, y no se asume en ningun caso (donde sus opiniones fueran solicitadas en materias no exclusivamente reglamentadas) las responsabilidades que correspondan a proyectistas, armadores, peritos de pruebas en obras, y toda persona o Entidad, obligada por la Ley o por contrato, a dar garantias; todos estos sujetos mantienen inalteradas sus correspondientes responsabilidades, incluso en el caso que se efectuen consultas por parte del RINA. Por lo que se refiere a las tareas directamente tomadas y desarrolladas, fuera de las que se delegan en el proximo inciso, el RINA responde en los terminos que estipula la Ley. En el ambito de las tareas que se refieran al RINA, en cuanto Delegado del Ministerio de la Marina Mercante, las eventuales responsabilidades, pueden ser supuestas solo en el caso de dolo o culpa grave de los funcionarios o de los sujetos engargados. En ningun caso la responsabilidad - cualquiera que sea el monto de daño lamentado - podra' exceder de cinco veces el monto de la remuneracion percibida por el RINA como retribucion por los servicios prestados, o por prestaciones, de las cuales se derive el daño lamentado.

The statement of class is issued on the basis of the requirements and conditions as specified in the RINA Rules of which the interested party has acquired full knowledge, accepting them unconditionally, with particular regard to the following clauses : RINA carries out its duties through officers or other persons it considers possess all the requirements of suitability and competence for the tasks which have been assigned to them. In its capacity as expert, RINA only expresses opinions and evaluations of compliance with its own rule requirements and does not, in any case whatsoever, (even if its opinions are requested on matters not expressly covered by Rules) assume the liabilities pertaining to the designers, shipowners, builders, test inspectors, shipyards or any person or organization responsible by law or contractually for providing guarantees for all of whom the respective liabilities remain unchanged even in the case of consultative actions by RINA. For what concerns the tasks taken on and carried out directly, other than those delegated in the following, RINA is answerable in law terms. Within the context of the tasks under the responsibility of RINA as delegate of an Administration, liability can only be recognized in the case of fraud or gross negligence by the officers or the persons encharged. In no case shall the liability, regardless of the amount of damage reported, exceed a value equal to 5 times the total of the fees received by RINA as consideration of the services rendered from which the damage reported derives.

Form CLASSE5-Dic-BG-10/92

Annex 17 (continued)
English translation of valuation

TAXO
Valuation

TAXO VALORACIÓN S.L.
C. Universidad 4, 1º 46003 Valencia
Phone (96) 353 1893 Fax (96) 351 8353

Report no.: PO-0004/01
Type: Shipping.
Valuer: F.C.V.

VALUATION OF THE M/V "GRAND PRINCE"

This valuation is issued at the request of Mr. Alberto Penelas, Lawyer, with address at Vigo, 11, Pintor Laxeiro Street, 2nd. A.

1.- IDENTIFICATION

The motor fishing vessel "Grand Prince" was a fishing stern trawler equipped with a ramp, that was converted to a long liner in 1998. Her flag is of Belize, she is registered in the Port of Belize, under registry number 07972047. Her owner is Paik Commercial Corp., with address at 35 A Regent Street, Belize City- Belize. Her IMO number is 6701656.

2. MAIN PARTICULARS AND DESCRIPTION.

2.1. Main particulars.

-Length overall	44,10 mts.
- Length between perpendiculars	37,00 mts.
- Breadth	10,00 mts.
- Draught	4,80 mts.
- Gross Tonnage	534,75 GT.

2.2. Hull.

She is a vessel with hull made of steel, built at Port Weeller Drydocks in Canada in the year 1966, prepared for stern trawler fishing; she has one deck; with forecastle from the midship section forward for crew accommodation; with a pilot bridge over the said forecastle deck. In 1998 M/V "Grand Prince" was converted, the whole trawl fishing unit was removed and that the bottom-line fishing unit was installed. The forecastle deck was lengthened to the stern and a second fishing hold was built abaft the old one.

2.3. Engine.

Her main engine is of General Motors make, with 12 cylinders, two stroke of 956 kw.

She also has three auxiliary sets of 75 kw.

Refrigerating plant: two refrigeration compressors with their corresponding condensers, pumps, receptacles. Three freezing tunnels with a freezing capacity of 8 tons/day, coils in both holds and cold-insulation.

2.4. Special fittings.

Fishing unit for bottom line fishing made up of line winch, conveyor belt and boxes.

2.5. Communication, Navigation and Fishing Electronic Equipment.

- 1 VHF Sailor PT 144 B
- 1 VHF Kenwood.
- 1 telephony ICON IC M710
- 1 radio telephone Furuno FS5000.
- 1 Fax Toshiba.
- 1 TR emergency SART
- 1 Radar ARPA Furuno.
- 1 Radar Simrad Auritsu.
- 1 Nautex JRC.
- 1 Gonio Koden KS 5131
- 1 Automatic pilot Robertson, AP9MK3.
- 1 direction heading RGC.
- 1 GPS Navigator Furuno.
- 1 Loran GPS 6700 Apelco.
- 1 Inmarsat Furuno Felcon 81.
- 1 Video plotter LG.
- 1 sonar sounding Furuno.
- 1 sonar sounding Koden.

3.- STATE OF MAINTENANCE.

At first impression, the vessel is in good condition as to crew accommodation and fittings for fishing and the conservation thereof.

It should be emphasised that engines and most of the hull and are thirty four years old. Nevertheless, the M/V "Grand Prince" keeps her class at RINA.

4. CERTIFICATES AND LICENCES.

The F/V "Grand Prince" has certificates from Belize which entitles her to navigate and has those from the Classification Society Registro Italiano Navale, under class 100-A-1, 1-Nav IL.

5. CRITICAL JUDGEMENT ON THE VESSEL FOR HER ACTIVITY.

Fundamentally the vessel is old. She is a vessel which has been adapted for her present method of fishing, therefore she lacks the optimal characteristics, such as size, general arrangement and power for her present fishing activity. The foregoing does not mean that the vessel is of no use, but that she does not meet the best conditions for bottom-line fishing.

6.- INFORMATION ABOUT MARKET.

The purchase of vessels similar to M/V "Grand Prince", of the same age is not common, other than for their breaking-up, therefore the valuer does not have data available which might be used to compare with this, given that, after all, the M/V "Grand Prince" is still serviceable for fishing, due to her modernisation in 1998.

7.- REPLACEMENT COST.

This is assessed as 2,585,000.00 € (EUROS TWO MILLION FIVE HUNDRED AND EIGHTY FIVE THOUSAND).

8.- NET REPLACEMENT COST.

Bearing in mind the age of M/V "Grand Prince", the replacement cost, depreciated by her age, and modernised in 1988 is 360,000.00 ∊ (EUROS THREE HUNDRED AND SIXTY THOUSAND).

9 VALUATION.

Bearing in mind the net replacement value, the modernisation undertaken in 1998 and the state and usefulness of the vessel, the appraisal cost of M/V "Grand Prince" is, to the best of the valuer's knowledge and ability, 360,000.00 ∊ (EUROS THREE HUNDRED AND SIXTY THOUSAND).

And for the record, I sign this valuation at Vigo, on the 16th of March, 2001.

Signed: Faustino Carceller Vilalta.
PhD. Naval Architect.

ATTACHMENTS.

- General Arrangement Drawing.
- Provisory Patent of Navigation.
- R.I.N.A.: Certificate of Class.
- R.I.N.A.: Declaration of Class.

Annex 18
Technical report and certificate of valuation of the *Grand Prince* from Mr Antonio Alonso Perez, Marine Surveyor (in Spanish) (not reproduced), with annexes:
– Bill of Sale (in Spanish) (not reproduced), with supporting documents (in Spanish and in English) (reproduced as Annex 2 of the Application)
– Provisional Patent of Navigation (reproduced as Annex 3 of the Application)
– drawings of the *Grand Prince*

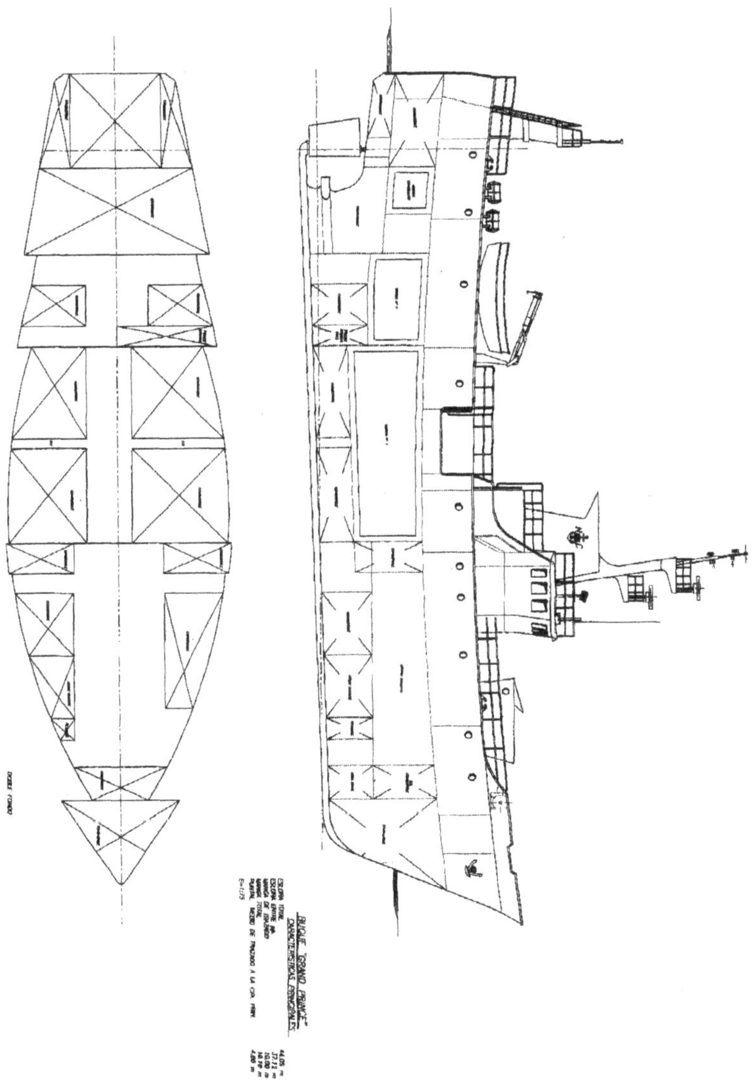

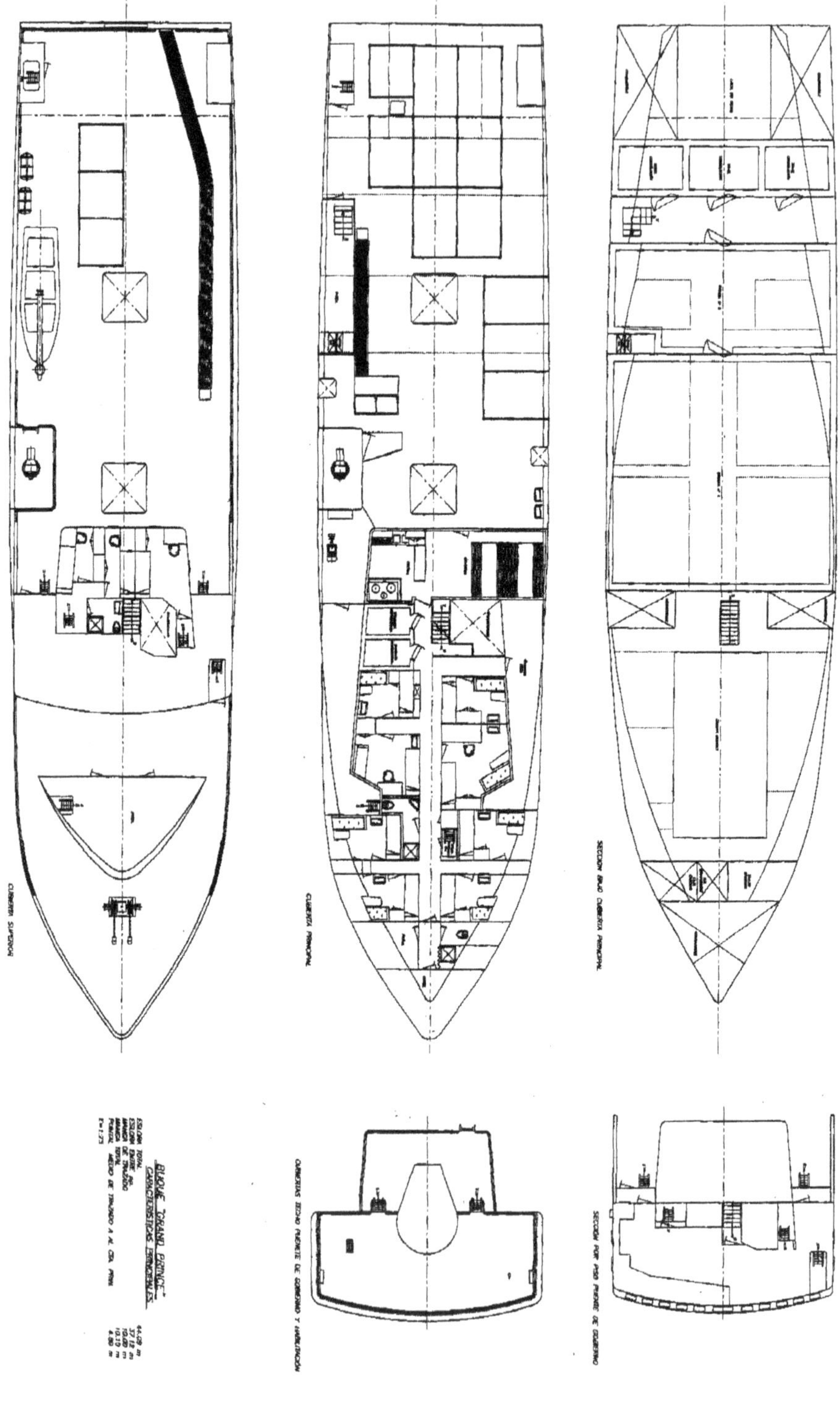
CUBIERTA SUPERIOR
CUBIERTA PRINCIPAL
SECCION BAJO CUBIERTA PRINCIPAL
BUQUE "GRAND PRINCE"
CARACTERISTICAS PRINCIPALES

Annex 18 (continued)
– ten colour prints of photographs of the *Grand Prince* and of parts of the equipment

GRAND PRINCE

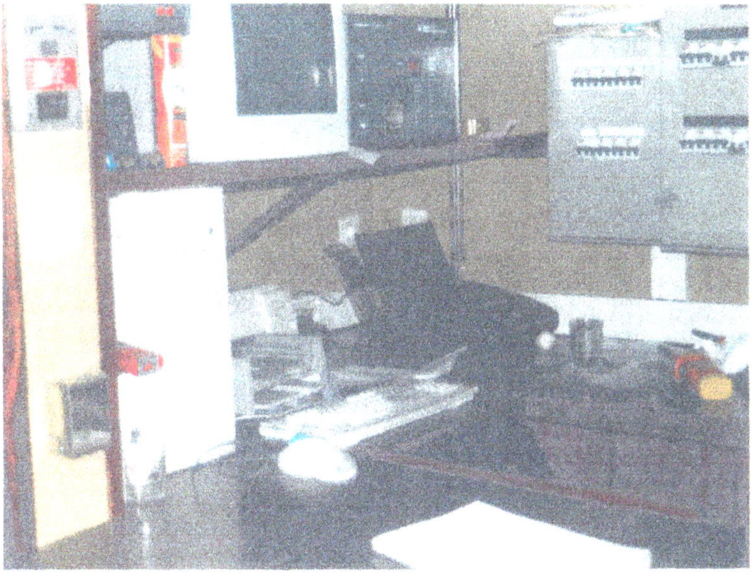

Annex 18 (continued)
English translation of the report and certificate

Captain Antonio Alonso Pérez
Marine Surveyor
Vigo.

TECHNICAL REPORT

M/V "GRAND PRINCE"

CERTIFICATE OF VALUATION

13TH. OF MARCH 2001

Captain Antonio Alonso Pérez
Marine Surveyor
Vigo.

PARTICULARS OF THE VESSEL

Name:	**M/V "GRAND PRINCE"**
IMO Number	6701656
Signal call	V3UJ7
Registry number	07972047
Shipowner	PAIK COMERCIAL CORP.
Flag	Belize
Port of Registry	Belize
Gross Tonnage	669
Net Tonnage	267
Year of building	1967
Shipyard	Port Séller Dry Docks Ltd. St. Catherines, Ontario
Hull	steel
Length overall	44,10 mts.
Length between perpendiculars	37,34 mts.
Moulded breadth	10,01 mts.
Draught	4,81 mts.
Type of vessel:	Engine. Frozen Fish Carrier.
Number of holds	2
Make of engine	General Motors
Principals:	Diesel 2SA 12 cyl. 230x 254 single reduction 1300 bhp (956kw)
Built by	General Motors Corp. La Grange
Auxiliary set:	2 x 75 kw 230 v. 60 Hz a.c.

Captain Antonio Alonso Pérez
Marine Surveyor
Vigo.

TECHNICAL REPORT

The undersigned, Mr. Antonio Alonso Pérez, Captain of the Merchant Navy, Average Agent, in the name and on behalf of SIRCAI VIGO, S.L. was requested by Mr. Alberto Penelas, on behalf of PAIK COMERCIAL CORP., to make a valuation of the vessel "GRAND PRINCE", which is kept detained by the Authorities of Reunion Island in the Indian Ocean.

From the attached documents and the informations received, all the following is inferred:

BUILDING

The vessel "Grand Prince", with hull made of steel, was built in the shipyard Port Séller Dry Docks Ltd. From St. Catherines, Ontario, Canada, in the year 1967, her particulars being those stated above.

The pilot bridge is placed forward and accommodations on the main deck forward of the vessel over the engine room.

The two holds are in the lower deck forward of the freezing tunnels and the fish-processing area is in the main deck, the fishing operation area and the bottom-line winch being on the upper deck.

This vessel was built as a cod-fishing stern trawler, she being subsequently converted to a deep-sea long liner; her trawling windlass, astern fishing unit, and ramp being dismantled, and a weather deck being installed.

Double bottom tanks are used for fuel and oils, and the forepeak for ballast, freshwater tanks being places both forward and astern.

The vessel is propelled by a General Motors main engine, with a single adjustable pitch propeller.

CAPACITY

Hold capacity	180 tons.
Diesel-oil capacity	285 tons.
Fresh water capacity	30 tons.

ENGINE

Main engine: General Motors, 1300 b.h.p. (956 kw)

Auxiliary set: 3 General Motors, of 75 kw, 230 v. 60 Hz a.c.

FREEZING SYSTEM

The main freezing plant is situated on the upper platform of the engine room, and uses FREON-22 as refrigerating gas.

The freezing capacity of the plant is 8 ton/day in three freezing tunnels placed on the lower deck abaft the holds, equipped with two compressors.

ELECTRONIC NAVIGATION SYSTEMS.

The navigation and communication equipment with which the vessel is equipped are as follows:

- 1 VHF SAILOR RT144B
- 1 VHF Kenwood
- 1 Radar ARPA Furuno
- 1 Radar Simrad Anritsu.
- 1 Navtex J.R.C. N.C.R. 300 A.
- 1 videoplotter LG Studioworks.
- 1 colour sounding Furuno.
- 1 colour sounding Koden CUS 8831.
- 1 Gonio Koden KS 5131
- 1 direction heading Robertson RGC and automatic pilot Robertson AP9MK3

- 1 GPS Navigator Furuno.
- 1 Loran GPS 6700 Apelco
- 1 inmarsat Furuno Felcon 81
- 1 telephony ICON IC M 710
- 1 radio telephone SSB Furuno FS5000
- 1 Fax Public Toshiba
- 1 TR emergency SART.

CRITERIA OF VALUATION.

In order to issue our opinion on the value of the vessel "Grand Prince", we shall bear in mind as follows:

1.- Technical specifications, design and condition of the vessel.
The vessel was built as a stern trawler with refrigerating well for the fishing of hake and cod, in 1967, her shipowner being Haskel Shipping & Properties Ltd.
In 1998, the vessel was remodelled, she being converted to a bottom-liner with the fitting of a bottom-line winch; her trawling windlass and astern ramp being dismantelled and a weather deck being built astern.

On the 27th of March 2000, the vessel was acquired by the firm PAIK COMERCIAL Corp., for an overall sum of 45,000,000 pesetas.

In my opinion, the vessel does not have the arrangement which is normally used in a modern automatic bottom-line vessel, and the powerful engine designed for trawling vessels has a high bunker consumption.

The pilot bridge is well organised with appropriate space and is provided with modern navigation electronic equipment.

2. Conditions of the International Market.

Fishing grounds for the catching of demersal fish with long-lines are few and far between, limited to reduced fishing areas, such as international waters and EU with a limited number of fishing licences.

At this moment, there is a lack of interest in buying these vessels, and the little existent interest is focused on modern existing vessels and brand-new vessels.

Some modern vessels have been for sale since 1999 and they have not been sold yet.

The quality of 'Grand Prince' is not appropriate to meeting the operational requirements of a long-liner in cold waters of the North Atlantic or Pacific, because she does not fulfill the requirements of resistance to ice and safety.
A possible buyer looking for a long-liner to fish tunny, swordfish, etc... in temperate waters will focus on vessels originally built to that end, such as those of Japan etc..., which can be obtained more cheaply, and which have an appropriate distribution, as well as higher safety and conditions of navigation.

It must also be borne in mind that Grand Prince lacks any kind of fishing licence whatsoever for the countries subject to quotas in areas such as NAFO, CAMELAR, JCAT, etc.

Should it be our intention to buy the vessel as a trawler, we would face the following problems:

A) The vessel has neither trawling windlass nor after ramp nor fishing gears. New sonars, receiving tanks, processing equipment, etc.. would have to be installed and the weather deck would have to be removed, which I deem an excessive cost for an old vessel with few amenities.

B) The market is glutted with trawlers for sale in good technical condition and ready to depart to the fishing grounds. There are some with reinforced hulls for ice, banks being more interested in financing this kind of vessels.

VALUATION OF THE VESSEL.

Grand Prince was sold in March 2000, to the firm PAIK COMERCIAL CORP. for an amount of 45,000,000 ptas, which bearing in mind the exchange rate of the French Franc at 25,36 pesetas, would be 1,774,448 French Francs which we understand is the scrap value of the vessel due to her age; nevertheless, and taking into account the good maintenance observed, as well as the investment in navigation gear and accommodation of the vessel, we understand that she has been revalued by 30%; therefore the vessel's value at present is:

58,500,000 pesetas.

Bearing in mind all the aforementioned, and the age of the vessel, and considering that both the hull and the engine are in good condition, without defects or damage, and bearing in mind that the price of a brand new vessel with the same particulars, is now approx. 425,000,000 and that the transformation cost could have approximately 30,000,000 pesetas.

Deduction factor: 0,08
Scrap value factor: 1-0,08= 0,92
Scrap value at 33 years = $0{,}92^{31}$= 0,075409
Vessel replacement cost: 0,075409 x 425,000,000 = 32,048,825 ptas.
Conditioning approx. cost: 30,000,000 ptas.
Vessel's cost: 62,048,825 ptas.
Scrap value in 3 years = $0{,}92^{3}$= 0,778688
Vessel replacement cost= 0,778688 x 62,048,825 ptas = 48,316,675 ptas.
Revaluation 30%=14,495,002 ptas.
Vessel's present value= 62,811,677 ptas.

Vigo, on the 15th of March 2001.
The Average Agent. (firma ilegible)

Captain Antonio Alonso Pérez

Marine Surveyor

Vigo.

CERTIFICATE OF VALUATION

The undersigned, Mr. Antonio Alonso Pérez, Captain of the Merchant Navy and Average Agent, in the name and on behalf of SIRCAI VIGO, S.L., at Vigo, at the request of Mr. Alberto Penelas,

CERTIFIES:

That he has undertaken the assessment of the deep sea long-liner called "GRAND PRINCE" and, bearing in mind the age of the vessel, her size, kind, class, speed, consumption and special particulars, as well as her present market price, I deem that the vessel replacement cost, in a condition free of damage and encumbrances is 60,655,838 pesetas (SIXTY MILLION SIX HUNDRED FIFTY FIVE THOUSAND EIGHT HUNDRED AND THIRTY EIGHT PESETAS).

Taking into account an exchange of 1FRF = 25,36 ptas.

The vessel replacement cost in a condition free of damage and encumbrances is 2,391,792 French Francs (TWO MILLION THREE HUNDRED AND NINETY ONE THOUSAND, SEVEN HUNDRED AND NINETY TWO FRENCH FRANCS).

And for the record to the appropriate effect, this present is issued at Vigo on the fifteenth of March of the year two thousand and one.

Vigo, on the 15th of March 2001.

The Average Agent. (illegible signature).

PLEADINGS - MÉMOIRES

OBSERVATIONS DU GOUVERNEMENT FRANÇAIS

1

OBSERVATIONS DU GOUVERNEMENT FRANÇAIS

relatives à la demande présentée au nom du Belize devant le

TRIBUNAL INTERNATIONAL DU DROIT DE LA MER

concernant le navire «Grand Prince»

Présentée comme une demande de «prompte mainlevée de l'immobilisation du navire de pêche "Grand Prince" au titre de l'article 292 de la Convention des Nations Unies sur le droit de la mer», la requête adressée le 21 mars 2001 au Tribunal international du droit de la mer par Me Alberto Penelas Alvarez au nom du Belize ne saurait être regardée comme introduisant une instance régie par les dispositions de l'article 292. La demande ainsi présentée au nom du Belize n'entre manifestement pas dans les prévisions de cet article.

Le Gouvernement de la République française considère qu'il n'a donc pas à présenter, en ce qui le concerne, l'exposé en réponse prévu à l'article 111, paragraphe 4 du Règlement du Tribunal.

Deux séries de raisons peuvent être invoquées à l'appui de cette position. Les unes tiennent à la nature même de la procédure de prompte mainlevée, les autres découlent des circonstances qui entourent la demande.

1 – Raisons tenant à la nature de la procédure de prompte mainlevée

La procédure prévue par l'article 292 a pour unique objet d'assurer la prompte mainlevée de l'immobilisation d'un navire dès le dépôt d'une caution raisonnable, en attendant l'aboutissement des procédures judiciaires intentées contre le capitaine ou le propriétaire du navire devant les juridictions de l'Etat ayant procédé à l'immobilisation. Aussi, lorsque les procédures judiciaires internes ont abouti et, plus particulièrement, lorsqu'elles ont conduit au prononcé d'une condamnation à la confiscation du navire, tout recours éventuel à la procédure de l'article 292 perd sa raison d'être. En pareil cas, une demande en prompte mainlevée est dépourvue d'objet.

Dès lors qu'un tribunal national a prononcé, à titre de sanction applicable, la confiscation du navire, l'ouverture d'une instance en mainlevée d'immobilisation devant le Tribunal international du droit de la mer non seulement n'est plus possible mais n'est même pas concevable. En effet, dans le cadre d'une instance de ce type, le Tribunal ne se prononce que sur le caractère raisonnable de la caution exigée pour ordonner la mainlevée de l'immobilisation du navire. Ce qui présuppose, d'une part, que de simples mesures provisoires aient été prises à titre conservatoire à l'égard du navire et, d'autre part, que ces mesures puissent être rapportées ou interrompues en échange d'une garantie d'exécution des éventuelles créances de l'Etat sur le propriétaire du navire. Or, la confiscation prononcée par une cour de justice nationale à titre de peine principale ou accessoire a pour effet de transférer autoritairement et de façon définitive à l'Etat le bien faisant l'objet de la confiscation. Le propriétaire du navire se trouve déchu de son titre par décision de justice et s'il souhaite recouvrer ses droits sur le bien, les voies de recours qui lui sont offertes ne peuvent plus consister en une action en mainlevée, puisqu'il ne peut plus être considéré comme titulaire d'un droit de propriété sur le navire.

De plus, on ne peut perdre de vue qu'en raison de la fonction particulière qui lui est assignée, la procédure de l'article 292 ne peut interférer avec les actions en justice engagées par l'Etat côtier intéressé en vue de réprimer les infractions à ses lois et règlements commises par le navire ayant fait l'objet d'une mesure d'immobilisation.

C'est ce qui résulte du paragraphe 3 de l'article 292 qui précise: «...le tribunal ... n'a à connaître que de la question de la mainlevée ou de la mise en liberté, **sans préjudice de la suite qui sera donnée à toute action** dont le navire, son propriétaire ou son équipage peuvent être l'objet **devant la juridiction nationale appropriée**». Le texte anglais de cette disposition indique: "without prejudice to **the merits** of any case before the appropriate domestic forum against the vessel, its owner or its crew". Dans toute instance pénale engagée à l'encontre du capitaine d'un navire de pêche étranger pour violation des lois et règlements de l'Etat côtier, la détermination de la peine applicable et la condamnation à cette pénalité font partie intégrante de ce que l'on appelle «the merits», c'est-à-dire **le fond** même de l'affaire soumise à un tribunal national comme l'indique clairement le texte espagnol de l'article 292, paragraphe 3 («sin prejuzgar **el fondo** de cualquier demanda interpuesta ante el tribunal nacional «).

Le Tribunal international du droit de la mer ne peut, par le biais d'une procédure en prompte mainlevée, s'immiscer ni dans le déroulement ni dans le résultat d'une instance judiciaire interne. Or, tel serait le cas si le Tribunal accueillait la demande qui lui a été présentée le 21 mars au nom du Belize. Il ne peut donc accueillir, pour en décider avec autorité de chose jugée, ladite demande.

2 – Raisons tenant aux circonstances de la demande

Le navire "Grand Prince", surpris en infraction dans la zone économique française, a été arraisonné et appréhendé le 26 décembre 2000 et conduit à l'île de La Réunion, où il est arrivé le 9 janvier 2001. Le Directeur des Affaires maritimes de La Réunion a prononcé la saisie conservatoire du navire, laquelle a été confirmée le 12 janvier par une ordonnance du Tribunal d'instance de Saint-Paul qui a, en outre, fixé le montant de la caution à verser pour permettre la mainlevée de cette saisie. D'autre part, le 11 janvier, le Substitut du Procureur de la République près le Tribunal de Grande Instance de Saint-Denis a dressé un procès-verbal d'interpellation à l'encontre du capitaine du navire et, considérant qu'en l'espèce l'ouverture d'une information n'était pas nécessaire, a décidé de citer directement l'intéressé à comparaître à l'audience du Tribunal correctionnel du 23 janvier, en application des articles 393 et suivants du code de procédure pénale (ANNEXE I). Le jugement du Tribunal correctionnel, rendu le jour même (ANNEXE II), a prononcé la confiscation du navire "Grand Prince" avec exécution immédiate (nonobstant un appel éventuel), par application de l'article 131-6,10° du code pénal et 471 dernier alinéa du code de procédure pénale (ANNEXE III). Il a en outre condamné le capitaine à une peine d'amende et à des dommages-intérêts.

Quels que soient les recours qui ont été ou pourraient être exercés par l'armateur ou le capitaine du navire dans l'ordre juridique français à l'encontre de ce jugement, l'Etat du pavillon ne peut plus désormais se fonder sur les dispositions de l'article 292 de la Convention des Nations Unies sur le droit de la mer pour attraire la France devant le Tribunal international du droit de la mer. Dans le cas particulier, le Tribunal ne pourrait pas, en effet, ordonner à la France de procéder à la prompte mainlevée de l'immobilisation du "Grand Prince" dès le dépôt d'une caution ou d'une autre garantie dont il fixerait le montant et la forme, car il s'ingérerait alors dans la substance même d'une affaire pénale qui a été tranchée par la juridiction française compétente; ce qui est expressément exclu par les dispositions mêmes de l'article 292, comme il a été rappelé précédemment.

La demande présentée au Tribunal le 21 mars 2001 reconnaît d'ailleurs incidemment qu'il ne peut plus être question désormais d'obtenir une quelconque mainlevée, que ce soit en fournissant une garantie raisonnable ou en versant la caution initialement fixée par le Tribunal d'instance de Saint-Paul: «As a result, the vessel could not be released neither upon posting a reasonable guarantee, nor upon posting the bond initially fixed by the First Instance Tribunal of Saint-Paul» (paragraphe 28 de la demande).

Aussi cette demande cherche-t-elle à surmonter cette impossibilité en avançant la prétention qu'il y aurait eu , de la part de la France, violation de la Convention de 1982 parce que, en décidant la confiscation du "Grand Prince" quelques jours seulement après la fixation du montant de la caution par le Tribunal d'instance de Saint-Paul, et en décidant en outre l'exécution provisoire de cette sanction en vue d'éviter toute mainlevée de saisie , le Tribunal correctionnel de Saint-Denis aurait imaginé un «artifice» pour se soustraire aux exigences de l'article 73, paragraphe 2 de la Convention (paragraphes 24 et 25 de la demande).

En invoquant «the artifice of deciding the confiscation of the vessel, and its provisional execution, with the enough celerity to prevent its release by posting of any kind of guarantee» (paragraphe 31), la demande qui a été formulée au nom de l'Etat du Belize, outre qu'elle repose sur un pur et simple procès d'intention sans aucun commencement de preuve, méconnaît que les décisions prises par les autorités judiciaires françaises l'ont été en pleine conformité avec les dispositions du droit national applicables. En réalité, cette demande tend à alléguer l'existence d'un différend portant sur la mise en œuvre par la France des pouvoirs qui lui sont reconnus par l'article 73 de la Convention. Le 1er paragraphe de cet article précise que, dans l'exercice de ses droits souverains sur les ressources biologiques de la zone économique exclusive, «d'Etat côtier peut prendre toutes mesures, y compris l'arraisonnement, l'inspection, la saisie et l'introduction d'une instance judiciaire, qui lui sont nécessaires pour assurer le respect des lois et règlements qu'il a adoptés conformément à la Convention».

Est-il besoin de rappeler que cette disposition laisse au législateur national le soin de définir à la fois les délits de pêche et les pénalités applicables aux auteurs de ces délits? Il appartient, en conséquence, au juge national saisi d'un cas concret de déterminer la peine à appliquer à la lumière des dispositions législatives en vigueur, des preuves qui lui sont apportées et des circonstances de l'affaire. La seule limite qui soit apportée à l'exercice du pouvoir de sanction d'un Etat côtier est celle énoncée au paragraphe 3 de l'article 73 qui exclut les peines d'emprisonnement et tout autre châtiment corporel.

De surcroît, il convient de souligner que la confiscation d'un navire de pêche étranger convaincu d'infraction aux lois et règlements en matière de pêche dans la zone économique est une sanction parfaitement licite au regard du droit international et qui est d'ailleurs expressément prévue non seulement par la législation française, mais aussi par de nombreuses autres législations nationales (par exemple: Barbade, Comores, Fidji, Grenade, Guyana, Indonésie, Jamaïque, Malaisie, Nouvelle Zélande, Norvège, Portugal, Russie, Tanzanie).

Il découle des considérations précédentes que ce qui est en fait invoqué dans la demande dont le Tribunal a été saisi concerne non plus une question de mainlevée mais un différend d'une autre nature portant sur l'exercice par la France de ses droits souverains, différend qui, en tout état de cause, n'entre pas dans les prévisions de l'article 292 de la Convention.

Or, si le Belize a donné pouvoir à une personne pour agir en son nom dans le cadre de l'article 292, le titulaire dudit pouvoir ne peut pas prétendre agir en dehors de ce cadre et notamment tenter de soumettre au Tribunal une question autre que celle faisant l'objet de cet article.

Le Gouvernement français est donc fondé à considérer non seulement que l'instance est mal engagée, mais encore que cette instance n'a pas lieu d'être. En d'autres termes, face à cette demande, le Tribunal devrait prononcer un non lieu.

Au surplus, s'agissant d'un différend du type de celui mentionné ci-dessus, le Gouvernement français serait en droit de faire valoir, conformément à l'article 297, paragraphe 3 a) de la Convention, qu'il n'est pas tenu d'accepter qu'un tel différend soit soumis à l'une des procédures prévues à la section 2 de la Partie XV de la Convention sur le droit de la mer et que, dans ces conditions, le Tribunal international du droit de la mer, non plus qu'aucune autre juridiction internationale, n'a compétence pour en connaître. En déposant son instrument de ratification, le Gouvernement français a d'ailleurs formulé une déclaration en ce sens, conformément à l'article 298 paragraphe 1 b) de la Convention.

Pour ces motifs,

Le Gouvernement de la République française prie le Tribunal international du droit de la mer, statuant par voie d'ordonnance et sans qu'il soit besoin de tenir d'audiences publiques à cet effet, de constater que la demande de mainlevée présentée le 21 mars 2001 au nom du Belize est sans objet, qu'elle doit par suite être écartée et qu'il n'y a dès lors pas lieu à ouvrir une instance.

Paris, le 28 mars 2001

Annexe 1
Code de procédure pénal français (extraits : articles 393 et 394)

ANNEXE I

Extraits du code de procédure pénale français

Art. 393 *(L. n° 83-466 du 10 juin 1983)* En matière correctionnelle, après avoir constaté l'identité de la personne qui lui est déférée, lui avoir fait connaître les faits qui lui sont reprochés et avoir recueilli ses déclarations si elle en fait la demande, le procureur de la République peut, s'il estime qu'une information n'est pas nécessaire, procéder comme il est dit aux articles 394 à 396.

Le procureur de la République informe alors la personne déférée devant lui qu'elle a le droit à l'assistance d'un *(L. n° 93-2 du 4 janv. 1993)* « avocat » de son choix ou commis d'office. L'avocat choisi ou, dans le cas d'une demande de commission d'office, le bâtonnier de l'ordre des avocats, en est avisé sans délai.

L'avocat peut consulter sur-le-champ le dossier et communiquer librement avec le prévenu.

Mention de ces formalités est faite au procès-verbal à peine de nullité de la procédure.

Art. 393-1 *(L. n° 2000-516 du 15 juin 2000, art. 115)* Dans les cas prévus à l'article 393, la victime doit être avisée par tout moyen de la date de l'audience.

Art. 394 *(L. n° 83-466 du 10 juin 1983)* Le procureur de la République peut inviter la personne déférée à comparaître devant le tribunal dans un délai qui ne peut être inférieur à dix jours, sauf renonciation expresse de l'intéressé en présence de son avocat, ni supérieur à deux mois. Il lui notifie les faits retenus à son encontre ainsi que le lieu, la date et l'heure de l'audience. Cette notification, mentionnée au procès-verbal dont copie est remise sur-le-champ au prévenu, vaut citation à personne.

L'avocat choisi ou le bâtonnier est informé, par tout moyen et sans délai, de la date et de l'heure de l'audience ; mention de cet avis est portée au procès-verbal. *(L. n° 93-2 du 4 janv. 1993)* « L'avocat » peut, à tout moment, consulter le dossier.

Si le procureur de la République estime nécessaire de soumettre le prévenu jusqu'à sa comparution devant le tribunal à une ou plusieurs obligations du contrôle judiciaire, il le traduit sur-le-champ devant le président du tribunal ou le juge délégué par lui, statuant en chambre du conseil avec l'assistance d'un greffier. Ce magistrat peut, après audition du prévenu, son *(L. n° 93-2 du 4 janv. 1993)* « avocat » ayant été avisé et entendu en ses observations, s'il le demande, prononcer cette mesure dans les conditions et suivant les modalités prévues par les articles 138 *(L. n° 93-2 du 4 janv. 1993)* « et 139 ». Cette décision est notifiée verbalement au prévenu et mentionnée au procès-verbal dont copie lui est remise sur-le-champ.

Annexe 2
Jugement correctionnel du tribunal de grande instance de Saint Denis en date du 23 janvier 2001

A N N E X E II

TRIBUNAL DE GRANDE INSTANCE de SAINT DENIS

CONTRADICTOIRE

JUGEMENT CORRECTIONNEL DU : 23 JANVIER 2001

N° de Jugement : 62/01
N° de Parquet : 01396

Appel Prévenu, MP, PC

A l'audience du **TRIBUNAL CORRECTIONNEL**, au Palais de Justice de SAINT DENIS le **VINGT TROIS JANVIER DEUX MILLE UN**

composé de **Monsieur BRUNET**, Président,,
Madame MARTINEZ, Juge Assesseur,
Monsieur PRADIER, Juge Assesseur,

assisté de **Monsieur GIMONET** Greffier,

en présence de **Monsieur SENECHAL**, Substitut du Procureur de la République a été appelée l'affaire

ENTRE :
Monsieur le PROCUREUR DE LA REPUBLIQUE, près ce Tribunal, demandeur et poursuivant,

- **ARMEMENT SAPMER** demeurant Darse de Pêche B.P 2012 97823 LE PORT, partie civile constituée par l'intermédiaire d'un avocat à l'audience, non comparante, représentée par Maître CREGUT, SCP BELOT - AKHOUN - CREGUT - HAMEROUX,

- **C.O.M.A.T.A.** demeurant 1 rue Ambroise CROIZAT 97420 LE PORT, partie civile constituée par l'intermédiaire d'un avocat à l'audience, non comparante, représentée par Maître CREGUT, SCP BELOT - AKHOUN - CREGUT - HAMEROUX,

- **ARMEMENT DES MASCAREIGNES**
- **ARMEMENT LE GARREC**
parties civiles constituées par l'intermédiaire d'un avocat à l'audience, non comparante, représentée par Maître CREGUT, SCP BELOT - AKHOUN - CREGUT - HAMEROUX,

- **COMITE REGIONAL DE PECHE MARITIME et ELEVAGES**

- 2 -

MARINS DE LA REUNION élisant domicile à l'étude d'avocat SCP BACH immeuble FUTURA 190 rue des deux canons à SAINTE CLOTILDE, partie civile constituée par l'intermédiaire d'un avocat à l'audience, non comparante, représentée par Maître CREGUT, SCP BELOT - AKHOUN - CREGUT - HAMEROUX,

ET :

NOM : **PEREZ NOVO Ramon Francisco**

DATE DE NAISSANCE : 05/10/1957
LIEU DE NAISSANCE : RIBIERA - ESPAGNE
FILIATION : de PEREZ NOVO José et de NOVO MARTINEZ Josépha
NATIONALITE : ESPAGNOLE
ADRESSE : RUA DA CARBALLEIRA 10 RIBIERA
VILLE : ESPAGNE
SITUATION FAMILIALE :
PROFESSION : Capitaine De Navire

Jamais condamné, libre sous contrôle judiciaire

Comparant et assisté de Maître ANTOINE, avocat au Barreau de Saint Denis,

Prévenu de :

DEFAUT DE SIGNALEMENT D'ENTREE DANS LA ZONE ECONOMIQUE EXCLUSIVE

PECHE ILLICITE

A l'appel de la cause, le Président a constaté l'identité du prévenu, a donné connaissance de l'acte saisissant le Tribunal et l'a interrogé ;

Les parties civiles étant régulièrement constituées pour l'audience de ce jour ;

Le conseil des parties civiles a déposé des conclusions et a été entendu en sa plaidoirie ;

Le Ministère Public a été entendu en ses réquisitions ;

- 3 -

Le prévenu et son défenseur ont présenté ses moyens de défense et le prévenu a eu la parole en dernier ;

Le Greffier a tenu note du déroulement des débats ;

Après en avoir délibéré conformément à la loi, le Tribunal a statué en ces termes :

Par l'intermédiaire d'une interprète de langue espagnole, Melle BAILLIF, laquelle a prêté serment d'apporter son concours à la justice en son honneur et sa conscience.

LE TRIBUNAL

Attendu que PEREZ NOVO Ramon Francisco a été renvoyé par décision du Procureur de la République en date du 11 Janvier 2001, régulièrement notifiée le même jour devant le Tribunal Correctionnel de ce siège, sur le fondement des dispositions des articles 395 et suivants du Code de procédure pénale ;

Attendu que le prévenu a comparu, qu'il y a donc lieu de statuer contradictoirement à son encontre ;

Attendu que **PEREZ NOVO Ramon Francisco** est prévenu :

d'avoir dans la zone économique exclusive des cotes du territoire de la République, en l'espèce au large des ILES KERGUELEN dans les Terres Australes et Antarctiques FRançaises,, courant décembre 2000 et notamment à compter du 24 décembre et depuis temps non prescrit, étant capitaine du navire ''LE GRAND PRINCE'', battant pavillon étranger (BELIZE), omis de signaler son entrée dans la zone économique exclusive et de déclarer le tonnage de poisson détenu à bord.''faits prévus et réprimés à l'article 1 de la loi du 01.03.1988 modifié par la loi du 05 juillet 1996, les articles 1, 2, 4, 9, 11 de la loi du 18 juin 1966 modifiée par la loi du 18 novembre 1997 et les articles 2 et 4 de la loi 83-582 du 05 juillet 1983.'''

d'avoir dans la zone économique exclusive des cotes du territoire de la République, en l'espèce au large des ILES KERGUELEN dans les Terres Australes et Antarctiques FRançaises, courant décembre 2000, notamment du 24 au 26 décembre 2000, depuis temps non prescrit, étant capitaine du navire ''LE GRAND PRINCE'', battant pavillon étranger (BELIZE), pratiqué la pêche sans avoir obtenu d'autorisation préalable des autorités compétentes.''faits prévus et réprimés à l'article 1 de la loi du 05 juillet 1996, les articles 1, 2, 4, 9, 11 de la loi du 18 juin 1966 modifiée par la loi

-4-

du 18 novembre 1997 et les articles 2 et 4 de la loi 83-582 du 05 juillet 1983.'"

SUR L'ACTION PUBLIQUE

Attendu qu'il résulte de la procédure et qu'il n'est pas contesté que le Grand Prince est entré dans la Zone Economique des Iles Kerguelen sans signaler son entrée et sans déclarer le tonnage de poissons détenu à bord et ce en violation de l'article 4 de la loi du 18 juin 1966 modifiée par la loi du 18 novembre 1997.
Attendu par ailleurs que lors de l'intervention de la frégate "Nivose" le navire était en action de pêche illicite, une quinzaine de palangres étant à l'eau, le commandant de l'hélicoptère de la frégate Nivose ayant constaté le 26.12.2000 à 8h53 la présence de 6 bouées à la mer à 450 mètres du navire.
Attendu qu'il n'est pas contesté que cette pêche illicite a été pratiquée de façon consciente par le prévenu.
Attendu que l'entrée sans déclaration dans la ZEE et l'action de pêche constatée sont suffisantes pour démontrer que les poissons se trouvant dans la cale provenaient d'une pêche illégale, les circonstances que le journal de navigation n'ait pas été rempli depuis le 23.12.2000 et que les légines encore fraîches se trouvaient à bord, constituant des présomptions concordantes.
Attendu qu'il convient en conséquence de déclarer Ramon PEREZ NOVO coupable des faits qui lui sont reprochés.
Attendu sur la peine, qu'il importe essentiellement dans ce type de délit dont la découverte nécessite la mise en place d'importants et coûteux moyens matériels, d'en éviter la réitération et d'empêcher les coupables puissent tirer profit de leur action délictuelle.
Qu'il convient donc d'ordonner la confiscation du navire et de ses accessoires ainsi que du matériel de pêche et du produit de la pêche actuellement saisi, à titre de peine de substitution à l'emprisonnement, l'exécution provisoire devant être ordonnée pour permettre l'effectivité de la peine.
Attendu cependant que le tribunal doit tenir compte de la loyauté et de la collaboration du prévenu et de son armateur, éléments qui permettent de limiter à la somme de 200 000 francs l'amende à imposer.
Attendu qu'à l'issue des débats le prévenu a sollicité la restitution de son passeport avec exécution provisoire.
Compte tenu de la peine prononcée et de l'absence d'opposition du ministère public sur ce point, il y a lieu de faire droit à cette demande.

SUR L'ACTION CIVILE

Attendu que ARMEMENT SAPMER, COMATA, ARMEMENT DES

- 5 -

MASCAREIGNES, ARMEMENT LE GARREC et le COMITE REGIONAL DE PECHE MARITIME et ELEVAGES MARINS DE LA REUNION se constituent régulièrement partie civile et sollicitent chacun la somme de 100 000 francs à titre de dommages et intérêts ;

Leurs constitutions de parties civiles sont recevables et régulières en la forme;

Il convient de constater que les armateurs acquittant d'importants droits pour pouvoir pêcher légalement dans la ZEE subissent un préjudice certain du fait de la concurrence illégale des pêcheurs pirates et du fait de l'épuisement de la réserve de légine qui détermine les quotas.

Compte-tenu des éléments de la procédure et des débats, le Tribunal dispose d'éléments suffisants pour déclarer le prévenu responsable du préjudice subi par les parties civiles, de recevoir ces constitutions et d'allouer la somme de 20 000 francs à chacun des armements à titre de dommages intérêts toutes causes de préjudice confondues ; ainsi que le franc symbolique au COMITE REGIONAL DE PECHE MARITIME et ELEVAGES MARINS DE LA REUNION dont la recevabilité de la partie civile n'est pas contestée et qui a subi un préjudice moral de principe indiscutable.

PAR CES MOTIFS

SUR L'ACTION PUBLIQUE

Statuant publiquement, en premier ressort et par jugement **contradictoire,** à l'égard de **PEREZ NOVO Ramon Francisco** ;

Déclare **PEREZ NOVO Ramon Francisco** coupable des faits qui lui sont reprochés.

Condamne **PEREZ NOVO Ramon Francisco** :

à 1 amende délictuelle de 200 000,00 francs (deux cents mille francs) ;

Ordonne la confiscation du navire et des accessoires comme chose ayant servi à commettre l'infraction avec exécution provisoire par application des articles 131-6, 10° du code pénal et 471 dernier alinéa du code de procédure pénale,

Par application de la loi du 5 juillet 1983, article 2 paragraphe 2, ordonne la confiscation du matériel de pêche saisi et article 4, des produits de la

- 6 -

pêche saisis,

Ordonne la restitution du passeport de Monsieur **PEREZ NOVO Ramon Francisco** avec exécution provisoire ;

SUR L'ACTION CIVILE

Statuant publiquement, en premier ressort et par jugement **contradictoire,** à l'égard **des armements SAPMER, COMATA, DES MASCAREIGNES et LE GARREC et du COMITE REGIONAL DE PECHE MARITIME et ELEVAGES MARINS DE LA REUNION** ;

Les déclare recevables en leur constitution de partie civile ;

Condamne **PEREZ NOVO Ramon Francisco** à payer à **la SAPMER, la COMATA, L'ARMEMENT DES MASCAREIGNES et L'ARMEMENT LE GARREC**

- la somme de 20 000,00 Francs à titre de dommages et intérêts à chacune de ces parties civiles ;

Condamne **PEREZ NOVO Ramon Francisco** à payer au **COMITE REGIONAL DE PECHE MARITIME et ELEVAGES MARINS DE LA REUNION** ;

- la somme de 1 Franc symbolique à titre de dommages et intérêts ;

La présente décision est assujettie à un droit fixe de procédure d'un montant de **six cents francs (600 Frs)** dont est redevable chaque condamné.

Le tout en application des articles 406 et suivants et 485 du Code de procédure pénale.

Et le présent jugement a été signé par le Président et le Greffier.

LE GREFFIER, LE PRESIDENT,

Suivent les signatures.

POUR COPIE CERTIFIÉE CONFORME
LE GREFFIER EN CHEF

TRIBUNAL DE GRANDE INSTANCE DE ST-DENIS (Réunion)

Annexe 3
Code pénal français (extrait : article 131-6)

ANNEXE III

Extraits du code pénal français (article 131-6) et du code de procédure pénale français (article 471)

Art. 131-6 Lorsqu'un délit est puni d'une peine d'emprisonnement, une ou plusieurs des peines privatives ou restrictives de droits suivantes peuvent être prononcées :– *Pén. 434-41.*

1° La suspension, pour une durée de cinq ans au plus, du permis de conduire, cette suspension pouvant être limitée, selon des modalités déterminées par décret en Conseil d'État, à la conduite en dehors de l'activité professionnelle ;– *V. infra, art. R. 131-1 s. – Pr. pén. 702-1.*

2° L'interdiction de conduire certains véhicules pendant une durée de cinq ans au plus ; – *V. infra, art. R. 131-3 s.*

3° L'annulation du permis de conduire avec interdiction de solliciter la délivrance d'un nouveau permis pendant cinq ans au plus ;

4° La confiscation d'un ou de plusieurs véhicules appartenant au condamné ;

5° L'immobilisation, pour une durée d'un an au plus, d'un ou de plusieurs véhicules appartenant au condamné, selon des modalités déterminées par décret en Conseil d'État ;– *V. infra, art. R. 131-5 s.*

6° L'interdiction de détenir ou de porter, pour une durée de cinq ans au plus, une arme soumise à autorisation ;

7° La confiscation d'une ou de plusieurs armes dont le condamné est propriétaire ou dont il a la libre disposition ; – *Pén. 131-21.*

8° Le retrait du permis de chasser avec interdiction de solliciter la délivrance d'un nouveau permis pendant cinq ans au plus ;

9° L'interdiction pour une durée de cinq ans au plus d'émettre des chèques autres que ceux qui permettent le retrait de fonds par le tireur auprès du tiré ou ceux qui sont certifiés et d'utiliser des cartes de paiement ; – *Pén. 131-19 s.*

10° La confiscation de la chose qui a servi ou était destinée à commettre l'infraction ou de la chose qui en est le produit. Toutefois, cette confiscation ne peut pas être prononcée en matière de délit de presse. – *Pén. 131-21.*

(L. n° 92-1336 du 16 déc. 1992) « 11° L'interdiction pour une durée de cinq ans au plus d'exercer une activité professionnelle ou sociale dès lors que les facilités que procure cette activité ont été sciemment utilisées pour préparer ou commettre l'infraction. Cette interdiction n'est toutefois pas applicable à l'exercice d'un mandat électif ou de responsabilités syndicales. Elle n'est pas non plus applicable en matière de délit de presse. »– *Pr. pén.* [illegible]*, 775, 777.*

Annexe 3 (suite)
Code de procédure pénale français (extrait : article 471)

ARTICLE 471 dernier alinéa du code de procédure pénale (*L. n° 83-466 du 10 juin 1983*) "Les sanctions pénales prononcées en application (*L. n° 92-1336 du 16 décembre 1992*) "des articles 131-6 à 131-11 du Code pénal" peuvent être déclarées exécutoires par provision."

Minutes of Public Sittings – Procès-verbal des audiences publiques

INTERNATIONAL TRIBUNAL FOR THE LAW OF THE SEA
TRIBUNAL INTERNATIONAL DU DROIT DE LA MER

MINUTES OF PUBLIC SITTINGS

MINUTES OF THE PUBLIC SITTINGS
HELD ON 5, 6 AND 20 APRIL 2001

The "Grand Prince" Case
(Belize v. *France), Prompt Release*

PROCÈS-VERBAL DES AUDIENCES PUBLIQUES

PROCÈS-VERBAL DES AUDIENCES PUBLIQUES
DES 5, 6 ET 20 AVRIL 2001

Affaire du « Grand Prince »
(Belize c. France), prompte mainlevée

For ease of use, in addition to the continuous pagination, this volume also contains, between square brackets at the beginning of each statement, a reference to the pagination of the uncorrected verbatim records.

En vue de faciliter l'utilisation de l'ouvrage, le présent volume comporte, outre une pagination continue, l'indication, entre crochets, au début de chaque exposé, de la pagination des procès-verbaux non corrigés.

Minutes of the Public Sittings held on 5, 6 and 20 April 2001

Procès-verbal des audiences publiques des 5, 6 et 20 avril 2001

"GRAND PRINCE"

PUBLIC SITTING HELD ON 5 APRIL 2001, 3.00 P.M.

Tribunal

Present: *President* CHANDRASEKHARA RAO; *Vice-President* NELSON; *Judges* CAMINOS, MAROTTA RANGEL, YANKOV, YAMAMOTO, KOLODKIN, PARK, MENSAH, BAMELA ENGO, AKL, ANDERSON, VUKAS, WOLFRUM, LAING, TREVES, MARSIT, EIRIKSSON, NDIAYE, JESUS; *Judge* ad hoc COT; *Registrar* CHITTY.

Belize is represented by:

Mr Alberto Penelas Alvarez,
Avocat, Bar of Vigo, Spain,

as Agent;

and

Mrs. Beatriz Goicoechea Fábregas,
Avocat, Bar of Vigo, Spain,

as Counsel.

France is represented by:

Mr François Alabrune,
Deputy Director of Legal Affairs of the Ministry of Foreign Affairs,

as Agent;

and

Mr Jean-Pierre Quéneudec,
Professor of International Law at the University of Paris I, Paris, France,

Mr Michel Trinquier,
Deputy Director for the Law of the Sea, Fisheries and the Antarctic, Office of Legal Affairs of the Ministry of Foreign Affairs,

Mr Jacques Belot,
Avocat, Bar of Saint-Denis, Réunion, France,

as Counsel.

AUDIENCE PUBLIQUE DU 5 AVRIL 2001, 15 H 00

Tribunal

Présents : M. CHANDRASEKHARA RAO, *Président*; M. NELSON, *Vice-Président*; MM. CAMINOS, MAROTTA RANGEL, YANKOV, YAMAMOTO, KOLODKIN, PARK, MENSAH, BAMELA ENGO, AKL, ANDERSON, VUKAS, WOLFRUM, LAING, TREVES, MARSIT, EIRIKSSON, NDIAYE, JESUS, *juges*; M. COT, *juge* ad hoc; M. CHITTY, *Greffier*.

Belize est représenté par :

M. Alberto Penelas Alvarez,
avocat, membre du barreau de Vigo, Espagne,

comme agent;

et

Mme Beatriz Goicoechea Fábregas,
avocate, membre du barreau de Vigo, Espagne,

comme conseil.

La France est représentée par :

M. François Alabrune,
directeur adjoint à la direction des affaires juridiques du Ministère des affaires étrangères,

comme agent;

et

M. Jean-Pierre Quéneudec,
professeur de droit international à l'Université de Paris I, Paris, France,

M. Michel Trinquier,
sous-directeur du droit de la mer, des pêches et de l'Antarctique à la direction des affaires juridiques du Ministère des affaires étrangères,

M. Jacques Belot
avocat à Saint-Denis de la Réunion, France,

comme conseils.

"GRAND PRINCE"

Opening of the Oral Proceedings
[PV.01/2, E, p. 4–6; F, p. 1–3]

The Registrar:
On 21 March 2001 an Application was filed on behalf of Belize against France for the prompt release of the fishing vessel *Grand Prince.*

The Application was made under article 292 of the United Nations Convention on the Law of the Sea.

The case has been named *The "Grand Prince" Case (Belize* v. *France)* and entered in the List of cases as case No. 8. Today the Tribunal will take up the hearing in this case.

Agents and Counsel for both Belize and France are present.

The President:
This public sitting is held pursuant to article 26 of the Statute of the Tribunal to hear the parties present their evidence and arguments in the *"Grand Prince" Case.*

I call on the Registrar to read out the submissions of Belize as contained in its Application.

The Registrar:
The Applicant requests the Tribunal:

1. To declare that the Tribunal has jurisdiction under article 292 of the United Nations Convention on the Law of the Sea to hear the present application.
2. To declare the present application admissible.
3. To declare that France failed to comply with article 73, paragraph 2, of the Convention, as the guarantee fixed for release of Grand Prince is not reasonable as to its amount, nature or form.
4. To declare that France failed to comply with article 73, paragraph 2, of the Convention by having evaded the requirement of prompt release under this article by not allowing the release of the vessel upon the posting of a reasonable, or any kind of, guarantee alleging that the vessel is confiscated and that the decision of confiscation has been provisionally executed.
5. To decide that France shall promptly release the Grand Prince upon the posting of a bond or other security to be determined by the Tribunal.
6. To determine that the bond or other security shall consist of an amount of two hundred and six thousand one hundred and forty nine (206,149) Euros or its equivalent in French Francs.
7. To determine that the monetary equivalent to (a) 18 tonnes of fish on board the Grand Prince held by the French authorities, and valued on 123,848 Euros (b) the fishing gear, valued on 24,393 Euros (c) the fishing materials valued on 5,610 Euros, totalling 153,851 Euros, shall be considered as security to be held or, as the case may be, returned by France to this party.
8. To determine that the bond shall be in the form of a bank guarantee.
9. To determine that the wording of the bank guarantee shall, among other things, state the following:

OPENING OF THE ORAL PROCEEDINGS – 5 April 2001, p.m.

A. In case France returns to the shipowner the concepts referred to under point 7 (of the present submissions):

"The bank guarantee it is issued in consideration of France releasing the Grand Prince, in relation to the incidents dealt with in the Order of 12 January 2001 of the Court of First Instance of Saint-Paul and that the issuer undertakes and guarantees to pay to France such sums, up to 206,149 Euros, as may be determined by a final and firm judgement or decision of the appropriate domestic forum in France or by agreement of the parties. Payment under the guarantee would be due promptly after receipt by the issuer of a written demand by the competent authority of France accompanied by a certified copy of the final and firm judgement or decision or agreement."

B. In case France does not return to the shipowner the concepts referred to under point 7 (of the present submissions):

"The bank guarantee it is issued in consideration of France releasing the Grand Prince, in relation to the incidents dealt with in the Order of 12 January 2001 of the Court of First Instance of Saint-Paul and that the issuer undertakes and guarantees to pay to France such sums, up to 52,298 Euros, as may be determined by a final and firm judgement or decision of the appropriate domestic forum in France or by agreement of the parties. Payment under the guarantee would be due promptly after receipt by the issuer of a written demand by the competent authority of France accompanied by a certified copy of the final and firm judgement or decision or agreement."

10. To determine that the bank guarantee shall be invoked only if the monetary equivalent of the security held by France is not sufficient to pay the sums as may be determined by a final and firm judgement or decision of the appropriate domestic forum in France.

The President:
On 22 March 2001, a copy of the Application was transmitted to the Government of France together with the Order of 21 March 2001, in which the President of the Tribunal fixed 5 and 6 April 2001 as the dates for the hearing of the case.

On 28 March 2001, the Government of France filed observations regarding the Application filed on behalf of Belize.

I now call on the Registrar to read out the submission of the Government of France in its Observations.

"GRAND PRINCE"

The Registrar:
The Respondent requests the Tribunal:

> by means of an Order and without need of holding public hearings for that purpose, to note that the Application for release lodged on 21 March 2001 on behalf of Belize is without object [*sans objet*], that it must therefore be rejected, and that there are thus no grounds to institute proceedings.

The President:
Copies of the Application and the Observations of the Government of France have been made available to the public.

The Tribunal notes the presence in court of Mr Alberto Penelas Alvarez, Agent of Belize, and Mr François Alabrune, Agent of France.

I now call on the Agent of the Applicant to note the representation of Belize.

Mr Penelas Alvarez:
Mr President, distinguished Members of the Tribunal, distinguished representatives of France, this is the first time that I and those on my team have acted before this international and relevant Tribunal, and I wish to say that this is a big honour for us. We also wish to thank very much the Registrar of the Tribunal for his helpful and kind assistance, which I hope has allowed us to make the application from a formal point of view in the most correct way.

As advanced to the Tribunal, the State of Belize has authorized me to act as an Agent, and Ms Beatriz Goicoechea to act as legal counsellor.

The President:
May I interrupt the Agent of the Applicant? I have called on you to introduce your delegation, the representatives of Belize. Will you please do that?

Mr Penelas Alvarez:
Yes, Mr President.

Beatriz Goicoechea will act as legal counsellor. She is a Spanish lawyer who specializes in international and maritime law. Carlos Pérez is also a lawyer and he will assist us in general matters. I will make the full representations. They will just assist me.

Thank you very much.

The President:
Thank you.

I now call on the Agent of the Respondent to note the representation of France.

M. Alabrune :
Je vous remercie, Monsieur le Président, permettez-moi de présenter à vous-mêmes et aux membres du Tribunal les membres de la délégation qui représente la France devant votre Tribunal.

Je nommerai en premier lieu le Professeur Jean-Pierre Quéneudec en qualité de conseil. Monsieur Michel Trinquier, sous-directeur du droit de la mer et de l'Antarctique à la direction des affaires juridiques au Ministère des affaires étrangères et Maître Jacques Belot, avocat, également en qualité de conseil.

Je vous remercie.

OPENING OF THE ORAL PROCEEDINGS – 5 April 2001, p.m.

The President:
Thank you.

Today both parties will address the Tribunal on admissibility and jurisdiction. Tomorrow the parties will address the Tribunal on the other issues.

I now give the floor to the Agent of Belize.

"GRAND PRINCE"

Argument of Belize

STATEMENT OF MR PENELAS ALVAREZ
AGENT OF BELIZE
[PV.01/2, E, p. 7–9]

Mr Penelas Alvarez:
Mr President, Members of the Tribunal, distinguished representatives of France, as agreed, I will refer this afternoon only to the concrete question of jurisdiction introduced by France in its letter of comments to the Application. However, in order to address this matter in a correct way, I will need to make some general reference to the facts of the case.

In our opinion, France is trying to avoid or obstaculize the present proceeding, arguing two different questions.

The first is that our Application is not admissible under article 292 of the Convention, in that the domestic court in La Réunion and the [criminal] court of Saint-Denis have decided to confiscate the vessel *Grand Prince* and to execute notwithstanding appeal the decision whilst the remedies of appeal are in course and obviously pendent of a final and firm decision.

In support of this allegation, France argues that this Tribunal can only deal with the matter of the reasonableness of the bond or guarantee and with nothing else. The Tribunal, according to France, will not have jurisdiction or competence to deal with a case where a coastal State, by application of a domestic precept, impedes prompt release of a vessel.

Secondly, France is arguing that the objective of the Application is not whether France complied or not with the request for prompt release, as stated under article 73, paragraph 2, of the Convention, but to question the legality of French domestic laws, which, as France has pointed out in its letter of comment, provide for confiscation of ships and imprisonment of crews. On this basis, France understands that the procedure we have chosen, article 292, is not suitable. Literally what France is arguing – and I read page 3 of its letter – is that: "the [only] limit given for the exercise of sanctioning powers of a coastal State is indicated in paragraph 3 of article 7[3], which excludes sanctions of imprisonment and corporal punishments". This is what France is saying, that the measures that a coastal State can take to prevent fishing have these limits only.

I think that without doubt it is very clear in our Application that the unique subject matter of the present case is whether France has respected or contravened article 73, paragraph 2, of the Convention. In other words, if in this case France provided the opportunity to release the *Grand Prince* and, if so, if the eventual bond is a reasonable one. That is the only subject matter of this case. Clearly, we are not questioning the merits of the case. That has been done in La Réunion where there will be an appeal and we are awaiting a date for that appeal.

We are not discussing the eventual legality of the sanctions that French law contemplates for these cases. We have pointed out in our application that among these sanctions is imprisonment of the crew. It is clear that is not in conformity with the Convention. Mr President, we are not dealing with or discussing that matter here.

France has forgotten, in its letter of comment, that the dispositions of the Convention relating to prompt release of vessels and crews prevail over any domestic precepts. As a consequence, a State cannot invoke a domestic law to justify a breach of this important article of the Convention.

Let me recall the jurisprudence of the case law of this Tribunal. In the Judgment in the "*Camouco" Case*, in paragraph 57, the Tribunal stated:

STATEMENT OF MR PENELAS ALVAREZ – 5 April 2001, p.m.

> Article 292 of the Convention is designed to free a ship and its crew from prolonged detention on account of the imposition of unreasonable bonds in municipal jurisdictions, or the failure of local law to provide for release on posting of a reasonable bond, inflicting thereby avoidable loss on a ship owner or other persons affected by such detention.

This paragraph is self-explanatory.

Point 59 of the Judgment in the *M/V "SAIGA" Case* reads as follows:

> For the purpose of the admissibility of the application for prompt release of the *M/V Saiga* it is sufficient to note that non-compliance with article 73, paragraph 2, … has been "alleged" and to conclude that the allegation is arguable or sufficiently plausible.

Point 7[1] of the same Judgment states:

> In light of the independent character of the proceedings for the prompt release of vessels and crews, when adopting its classification of the laws of the detaining State, the Tribunal is not bound by the classification given by such State.

The precepts of the Convention and the case law of the Tribunal is also in line with other relevant international conventions. Let me refer to the Vienna Convention on the Law of Treaties, which in Article 27 states that "a State cannot invoke the dispositions of its domestic law as justification of the breach of treaties".

In our case, what is very clear is that France is alleging, in support of its non-compliance with the prompt release of a vessel, several articles of its [Penal] Code, copies of which were annexed to France's letter of comment.

I feel that France should also inform this Tribunal about the content of Article 55 of its Constitution, which consecrates all these principles, and the universal principle of the superiority of international treaties over domestic laws or regulations. The article reads as follows: "Treaties or agreements regularly ratified or approved have, upon their publication, authority superior to internal laws."

Mr President and distinguished Members of the Tribunal, the sole subject matter of these proceedings is to determine whether France acted in conformity with article 73.2 of the Convention, and consequently the Tribunal has very clear jurisdiction and competence to deal with the case by virtue of article 292.

Thank you very much, Mr President, distinguished Members of the Tribunal, for your kind attention.

The President:
Thank you.

There will now be a 15-minute break and then France will advance its arguments when we reassemble.

Short recess from 3.23 to 3.45 p.m.

The President:
I now invite the Agent of France to make his statement.

« GRAND PRINCE »

Plaidoirie de la France

EXPOSÉ DE M. ALABRUNE
AGENT DE BELIZE
[PV.01/2, F, p. 5–6]

M. Alabrune :
Monsieur le Président, Messieurs les Juges, je ressens comme un grand honneur la charge que le Gouvernement de la République française m'a confiée de le représenter en qualité d'agent devant votre Tribunal.

Monsieur le Président, Messieurs les Juges, la France estime que la seule question qui se pose en l'espèce est une question préalable : celle de savoir si votre Tribunal peut valablement connaître de la demande présentée au nom de Belize. Il s'agit là d'une question importante. Elle est en effet dépourvue de précédent et votre Tribunal va être amené à prendre sur ce sujet une décision de principe.

Votre décision confirmera les limites que la Convention des Nations Unies sur le droit de la mer a fixées pour le recours à son article 292. Cette décision déterminera donc la portée que votre Tribunal donne, en conformité avec la Convention, à la procédure en prompte mainlevée prévue par cet article.

La différence entre la demande présentée au nom du Belize et les affaires concernant la France sur lesquelles votre Tribunal s'est déjà penché, celle du *« Camouco »* ou celle du *« Monte Confurco »*, cette différence est capitale. Dans ces deux affaires précédentes, votre Tribunal avait en effet à connaître de demandes de mainlevée présentées à un moment où les procédures introduites devant les juridictions nationales étaient en cours et ces procédures n'avaient pas abouti à un jugement sur le fond.

C'était le cas dans l'*Affaire du « Camouco »* dans laquelle, vous vous en souvenez, la procédure judiciaire engagée contre le capitaine était encore au stade de l'instruction lorsque vous vous êtes prononcés. C'était aussi le cas dans l'*Affaire du « Monte Confurco »* dans laquelle l'audience sur le fond devant le juge national ne devait avoir lieu qu'après le déroulement de la procédure en prompte mainlevée devant votre Tribunal.

Dans le cas présent, au contraire, et pour la première fois, on entend saisir votre Tribunal d'une demande en mainlevée alors que l'action judiciaire devant les juridictions nationales compétentes a déjà abouti à un jugement sur le fond de condamnation et alors même que cette condamnation consiste notamment en une mesure de confiscation du navire immobilisé. Voilà la différence majeure entre la présente espèce et les deux affaires précédentes.

Dans ce contexte, une action en mainlevée n'est plus possible et elle n'est même pas concevable. Les raisons en ont été exposées de manière synthétique, de manière résumée, dans les observations écrites qui ont été présentées au Tribunal par le Gouvernement de la République française, et ces raisons vont être à présent développées de manière plus détaillée par le Professeur Jean-Pierre Quéneudec, auquel, Monsieur le Président, je vous serais reconnaissant de bien vouloir donner la parole.

Je vous remercie, Monsieur le Président.

EXPOSÉ DE M. QUÉNEUDEC
CONSEIL DE BELIZE
[PV.01/2, F, p. 6–15]

M. Quéneudec :
Monsieur le Président, Messieurs les Juges, c'est assurément un honneur de s'adresser à nouveau au nom de la France au Tribunal international du droit de la mer. Cet honneur se double évidemment du plaisir de retrouver un cadre qui nous est désormais familier. Qu'il me soit permis d'ajouter cependant que, à force de se renouveler trop fréquemment, ce plaisir risque de s'émousser.

Monsieur le Président, il me revient d'entretenir votre haute juridiction du problème essentiel qui se trouve posé par la demande présentée au nom du Belize sur le fondement apparent de l'article 292 de la Convention des Nations Unies sur le droit de la mer concernant la situation du navire de pêche le *Grand Prince*. Cette demande soulève en effet une question préalable, comme l'a dit à l'instant l'agent du Gouvernement français, question préalable qui est celle de savoir si le Tribunal peut valablement connaître de la requête qui lui a été présentée.

Selon nous, la demande soumise au Tribunal le 21 mars, tendant à ouvrir une instance en mainlevée de l'immobilisation du navire le *Grand Prince*, n'entre pas dans les prévisions de l'article 292 de la Convention et ne saurait donc être accueillie par votre Tribunal. C'est ce que je voudrais m'attacher à démontrer. Aux fins de cette démonstration, je n'entends pas entrer dans l'examen du fond de la demande du Belize puisque la présente audience est consacrée aux problèmes de compétence et de recevabilité.

La requête dont on vous a saisi soulève en effet une question qui est tout à fait préliminaire, pour ne pas dire une question pré-préliminaire, sur laquelle devra nécessairement porter d'abord votre délibéré. Je vais donc m'en tenir à l'exposé des raisons pour lesquelles la demande du Belize ne peut pas être regardée comme relevant de l'article 292. Les membres du Tribunal savent mieux que personne que, dans le cadre de la procédure particulière prévue par l'article 292, il existe des limites strictes, non seulement quant à ce qui peut être demandé par l'auteur de la requête, mais aussi quant à ce qui peut être décidé par le Tribunal.

Rappelons simplement que cette procédure tourne tout entière autour de deux éléments, et de deux éléments seulement, à savoir :

- d'une part l'appréciation du bien-fondé de l'allégation avancée par l'Etat du pavillon, allégation selon laquelle l'Etat côtier n'aurait pas respecté une disposition spécifique de la Convention prévoyant la prompte mainlevée de l'immobilisation d'un navire dès le dépôt d'une caution suffisante;
- d'autre part, deuxième élément, l'appréciation du caractère raisonnable de la caution, si l'allégation précédente paraît fondée, et la détermination éventuelle du montant et de la forme de la caution dont le dépôt doit conduire l'Etat côtier à procéder sans délai à la mainlevée de l'immobilisation du navire.

En outre, comme le précise le paragraphe 3 de l'article 292, lorsque cette procédure particulière est mise en oeuvre, le Tribunal ne peut connaître que de la question de la mainlevée, et je cite la suite du paragraphe : « sans préjudice de la suite qui sera donnée à toute action dont le navire, son propriétaire ou son équipage, peuvent être l'objet devant la juridiction nationale appropriée *(without prejudice to the merits of any case before the appropriate domestic forum)* ». Ce qui signifie que le fond de l'affaire dans laquelle est impliqué le navire ou son capitaine devant une juridiction nationale échappe au domaine couvert par cet article 292.

« GRAND PRINCE »

Par conséquent, la recevabilité d'une demande de mainlevée et la compétence du Tribunal pour en connaître, rencontrent une importante limite *ratione materiae*. Il est inutile bien entendu d'insister sur ce point sur lequel le Tribunal a lui-même eu déjà une série de prononcés antérieurement à la présente instance.

Ce n'est cependant pas le seul type de limites apporté à une instance en mainlevée. Il en existe semble-t-il au moins une autre qui tient à la survenance d'un événement prenant place entre la date de l'immobilisation du navire et le moment où l'on prétend introduire une instance en mainlevée, lorsque cet événement est de nature à rendre vaine toute requête sur le fondement de l'article 292. Il ne s'agit donc pas d'une limite de nature temporelle, qui découlerait de l'écoulement du temps ou de l'existence d'un quelconque délai de forclusion. D'ailleurs, dans l'*Affaire du « Camouco »*, le Tribunal avait précisé que l'article 292 n'imposait pas de limite ou de condition *ratione temporis* et il avait déclaré, je cite le paragraphe 54 de l'arrêt : « l'article ne requiert pas de l'Etat du pavillon de soumettre une demande à un moment particulier après l'immobilisation du navire ».

Il ne s'agit donc pas d'une limite de nature temporelle. La limite à laquelle je me réfère apparaît plutôt comme une limite que l'on pourrait qualifier, pardon pour ce néologisme, de limite *ratione eventus*. Une telle limite *ratione eventus* n'est certes pas expressément inscrite dans les textes, mais elle est nécessairement impliquée par la fonction assignée à la procédure de mainlevée.

Le Tribunal n'a pas eu à s'en préoccuper dans les trois affaires de prompte mainlevée dont il a été saisi jusqu'à présent parce que le problème ne se posait pas. Pour la première fois, il doit y faire face aujourd'hui et prendre sur ce point une décision qui, nous n'en doutons pas, sera une décision de principe appelée, comme on dit, à faire jurisprudence. C'est précisément cette limite, que je me permets de qualifier de limite *ratione eventus*, à laquelle se heurte en premier lieu la demande présentée au nom du Belize et qui fait apparaître cette demande comme absolument irrecevable. Ce sera la le premier point que je développerai dans mon exposé.

Mais cette demande rencontre, d'autre part, un deuxième obstacle qui tient à ce que le Tribunal ne dispose pas de la compétence nécessaire pour pouvoir connaître de la requête, telle qu'elle a été présentée. Je traiterai de cet aspect dans un deuxième point de ma présentation.

Il est enfin un troisième aspect qui découle des considérations précédentes et sur lequel le Gouvernement français a insisté dans les observations écrites qu'il a adressées au Tribunal le 28 mars : l'instance que prétend introduire la requête du Belize n'a pas lieu d'être. Elle est proprement inexistante. Ma plaidoirie se terminera, Monsieur le Président, par la présentation de ce troisième point.

Je vais donc envisager à présent successivement, d'abord l'irrecevabilité de la demande, puis l'incompétence du Tribunal pour en connaître, et enfin, en troisième lieu, l'inconsistance en l'espèce d'une instance au titre de l'article 292.

Tout d'abord, l'irrecevabilité de la demande. La requête du Belize doit être regardée comme irrecevable parce qu'elle a été soumise au Tribunal le 21 mars dernier alors qu'était intervenu, deux mois auparavant, le 23 janvier, un jugement de condamnation faisant suite à l'action dont le capitaine du navire *Grand Prince* avait fait l'objet devant la juridiction française appropriée. Or, l'institution de la procédure de mainlevée de l'article 292 apparaît liée à l'existence d'une instance judiciaire à venir ou déjà en cours devant les tribunaux internes de l'Etat côtier, bien qu'elle soit pourtant entièrement distincte de cette action judiciaire interne.

La procédure de l'article 292 présuppose en effet que l'instance judiciaire interne, ou bien n'ait pas encore été formellement ouverte, comme c'était le cas dans les affaires du *« SAIGA »* et du *« Camouco »*, ou bien que cette instance interne soit encore pendante devant les juridictions nationales, comme dans l'*Affaire du « Monte Confurco »*, c'est-à-dire que la procédure de l'article 292 présuppose que l'instance judiciaire interne n'ait pas encore abouti à une décision sur le fond.

Lorsque l'Etat du pavillon d'un navire de pêche est amené à recourir à la procédure de l'article 292, c'est dans un but bien précis. C'est afin de permettre au propriétaire ou à l'armateur de récupérer le navire sans avoir à attendre l'aboutissement d'une action judiciaire introduite par les autorités de l'Etat côtier.

Aussi peut-on dire, a contrario, que lorsque cette action judiciaire interne a abouti, c'est-à-dire lorsque l'instance judiciaire interne n'est plus pendante devant un tribunal national, le recours à la procédure de l'article 292 tend à perdre non seulement tout intérêt, mais même à perdre toute raison d'être.

Ce n'est pas une affirmation gratuite. C'est ce qui est impliqué par le texte même de l'article 292. Le paragraphe 3 de cet article 292 utilise l'expression, je cite, « sans préjudice de la suite qui sera donnée à toute action ». L'utilisation du futur indique on ne peut plus clairement que l'on se place bien dans la perspective d'un jugement qui sera rendu ultérieurement par le tribunal national compétent.

De même, la formule « sans préjudice » elle-même ne peut se comprendre que dans le sens « sans préjuger », comme le montre d'ailleurs plus nettement le texte anglais : « *without prejudice to the merits of any case* ». Ce qui signifie qu'il ne saurait être question de décider d'avance de porter un jugement prématuré ou de prévoir par conjecture.

Mais c'est aussi ce qui résulte du Règlement du Tribunal lui-même. L'article 114 du Règlement du Tribunal consacré au dépôt d'une caution auprès du Tribunal lui-même et dans le paragraphe 2 précise, je cite :

> Le Greffier endosse ou transmet la caution ou autre garantie financière à l'Etat qui a immobilisé le navire, pour autant qu'elle est requise pour qu'il soit donné suite à l'arrêt, sentence ou décision définitive de l'autorité compétente de l'Etat qui a procédé à l'immobilisation.

Au seul vu des textes, il est donc bien évident que la saisine du Tribunal au titre de l'article 292 est conçue comme devant intervenir avant que les procédures internes engagées contre le navire ou son capitaine aient elles-mêmes abouti à une décision sur le fond. Dès lors, on voit mal comment la saisine du Tribunal sur la base de cet article pourrait prendre place après qu'une décision sur le fond a été prise par la juridiction interne appropriée.

Monsieur le Président, cette lecture des textes applicables se trouve d'autre part confirmée par l'interprétation qu'en a donnée et l'application qu'en a faite le Tribunal lui-même dans les affaires de mainlevée dont il a été saisi jusqu'ici. Ainsi, dans l'*Affaire du navire « SAIGA »*, l'arrêt du 14 décembre 1997 précisa, à propos précisément des rapports entre la procédure de l'article 292 et les procédures nationales, et je cite un passage du paragraphe 49 de cet arrêt :

> si les Etats qui sont parties à la procédure devant le Tribunal sont liés par l'arrêt adopté par le Tribunal pour ce qui est de la mainlevée et de la caution ou autre garantie, les juridictions nationales ne sont pas, lors de l'examen de la question quant au fond, liées par les constatations de fait ou de droit que le Tribunal a pu faire pour aboutir à ses conclusions.

Monsieur le Président, comment pourrait-on affirmer que les tribunaux nationaux ne sont pas tenus par les constatations faites par votre Tribunal, si on ne partait pas du présupposé logique que l'intervention de ces tribunaux nationaux est postérieure à un arrêt rendu par vous en matière de mainlevée ?

Cela fut rappelé sous une autre forme dans l'arrêt rendu dans l'*Affaire du « Monte Confurco »* où le Tribunal, reprenant les termes de l'article 292, indiqua, je cite encore :

> La procédure prévue à cet article … ne saurait, par conséquent, concerner que la question de la mainlevée et de la libération, sans préjudice de la suite qui sera donnée à toute action dont le navire, son propriétaire ou son équipage peuvent être l'objet devant la juridiction nationale appropriée.

On en trouve également un écho dans la décision rendue par le Tribunal dans l'*Affaire du « Camouco »* où il était relevé, je cite encore, et il s'agit cette fois du paragraphe 58 de l'arrêt *« Camouco »* :

> l'article 292 autorise la soumission d'une demande de mainlevée après une courte période à compter du moment de l'immobilisation et, dans la pratique, les recours internes ne peuvent normalement pas être épuisés dans un délai aussi court.

Bien que formulée à propos de la non-applicabilité de la règle de l'épuisement préalable des recours internes dans le cadre de l'article 292, cette observation de l'arrêt *« Camouco »*, l'observation ainsi faite par votre Tribunal, traduisait pourtant, semble-t-il, la conviction qu'une action au titre de l'article 292 prend nécessairement place en attendant l'aboutissement des actions judiciaires engagées dans l'ordre interne.

Il est donc permis d'affirmer qu'une demande présentée en vertu de l'article 292 n'est plus recevable à partir du moment où un tribunal interne a statué et adopté une décision sur le fond de l'action intentée contre le capitaine du navire. En pareil cas, on peut dire qu'une demande de mainlevée soumise au Tribunal se heurte à une fin de non-recevoir qui représente un obstacle définitif à l'ouverture ou à la poursuite de l'instance régie par l'article 292. Sinon, il faudrait admettre que le Tribunal, en se prononçant sur une demande de mainlevée, aurait le pouvoir de transformer l'action en mainlevée en une action en réformation d'un jugement national, ce qu'il n'a évidemment pas le pouvoir de faire, comme il fut clairement précisé dans le dernier arrêt de ce tribunal, je cite un extrait du paragraphe 72 de l'arrêt *« Monte Confurco »* du 18 décembre 2000 : « aux termes de l'article 292 de la Convention, il [le Tribunal] n'est pas une instance d'appel à l'encontre d'une décision rendue par une juridiction nationale ».

Le moyen que nous avançons ainsi, à l'appui de la thèse soutenue par la France de l'irrecevabilité de la demande, ne consiste pas à tenter de faire prévaloir une décision judiciaire nationale sur une obligation internationale découlant d'une convention en vigueur, contrairement à ce que semblait dire la partie adverse dans ses écritures et contrairement à ce qu'a dit l'agent du Belize tout à l'heure. Le moyen que nous invoquons découle en réalité de la lettre et de l'esprit de la disposition conventionnelle relative à la prompte mainlevée telle qu'elle a été interprétée par la jurisprudence du Tribunal.

De surcroît, dans le cadre de la procédure de mainlevée, lorsqu'il est amené à évaluer le montant raisonnable d'une caution, le Tribunal se fonde sur une série d'éléments et tient compte notamment des peines susceptibles d'être encourues, comme par exemple, le montant possible des amendes ou encore la confiscation éventuelle du navire et des engins de pêche. Mais la prise en compte des pénalités encourues, possibles, éventuelles, pour déterminer le montant de la caution est la simple traduction du fait que la caution a aussi pour objet d'apporter à l'Etat côtier une garantie qui lui permettra, en cas de besoin, d'assurer l'exécution effective des peines lorsque celles-ci seront prononcées. Comment, dès lors, pourrait-on concevoir la saisine du Tribunal pour qu'il fixe une caution apportant une telle garantie d'exécution des peines à venir, lorsque ces dernières ont déjà été prononcées, et surtout lorsque la confiscation du navire constitue l'une de ces peines ? Monsieur le Président, pour toutes ces raisons, nous considérons que la requête du Belize est irrecevable et nous prions le Tribunal de déclarer qu'elle n'est pas recevable.

Cette requête ne soulève toutefois pas uniquement un problème de recevabilité, elle butte aussi sur un autre obstacle qui consiste en ce que le Tribunal n'est pas compétent pour connaître de cette demande telle qu'elle a été formulée.

J'en viens maintenant, Monsieur le Président, au deuxième point de mon exposé consacré à l'incompétence du Tribunal.

Soutenir l'argument de l'incompétence de la juridiction internationale à laquelle on s'adresse n'est pas toujours un exercice agréable pour celui qui plaide, ni d'ailleurs pour les juges qui lui font l'honneur de l'écouter. Fort heureusement, si l'exercice n'est pas agréable, dans ce cas particulier, il est relativement facile à accomplir, car ici l'incompétence du Tribunal est tellement manifeste qu'elle s'impose presque comme une évidence et n'appellera donc pas une longue démonstration.

Aux yeux du Gouvernement français, en effet, le Tribunal ne saurait trouver dans l'article 292 de la Convention une base de compétence pour connaître de la requête du Belize telle qu'elle a été présentée, et il n'existe par ailleurs aucune base de compétence sur laquelle le Tribunal pourrait se fonder si, par extraordinaire, il décidait de re-qualifier la requête présentée par Belize. Il convient donc d'envisager successivement ces deux aspects : l'incompétence du Tribunal d'une part dans le cadre de l'article 292, et d'autre part l'incompétence du Tribunal en dehors du cadre de cet article.

Tout d'abord, dans le cadre de l'article 292 de la Convention. Dans les trois affaires précédentes relatives à des demandes de prompte mainlevée, le Tribunal a toujours pris soin de vérifier que sa compétence pour connaître de ces demandes était établie en s'assurant en particulier de la qualité de Parties à la Convention des Nations Unies sur le droit de la mer des deux Etats concernés.

Dans le cas présent, le Belize et la France sont des Etats Parties à la Convention et sont, de ce fait, soumis à la juridiction du Tribunal prévue par l'article 292 de cette Convention. Toutefois, lorsqu'il est saisi en application de cet article, le Tribunal doit aussi vérifier que la question qui lui est soumise possède bien les qualifications particulières qui sont requises par le titre de juridiction invoqué.

Or, bien que du point de vue procédural, le Tribunal ait été apparemment saisi en application de l'article 292, la requête qui lui est présentée recouvre en réalité un différend plus large qu'une demande en prompte mainlevée. Ce qui est en cause, en effet, c'est la question de savoir si l'application de la loi française par les autorités judiciaires françaises correspond à ce qui est permis par la Convention sur le droit de la mer. En particulier, le requérant cherche à faire dire et juger par le Tribunal que la loi française prévoyant la confiscation des navires de pêche coupables d'infractions et l'application qui a été faite de cette loi par le tribunal correctionnel de Saint-Denis de la Réunion ne sont pas conformes à la Convention. D'autre part, le requérant tend à demander au Tribunal de statuer sur le déroulement des procédures judiciaires françaises qui ont abouti à la condamnation du capitaine du *Grand Prince* et à la confiscation de ce navire.

Une illustration en a été fournie dans la prétendue réplique que, de façon assez surprenante, le requérant s'est cru autorisé à adresser au Tribunal, en réponse aux Observations écrites du Gouvernement français, et qui, je le signale en passant, est en contradiction flagrante avec les dispositions de l'article 111, paragraphe 6, du Règlement, alors pourtant que le requérant prétend se situer uniquement dans le cadre de la procédure de mainlevée organisée par cette disposition du Règlement. Cette réplique ou soi-disant réplique insiste sur la prétention selon laquelle il y aurait eu de la part de la France, je cite, une violation grave et flagrante de la Convention résultant de la tenue d'un procès rapide et sommaire.

Il ne s'agit plus, on le voit, d'une simple allégation selon laquelle les autorités françaises n'auraient pas respecté les dispositions de la Convention prévoyant la prompte mainlevée de l'immobilisation du navire dès le dépôt d'une caution suffisante. La demande du Belize tend en fait, par le biais de l'article 292, à porter devant le Tribunal une question que, dans les droits anglo-saxons, on pourrait nommer : « *denial of procedural fairness and of due process in relation to judicial proceedings* ».

Dans le cadre de l'article 292, le Tribunal n'est certainement pas compétent pour se prononcer sur de telles demandes qui n'entrent pas dans les prévisions de cet article. Les termes mêmes employés dans la requête en sont la meilleure illustration que l'on puisse donner. Le requérant a en effet cru bon d'affirmer que les autorités judiciaires françaises avaient usé, je cite, « d'artifice », qu'elles avaient eu recours à un subterfuge et que leur action s'apparentait à une fraude à la loi.

Ces propos sont en eux-mêmes révélateurs. Ils suffisent à montrer que nous sommes ici bien loin d'une simple question de mainlevée. Dès lors le Tribunal, je le répète, ne dispose pas, en vertu de l'article 292, d'une compétence pour apprécier les éléments sur lesquels repose la demande du Belize. S'il décidait néanmoins de retenir la requête qui lui a été soumise, ne risquerait-il pas de s'exposer aux risques de commettre un excès de pouvoir et de se voir reprocher un « *misuse of power* » ?

Il existe toutefois une autre raison à l'incompétence du Tribunal pour connaître de cette demande. Cette autre raison se situe en dehors du cadre de l'article 292 et il convient d'en dire simplement quelques mots.

Puisque les éléments sur lesquels repose la demande du Belize n'entrent pas dans le cadre de l'article 292 sur la prompte mainlevée, et que par conséquent le Tribunal n'a pas compétence pour examiner la requête au titre de cet article, il est nécessaire de se poser la question de savoir s'il peut exister une autre base de compétence qui pourrait être avancée compte tenu du but poursuivi par cette requête.

Comme on l'a vu, cette requête met plus ou moins directement en cause les conditions d'exercice par la France en tant qu'Etat côtier de ses droits souverains et de sa juridiction dans la zone économique exclusive. En d'autres termes, derrière l'apparence d'une anodine demande de mainlevée, se dissimule en réalité un différend d'ordre plus général. Or, le Tribunal n'a absolument pas compétence pour connaître d'un tel différend.

Il n'est pas contesté en effet que, en tant qu'Etat côtier, la France dispose du pouvoir souverain d'édicter des règles relatives à la pêche dans sa zone économique, au nom de ce que l'on peut appeler sa « *jurisdiction to prescribe* ». Il est également incontestable que la France est en droit de poursuivre l'exécution forcée de ces règles au moyen de décisions judiciaires en vertu de sa « *jurisdiction to adjudicate* ». Il n'est pas non plus douteux que, dans le cas présent, ce qui a été réalisé par les autorités françaises est un acte judiciaire d'exécution forcée dans l'exercice des droits souverains que détient l'Etat côtier sur la zone économique exclusive.

Or, au moment de la ratification de la Convention des Nations Unies sur le droit de la mer, le Gouvernement français a déposé une déclaration, conformément à l'article 298, paragraphe 1 b), de ladite Convention, déclaration par laquelle il faisait savoir qu'il n'acceptait aucune des dispositions de la Partie XV, section 2, de la Convention au sujet, je cite : des « différends qui concernent les actes d'exécution forcée accomplis dans l'exercice de droits souverains ou de la juridiction, et que l'article 297, paragraphe 2 ou 3, exclut de la compétence d'une cour ou d'un tribunal ». Il en résulte qu'en tout état de cause, le Tribunal ne disposerait pas, à l'égard de la France, de la compétence pour connaître d'un éventuel différend relatif à un acte d'exécution forcée.

Il me reste, Monsieur le Président, à envisager, le troisième et dernier aspect soulevé par la demande présentée au nom du Belize et qui est constitué par la circonstance qu'en l'occurrence il n'y a pas et il ne peut pas y avoir à proprement parler d'affaire en prompte mainlevée.

Monsieur le Président, il me faut de 5 à 10 minutes pour traiter de ce point. Me permettez-vous de poursuivre, en allant jusqu'à la pause ?

The President:
Please do continue.

M. Quéneudec :
J'en viens donc à ce troisième et dernier point concernant l'inexistence d'une instance au titre de l'article 292. On ne peut guère envisager ici l'existence d'une affaire et donc d'une instance en mainlevée de l'immobilisation d'un navire parce que, tout simplement, la demande présentée par le Belize est en fait dépourvue d'objet.

La requête du Belize est dépourvue d'objet, eu égard à la circonstance que le navire pour lequel elle demande le prononcé d'une mainlevée d'immobilisation a fait l'objet d'une mesure de confiscation décidée par le tribunal compétent à titre de peine et eu égard au fait que cette peine a été assortie d'une mesure d'exécution immédiate.

L'immobilisation du navire dont elle demande la mainlevée n'est pas en l'espèce une mesure provisoire analogue au procédé de la saisie conservatoire, qui est relativement fréquente dans le droit maritime, où l'on est porté à s'inspirer toujours de la maxime « Mieux vaut tenir que courir », droit maritime où l'on se préoccupe davantage de procédure au nom du fameux adage « *Remedies precede rights* ».

Une saisie conservatoire – en anglais, *arrest* ou *attachment*, selon le cas – permet de retenir un navire à titre de gage ou de sûreté en attendant le règlement d'un litige. Prise avec l'autorisation d'un juge, cette mesure provisoire peut être également levée sur autorisation de l'autorité judiciaire compétente « lorsqu'une caution ou une garantie suffisante auront été fournies », pour reprendre ici l'expression utilisée dans l'article 5 de la Convention de Bruxelles de 1952 sur la saisie conservatoire des navires de mer, dont les termes ont influencé en partie la rédaction de l'article 292 de la Convention sur le droit de la mer.

L'immobilisation ici en cause, s'agissant du *Grand Prince*, est tout à fait différente. Elle résulte d'une décision de justice qui a prononcé la confiscation du navire concerné en tant que peine applicable, conformément aux dispositions du droit national prévoyant la répression de délits, comme le délit de pêche illicite dans les eaux sous juridiction française. Contrairement à ce que prétend la partie requérante, le fait de prononcer la confiscation d'un navire de pêche battant pavillon étranger ne constitue en rien une violation de la Convention sur le droit de la mer. Cette Convention laisse chaque Etat Partie totalement libre de définir les infractions à ses lois et règlements en matière de pêche, de même que cette Convention laisse chaque Etat Partie libre de déterminer les sanctions susceptibles d'être appliquées aux auteurs de ces infractions, sous la réserve de l'article 73, paragraphe 3, bien entendu.

Le Tribunal n'ignore pas que ce type de sanction, la confiscation, est prévu par la législation nationale de nombreux Etats côtiers, dont les tribunaux n'hésitent pas à appliquer la peine de confiscation du navire, qui est une peine particulièrement grave lorsqu'il s'agit de réprimer des délits de pêche d'une particulière gravité. Il suffit, pour s'en convaincre, de consulter, dans la série *The Law of the Sea* publiée par la Division des affaires maritimes et du droit de la mer du Bureau des affaires juridiques du Secrétariat des Nations Unies, le volume consacré aux législations nationales sur la zone économique exclusive.

« GRAND PRINCE »

Le navire *Grand Prince* ayant été confisqué avec effet immédiat à titre de sanction pénale, il se trouve de fait immobilisé, mais cette immobilisation n'a rien de comparable à l'immobilisation qui résulte d'une mesure de saisie autorisée par un juge dans le cadre d'une procédure civile ou pénale engagée contre le propriétaire ou le capitaine du navire. Alors qu'une saisie de type conservatoire a pour seul effet d'empêcher le départ du navire et ne porte aucune atteinte aux droits du propriétaire, une confiscation prononcée par décision de justice, qui s'apparente ici, pour conserver ce parallèle avec le droit maritime, à une saisie exécution, entraîne le transfert au profit de l'Etat du droit de propriété sur le navire. Il s'agit de ce que les droits d'inspiration anglo-saxonne désignent sous le nom de « *forfeiture* », laquelle est généralement définie, je cite : « *loss of property as a penalty for some illegal act* ». En pareil cas, le titulaire du titre sur le navire n'est plus la personne physique ou morale qui en était propriétaire jusqu'à l'intervention de la mesure judiciaire de confiscation.

Dans ces conditions, si l'ancien propriétaire, dont le navire a été confisqué par décision de justice, souhaite recouvrer son titre sur le navire et retrouver la libre disposition de ce navire, il ne peut le faire qu'en contestant la régularité de la décision judiciaire qui a ordonné la confiscation. La voie normale consiste alors, pour lui, à recourir à une juridiction supérieure d'appel, en l'espèce, la cour d'appel de Saint-Denis de la Réunion. Cet ancien propriétaire ne peut pas prétendre soumettre ou faire soumettre cette question au Tribunal international du droit de la mer en se fondant sur l'article 292 de la Convention, parce que c'est une question qui concerne le fond de l'affaire, « *The merits of the case* », et qui est, en tant que telle, exclue du champ d'application de l'article 292, nous l'avons vu. Et d'ailleurs, cette question ne pourrait éventuellement être déférée à une juridiction internationale ayant compétence pour en connaître, qu'après épuisement préalable des voies de recours internes.

D'un autre côté, lorsque l'ancien propriétaire, au lieu de contester devant les tribunaux français la régularité ou le bien-fondé de la confiscation, cherche à récupérer son titre sur le navire par le biais d'une demande de mainlevée devant votre Tribunal, il se heurte à une autre impossibilité, puisque dans le cadre de l'article 292 le Tribunal ne se prononce que sur une question de mainlevée d'immobilisation. Dans ce cadre, le Tribunal peut ordonner à l'Etat côtier de procéder à la prompte mainlevée, c'est-à-dire que sa décision permet normalement au propriétaire de retrouver l'usage de son navire.

Donc, par suite de la confiscation, le titre de propriété se trouve entre les mains de l'Etat français. En ordonnant la prompte mainlevée, le Tribunal risquerait d'être conduit à ordonner aux autorités judiciaires françaises de restituer le navire à son propriétaire, étant donné que jusqu'à une décision de justice éventuellement contraire, le propriétaire actuel du navire est l'Etat français, une décision du Tribunal ordonnant la remise du navire à son propriétaire n'aurait aucun sens. Si, au contraire, le Tribunal ordonnait à la France de procéder à la mainlevée au profit de l'ancien propriétaire, outre le fait qu'il serait ainsi amené à réformer irrégulièrement un jugement rendu par une juridiction interne, surgirait inévitablement le problème de la suite qui pourrait être donnée à l'arrêt du Tribunal.

Il n'est pas douteux que la décision que pourrait prendre le Tribunal ordonnant à la France de restituer le navire *Grand Prince* à son ancien propriétaire, cette décision que pourrait prendre le Tribunal serait dépourvue de tout effet pratique.

En tant que juridiction internationale, le Tribunal ne peut pas se permettre de tenter de trancher une question qui finalement est vide de sens et que l'on peut qualifier du terme anglais ou américain « *moot* », selon la définition qu'en donnait Sir Gerald Fitzmaurice dans son opinion individuelle jointe à l'arrêt de la Cour internationale de Justice dans l'affaire du *Cameroun septentrional*. Une question peut être ou devenir « *moot* » lorsqu'elle apparaît comme « *pointless or without object* ». Et d'ailleurs, dans cette affaire, dans son arrêt du 2 décembre 1963, la Cour avait souligné, je cite :

> L'arrêt de la Cour doit avoir des conséquences pratiques en ce sens qu'il doit pouvoir affecter les droits et obligations juridiques existants des parties, dissipant ainsi toute incertitude dans leurs relations juridiques.

Monsieur le Président, on le voit, de quelque côté que l'on retourne la question, on débouche constamment sur une impasse. La raison en est simple. La demande est sans objet et le Tribunal ne saurait donc y faire droit. Et, comme toute juridiction soucieuse de sauvegarder l'intégrité de la fonction judiciaire, le Tribunal a donc ici la possibilité de faire usage de son pouvoir inhérent de constater que, dans les circonstances de l'espèce, il ne peut pas statuer sur la demande qui lui a été présentée au nom de l'Etat du Belize et qu'il convient en conséquence de déclarer le non-lieu.

Telles sont, Monsieur le Président, les différentes raisons qui nous conduisent à vous demander de déclarer que la requête du Belize doit être écartée.

Monsieur le Président, Messieurs les Juges, je souhaiterais en terminant, vous remercier de votre aimable attention.

The President:
Have you concluded your arguments on jurisdiction and admissibility?

M. Quéneudec :
J'ai terminé.

The President:
Thank you.

(*To the Agent of Belize*) Are you ready to give your reply or would you like a 15-minute break as agreed earlier?

Mr Penelas Alvarez:
I would appreciate a short break to prepare my reply.

The President:
Yes. We will meet again at 5 o'clock.

Short adjournment from 4.45 to 5.05 p.m.

The President:
I now invite the Agent of Belize to make his statement.

"GRAND PRINCE"

Argument of Belize (continued)

STATEMENT OF MR PENELAS ALVAREZ
AGENT OF BELIZE
[PV.01/2, E, p. 19–20]

Mr Penelas Alvarez:
It is curious to see that the allegations made by the French representatives are purely directed to justify invoking certain domestic regulations, obviously not [the French] Constitution, and also domestic proceedings, to justify a breach of article 73.2 of the Convention. I insist that that is not admissible.

I thought that today we were dealing only with the matters of jurisdiction and admissibility. However, I note that the representatives of France went through the merits of the case. Therefore, I wish very briefly to mention the facts of the arrest of the *Grand Prince*.

The vessel was detained on 26 December 2000. On 12 January 2001, 17 days after the detention, the court of first instance of Saint-Paul in La Réunion fixed a guarantee for release of the vessel and the Captain which allowed only the form of a cheque or a payment in cash in the amount of 11,400,000 FF. A bank guarantee was not allowed.

On 23 January 2001, which is only one week after the notification of the order to the Captain, neither the shipowner nor Belize was notified until France received the present Application. The shipowner was trying to make arrangements to try to place the bond and to avoid the disaster of paralyzing the ship. The [criminal] court of Saint-Denis, as France has recognized, decided effectively to confiscate the ship and to impose a fine on the Captain in the amount of 200,000 FF. The court also decided to execute the confiscation notwithstanding appeal. The said decision has been appealed, as you can see in the file, before the court of appeal of Saint-Denis, pending a date for a hearing.

On that basis, France actually impeded the release of the ship, neither with a reasonable bond nor with what was in our opinion the unreasonable bond fixed by the first instance court. As a result, the reality of all that is that the vessel remains detained in La Réunion. Those are the simple facts of our case.

Paragraph 1 of article 73 states that the coastal State can arrest and carry out judicial proceedings to ensure compliance with the laws and regulations adopted by it, but always in conformity with the Convention. Paragraph 2 of the same article establishes an important limit with regard to the power given to the coastal States under paragraph 1 of the same article, that the crews and vessels must in every case be released without delay against a reasonable bond. The Convention gives the same treatment to the crews and the vessels. They must not be detained while the judicial proceedings are pending.

Although I am conscious that the Tribunal has a clear and superior criterion of the aim and meaning of "prompt release" under article 73 of the Convention, I wish to recall a paragraph of the Judgment pronounced in the *"Monte Confurco" Case*, where the Tribunal masterfully expressed the meaning of the said relevant precept:

> Article 73 identifies two interests, the interest of the coastal State to take appropriate measures as may be necessary to ensure compliance with the laws and regulations adopted by it on the one hand and the interest of the flag State in securing prompt release of its vessels and their crews from detention on the other. It strikes a fair balance between the two interests. It provides for release of the vessel and its crew upon the posting of a bond or other security, thus protecting the interests of the flag State and of other

persons affected by the detention of the vessel and its crew. The release from detention can be subject only to a "reasonable" bond.

That was held by the Tribunal in the *"Monte Confurco" Case* and is absolutely clear.

I wonder where, in our case, is the said balance of interests between the two States? Where is the protection of the shipowner, the flag State, the creditors of the ship, the workers, the ship agents or other people with an interest in the ship? Where is that protection? If we follow the theory of France, every State could perfectly avoid the requirement of prompt release of vessels and crews. That is easy: you modify your domestic law, like France, to contemplate confiscation of ships, vessels, imprisonment of crews, execution notwithstanding appeal and a speedy proceeding. The proceedings can take place even after arrival of the ship at port. That is very easy. You can have a decision very quickly and then argue that as long as the decision is executed notwithstanding appeal, you do not have to release the ship.

It does not matter if, after an appeal based on law, it is decided that the decision was not correct. The crew can be taken out of prison and the vessel, if it still exists, can be returned to the shipowner. That is simple. That way one can avoid the requirements of prompt release under article 73.2 of the Convention.

France is trying to introduce a new concept in international law; a new concept in the Convention. I shall call it "prompt confiscation and prompt imprisonment". That concept would prevail over prompt release. If the Tribunal accepted such a position, article 73.2 would become in practice "dead letters", wet paper. It would be an open door for all kinds of subterfuge and strategies to evade compliance with the Convention.

Therefore, it is clear – I reproduce here the arguments of the Application – that the Tribunal has a clear jurisdiction in this case and that the Application is admissible.

Thank you very much, Mr President, and honourable Judges, for your kind attention.

The President:
I presume that you have concluded your arguments on jurisdiction?

Mr Penelas Alvarez:
That is correct, Mr President.

The President:
Thank you.

Would the Agent of France like to make a further statement?

« GRAND PRINCE »

Plaidoirie de la France (suite)

EXPOSÉ DE M. ALABRUNE
AGENT DE BELIZE
[PV.01/2, F, p. 17]

M. Alabrune :
Monsieur le Président, Messieurs les Juges, nous arrivons au terme de l'audience que votre Tribunal a bien voulu consacrer à la question préalable soulevée par la France et relative à la recevabilité de la demande et à la compétence du Tribunal pour connaître de cette demande présentée au nom du Belize.

Au cours de cette audience, la France a exposé ses arguments sur cette question et, contrairement à ce que vient d'affirmer l'autre partie, elle est restée à l'intérieur de la question de la recevabilité et de la compétence et n'en a pas débordé.

A l'issue de cette discussion au cours de laquelle les deux parties se sont exprimées, je souhaite déposer, sur cette question préalable de la recevabilité et de la compétence, les conclusions du Gouvernement de la République française, qui se lisent comme suit, et je cite :

> Le Gouvernement de la République française prie le Tribunal, rejetant toute conclusion contraire présentée au nom de l'Etat du Belize, de constater que la demande de mainlevée déposée le 21 mars 2001 au nom du Belize est irrecevable, et, qu'en tout état de cause, le Tribunal n'a pas compétence pour en connaître et que cette demande doit, dès lors, être écartée.

Je remets au greffe, sur cette question préalable, les conclusions du Gouvernement de la République française et j'ajoute évidemment, Monsieur le Président, que ces conclusions ne portent que sur la question préliminaire et que, bien entendu, la France déposera demain des conclusions finales à l'issue des débats du Tribunal.

Je vous remercie, Monsieur le Président.

The President:
Thank you.

The meeting is now adjourned. We will meet again at 10.00 a.m. tomorrow.

Adjournment at 5.20 p.m.

PUBLIC SITTING HELD ON 6 APRIL 2001, 10.00 A.M.

Tribunal

Present: *President* CHANDRASEKHARA RAO; *Vice-President* NELSON; *Judges* CAMINOS, MAROTTA RANGEL, YANKOV, YAMAMOTO, KOLODKIN, PARK, MENSAH, BAMELA ENGO, AKL, ANDERSON, VUKAS, WOLFRUM, LAING, TREVES, MARSIT, EIRIKSSON, NDIAYE, JESUS; *Judge* ad hoc COT; *Registrar* CHITTY.

For Belize: [See sitting of 5 April 2001, 3.00 p.m.]

For France: [See sitting of 5 April 2001, 3.00 p.m.]

AUDIENCE PUBLIQUE DU 6 AVRIL 2001, 10 H 00

Tribunal

Présents : M. CHANDRASEKHARA RAO, *Président*; M. NELSON, *Vice-Président*; MM. CAMINOS, MAROTTA RANGEL, YANKOV, YAMAMOTO, KOLODKIN, PARK, MENSAH, BAMELA ENGO, AKL, ANDERSON, VUKAS, WOLFRUM, LAING, TREVES, MARSIT, EIRIKSSON, NDIAYE, JESUS, *juges*; M. COT, *juge* ad hoc; M. CHITTY, *Greffier*.

Pour Belize : [Voir l'audience du 5 avril 2001, 15 h 00]

Pour la France : [Voir l'audience du 5 avril 2001, 15 h 00]

The President:
I now invite the Agent for the Applicant to make his statement.

Argument of Belize (continued)

STATEMENT OF MR PENELAS ALVAREZ
AGENT OF BELIZE
[PV.01/3, E, p. 4–8]

Mr Penelas Alvarez:
Mr President, honourable Judges, I shall today deal with the merits of the present case, starting with a brief introduction of the facts. The *Grand Prince* was carrying out a fishing campaign in the international waters in the so called "Williams Bank" outside the exclusive economic zone of the Kerguelens and outside the CCAMLAR area. After that campaign, the vessel was going to proceed to Brazil where it was allocated a fishing licence through a joint venture with a company from Brazil.

This is a case where, by an unfortunate decision of its Captain working for the first time on board, the fishing vessel entered the exclusive economic zone of the Kerguelens with, according to the Captain, the intention of fishing. It had no time to fish because it was caught on the same day it entered the zone. The vessel has never before been involved in illegal fishing and the Captain had clear instructions from the shipowner not to fish outside the allowed waters. When it was caught, the vessel had on board 18 tonnes of toothfish and 200 kilos of lobster.

On 26 December 2000 the vessel was detained by a French frigate and was taken to Port-des-Galets in La Réunion, where it arrived on 9 January 2001. On 12 January 2001 the court of first instance of Saint-Paul issued an order fixing a bond for release. The bond consisted of a payment by cheque or in cash, which is practically the same, in the amount of 11,400,000 French francs, which exceeds three times the value of the ship and is close to the price of a new modern vessel.

The order was notified to the Captain of the vessel on 15 January 2001. On the following days, myself, together with the shipowner's lawyer in La Réunion, Alain Antoine, had several contacts with the Director of the Direction of Maritime Affairs in La Réunion, Eric de Chavanes, and also with Vicent Esclapez, a person working in his department. We informed them that the shipowner was making all the financial arrangements to try to place a bank guarantee in the amount required by the court in order to avoid the unforeseeable loss caused by the detention of the ship.

We also informed them that it was our intention to discuss its reasonableness, independently of placing the bond, before this international Tribunal. The reason for saying that was that we felt that the amount of the bond and also the form was exorbitant compared to the possible fines which could be imposed on the Captain. In the light of these conversations, the crew of the vessel remained on board pending the release of the ship.

As you will understand, Mr President, a bond in such an amount, 11,400,000 French francs, cannot be obtained within a few days, especially when we are speaking of a small company which owns only the *Grand Prince*. That answers question number 5 posed by the Tribunal to Belize.

On 23 January 2001, only one week after the notification of the order fixing the amount of the bond to the Captain, the [criminal] court of Saint-Denis held a hearing and after one hour decided to confiscate the ship and to impose a fine on the Captain in the amount of 200,000 French francs. As we already know, the court also decided to execute the confiscation notwithstanding appeal. As a consequence, we were informed that the vessel could not be released, neither by posting the bond required by the first instance court nor with any other kind of bond. It was not possible to release the vessel. That was five or six days after the day the bond was fixed.

STATEMENT OF MR PENELAS ALVAREZ – 6 April 2001, a.m.

Yesterday it was mentioned that that decision has been appealed. The date for the appeal is pending. I should clarify that the appeal relates only to the merits of the case. We understand that the sanction of confiscation is absolutely disproportionate to the offence, as is shown by the low amount of the fine imposed upon the Captain. We are confident that the court of appeal will revoke the decision of confiscation. Obviously, Mr President, prompt release is not the objective or the subject matter of the appeal. Nothing rests on the decision in this respect. That answers the second question posed by the Tribunal to both parties.

The shipowner's lawyer in La Réunion and myself held a meeting on 24 January 2001 with the Maritime Director, Eric de Chavanes, where we again explained that the vessel could not be detained and that it should be released upon a reasonable guarantee. We further explained that the detention of the vessel was causing grave and unforeseeable damages including the loss of the fishing licence in Brazil. We also pointed out that if the vessel was not released, we would bring the matter before this Tribunal.

In order to solve matters in a normal way, we tried to convince the authorities in La Réunion of the need for the release of the vessel. We hoped that they would reconsider the position. At their request, we sent them information justifying the consequences of the vessel being detained. As evidence of that context, I enclosed document number 14 of our Application, a fax sent by me to Eric de Chavanes giving details of the fishing licence in Brazil and especially informing him of the deadline to take the licence. That was on 7 February 2001. We had many other contacts by phone. That answers question number 7 posed by the Tribunal to Belize. After several contacts and discussions with the authorities in La Réunion it was finally decided not to release the vessel. That is the way in which France impeded the release of the vessel.

In order to have some kind of evidence of proof of that situation we filed a request before the court of first instance of Saint-Paul asking for the release of the ship against a bank guarantee in the amount fixed by the same court. The request was rejected on 22 February on the basis that the [criminal] court had confiscated the vessel and executed the confiscation notwithstanding appeal. We enclose a copy of the request and the order of the court as documents 15 and 16 of our Application.

Under those circumstances, the shipowner explained the case to Belize and after a careful study of the matter it was decided to bring it before this international court. They are the reasons why we commenced preparation of the case and completed documentation at the beginning of March. We informed this Tribunal on 6 March 2001 of our intention to submit this matter to the Tribunal. That answers question number 6 posed to this party.

Our Application is based on two different matters. The first relates to the way in which France avoided the release of *Grand Prince* by posting any kind of guarantee, reasonable or not reasonable. The second matter, which is independent of the first, relates to whether the order fixed initially by the first instance court of Saint-Paul, document number 13 of the Application, can be considered reasonable as to its form, nature and amount in the light of article 73 of the Convention and the case law of this Tribunal. I shall deal with each question separately.

As regards the first question, I shall not tire the Tribunal by repeating the arguments I stated yesterday. I shall only remind the Tribunal of two facts, which are not under discussion. On 12 January 2001 the Court of First Instance of Saint-Paul fixed a guarantee for release of the vessel and the Captain against a bond in the form of a cheque or cash, which is the same, and in the amount of 11,400,000 French francs. That was notified to the Captain on 15 January 2001. Only one week after the notification to the Captain, on 23 January 2001, the [criminal] court of Saint-Denis decided, within one hour, to confiscate the vessel and execute the confiscation notwithstanding appeal, stating that there was no possibility of releasing the vessel. Those are the clear facts of the case.

Perhaps I may put some questions to the Tribunal. Is it reasonable that a bond consisting of a payment in cash should be of an amount exceeding three times the value of the ship? Is it reasonable that such a bond can be obtained and posted in La Réunion in a few days or only one week, especially in the case of a small company? Is it not a breach of article 73.2 of the Convention to avoid release against the posting of a reasonable bond by carrying out what I called yesterday "a prompt confiscation proceeding"? I think that the response to those questions is clearly "no".

I have already stated that the provisions of the Convention regarding prompt release are independent of and prevail over domestic laws and regulations and that as a consequence, a state cannot allege a domestic precept or law to justify a breach of the requirement for prompt release sanctioned by article 73.2 of the Convention.

For all those reasons, Mr President, and Members of the Tribunal, the formula used by France to evade prompt release of *Grand Prince* is unacceptable, extremely grave and constitutes a flagrant breach of the Convention.

I shall now refer to the second question: that is, whether or not the bond initially fixed by France was reasonable. As to the form and nature of the bond, I feel that it is unnecessary to go over again the arguments stated in our Application. I shall just mention that the Tribunal has made clear in previous cases that a bond consisting of a bank cheque or payment in cash is not a reasonable bond and that a bank guarantee or letter of credit must be allowed.

As to the amount, in the previous cases – *"SAIGA"*, *"Camouco"* and *"Monte Confurco"* – the Tribunal specified a number of relevant factors to be taken into account when assessing the reasonableness of the bonds, which include the gravity of the alleged offences, the penalties imposed, or imposable, under the laws of the detaining State – and I repeat imposed, because that is our case – the value of the detained vessel and the cargo seized, and the quantity of fish carried on board.

Belize, as a State Party to the Convention, wishes France to have a reasonable and sufficient guarantee to make effective a possible conviction in a final and firm judgment in the French courts. This is the aim of article 73, which is balanced by the request of prompt release.

Mr President, let us contemplate the worst scenario for the shipowner. Let us see what is the value of the *Grand Prince*, a ship of 36 years of age, bought two years ago for a price of 45 million pesetas, 271,000 euro, which was originally built as a stern trawler and then converted to a bottom liner, without at the moment any stable fishing possibilities.

With your permission, Mr President, I would like the Tribunal to hear the evidence of our experts, commencing with Faustino Carceller, a prominent naval engineer and marine surveyor with very great experience in the fishing vessels market. The Tribunal or the French delegation may also wish to ask him questions about the vessel.

Can I call the witness, Mr President?

The Registrar:
Mr President, before the expert is called upon to make the solemn declaration, I call upon the interpreters provided by Belize to interpret the testimony of the experts from Spanish into the official languages of the Tribunal to make the solemn declaration under article 85 of the Rules of the Tribunal. I will now call upon Ms Kathryn Smart to make the solemn declaration.

Interpreter sworn in (in English)

The Registrar:
Thank you.

I now call upon Mr Julio Quijano to make the solemn declaration.

Interpreter sworn in (in English)

The Registrar:
Thank you.

The interpreters will now take their positions in the interpretation booths. We shall need to wait until they have taken their places in the booths before we can proceed with the solemn declaration of the first expert called by Belize. An expert is required to make the solemn declaration under article 79 of the Rules of the Tribunal before making any statement before the Tribunal.

I have just received the signal that the interpreters have taken their place and that we can proceed.

I call upon Mr Antonio Alonso Perez to make the solemn declaration.

Mr Penelas Alvarez:
Excuse me. This witness is not Antonio Alonso Perez. He is Faustino Carceller.

The Registrar:
In that event, Mr President, I call upon Mr Faustino Carceller Vilalta to make the solemn declaration. Perhaps the expert may give his name and then proceed to take the oath.

Mr Penelas Alvarez:
I will ask him his name. Mr Carceller, could you kindly introduce yourself to the court?

The President:
Let him give his name and make the declaration.

Mr Faustino Carceller Vilalta sworn in (in Spanish)

"GRAND PRINCE"

Examination of experts

EXAMINATION OF MR CARCELLER VILALTA
BY MR PENELAS ALVAREZ (BELIZE)
[PV.01/3, E, p. 8–10]

Mr Penelas Alvarez:
Mr Carceller, would you kindly introduce yourself to the court?

Mr Carceller Vilalta (Interpretation from Spanish):
I am a naval engineer; I have a doctorate; I am also a marine surveyor. My professional experience consists of 22 years as a naval engineer working in the docks, where I worked in construction, the technical department, and for the last 10 years in a management position in the docks. Since 1988 I have run my own business, working on projects and valuations of vessels of all kinds, especially fishing vessels. During my career at the docks I worked on budgets for the construction of new vessels. I checked and reviewed budgets drawn up by others when I was in a management position, and I had the opportunity to compare the different finance plans for vessels built.

I have also worked as an independent consultant, in which I have done valuations for the Spanish Federation of Building Societies, which is a property valuation company in Spain. That company then decided to set up a new company particularly devoted to valuations. I form part of that company and I run and manage the valuation of vessels. During that time we have done hundreds of valuations of vessels, particularly fishing vessels. I belong to the following associations: the Association of Naval Engineers of Spain, the Society of Naval Architects and Engineers of the United States of America, and the Spanish Association of Shipping Arbitration.

Mr Penelas Alvarez:
Mr Carceller, do you ratify the full content and conclusions of your valuation report of *Grand Prince* dated 16 March 2001?

Mr Carceller Vilalta (Interpretation from Spanish):
Yes, of course.

Mr Penelas Alvarez:
Do you have any kind of link with the parties in this case, or any interest in the same?

Mr Carceller Vilalta (Interpretation from Spanish):
No, none at all.

Mr Penelas Alvarez:
Do you have an habilitation to act in front of Spanish courts?

Mr Carceller Vilalta (Interpretation from Spanish):
I have my qualifications as a naval engineer and doctor of naval engineering, and also my qualification as a marine surveyor. These enable me to speak before the Spanish courts at any level to report on matters relating to my technical competence. In fact, I have spoken before the Spanish courts in many cases related to shipping matters and fishing vessels.

EXAMINATION OF EXPERTS – 6 April 2001, a.m.

Mr Penelas Alvarez:
Have you ever acted as an arbiter in maritime cases?

Mr Carceller Vilalta (Interpretation from Spanish):
Yes. I was a sole arbiter and I was a member of a panel under the Spanish Institute of Marine Arbitration.

Mr Penelas Alvarez:
What is your experience of vessels of the characteristics of *Grand Prince*?

Mr Carceller Vilalta (Interpretation from Spanish):
Since I have had my own business and have been a consultant, I have worked on conversion projects for shipbuilders for a number of different vessels similar to the *Grand Prince*.

Mr Penelas Alvarez:
Do you have experience in the marketing of fishing vessels such as the *Grand Prince*, and, if so, what is your experience?

Mr Carceller Vilalta (Interpretation from Spanish):
My experience is restricted to valuations for a number of shipowners in an advisory capacity. I have not been involved directly in buying and selling as a main party, but as an adviser to those buying and selling.

Mr Penelas Alvarez:
What are the main premises to be taken into account when evaluating the price of a vessel?

Mr Carceller Vilalta (Interpretation from Spanish):
The age of the vessel, the state of maintenance, any modernization or repairs that have been carried out on the vessel, fishing licences, if any, in the case of a fishing vessel, the adaptation for the type of fishing concerned, and, of course, the demand for the type of vessel concerned.

Mr Penelas Alvarez:
Has the age of a vessel a relevant influence on its value?

Mr Carceller Vilalta (Interpretation from Spanish):
Yes. I would say that it is perhaps the most important factor, not just because age itself has an impact on the state of the boat, but because of the possible obsolescence of the vessel and its equipment.

Mr Penelas Alvarez:
What would be your opinion of the market price of *Grand Prince* at the present moment?

Mr Carceller Vilalta (Interpretation from Spanish):
As I said in my valuation, the market price is about 360,000 euro.

Mr Penelas Alvarez:
How do you arrive at that price?

"GRAND PRINCE"

Mr Carceller Vilalta (Interpretation from Spanish):
There are two main procedures of approximation, based on the cost price of a similar vessel newly-built and the price depreciating in time, and comparing that current depreciated value with the market value now for similar vessels. That is how I arrived at the estimated construction price of 2.585 million euro. I arrived at the conclusion that the current value, as I said before, would be 360,000 euro. I would say that it would be difficult to obtain such a price on the market today, because there is more supply than demand, but I think that would still be a reasonable price.

Mr Penelas Alvarez:
In your opinion, what is the natural destiny, in a short term period, of a vessel of the characteristics and age of *Grand Prince*?

Mr Carceller Vilalta (Interpretation from Spanish):
The *Grand Prince* is 35 years old, so I think that its only value is for scrap.

Mr Penelas Alvarez:
The maritime authorities in La Réunion valued this ship at 13,000,000 French francs, or [1,981,837] euro. Do you find that to be an accurate value?

Mr Carceller Vilalta (Interpretation from Spanish):
It seems completely illogical and unreasonable. It is impossible to achieve this price because a 35-year-old vessel has an old hull. Even though there may have been considerable modernizations and some of the hull might have been repaired, it is still old, and other parts of the boat are old, too. Also, the quality of the materials used is not as good as today. The engines are old. So I do not think that this price is logical at all. It is not the price of the vessel. I think that it would be impossible to achieve that price in any purchase agreement. For any buyer of a vessel through a shipbuilder, it is unthinkable that there could be any agreement based on that price.

Mr Penelas Alvarez:
The final question is: Could you please inform the Tribunal of the approximate cost of a newly-built vessel similar to *Grand Prince?*

Mr Carceller Vilalta (Interpretation from Spanish):
My estimate, as I have said in my evaluation, is 2,585,000 euro. Of course that depends on the specification but that is my estimate for a newly-built vessel similar to the *Grand Prince*.

Mr Penelas Alvarez:
Mr President, I have no further questions for this expert. I will ask you now to hear our second expert, the marine surveyor Mr Antonio Alonso Perez.

The President:
Let me ask France whether they wish to cross-examine.

(To the Agent of France) The expert is now available to you, you may wish to cross-examine.

AUDITION DES EXPERTS – 6 avril 2001, matin

CONTRE-INTERROGATOIRE DE M. CARCELLER VILALTA
PAR M. QUÉNEUDEC (FRANCE)
[PV.01/3, F, p. 7, E, p. 10]

M. Quéneudec :
Monsieur le Président, j'aurais deux questions à poser à M. Carceller en tant qu'expert cité par la partie adverse.

Première question : Monsieur Carceller, vous avez établi un rapport d'évaluation du *Grand Prince* le 16 mars 2001. Pourriez-vous dire au Tribunal à la demande de qui vous avez procédé à cette évaluation ?

Mr Carceller Vilalta (Interpretation from Spanish):
The lawyer of the shipowner, Mr Alberto Penelas.

M. Quéneudec :
Vous l'avez fait sur la base d'un dossier qui vous a été soumis. A partir de ce dossier, pourriez-vous indiquer au Tribunal quelle était à la date à laquelle vous avez procédé à l'évaluation le nom du propriétaire véritable du navire ?

Mr Carceller Vilalta (Interpretation from Spanish):
I was not given any report asking me to do the valuation. Mr Penelas asked me to provide a valuation. I know this boat because the shipyard carrying out the conversion of this vessel asked me to do a project for it in connection with the shipyard where I was asked to do it. I do not know the shipowner. I have no knowledge whatsoever of who the shipowner is.

M. Quéneudec :
Merci, Monsieur le Président.

The President:
Thank you very much.

(*To the Agent of Belize*) You can proceed with your next expert.

Mr Antonio Alonso Perez sworn in (in Spanish)

"GRAND PRINCE"

EXAMINATION OF MR ALONSO PEREZ
BY MR PENELAS ALVAREZ (BELIZE)
[PV.01/3, E, p. 10–12]

Mr Penelas Alvarez:
Mr Alonso, would you kindly introduce yourself to the court?

Mr Alonso Perez (Interpretation from Spanish):
My name is Antonio Alonso Perez. I am a captain in the Spanish merchant navy. I am also a marine surveyor. I am an inspector for the certification of vessels for the provision of flags and certification for the vessels of Honduras and Costa Rica. I am also the chief of security of the Port of Vigo in Spain.

Mr Penelas Alvarez:
Do you ratify the full content and conclusions of your evaluation report on *Grand Prince* dated 13 March 2001?

Mr Alonso Perez (Interpretation from Spanish):
Yes.

Mr Penelas Alvarez:
Do you have any kind of link with the parties in this case or any interest in the same?

Mr Alonso Perez (Interpretation from Spanish):
No.

Mr Penelas Alvarez:
Do you have the habilitation to act before the Spanish courts?

Mr Alonso Perez (Interpretation from Spanish):
As a captain of the merchant navy and as a marine surveyor, yes, I am entitled to do so. In fact, I have already acted as expert in a number of cases for the evaluation of vessels, equipment and hulls and in marine surveying matters.

Mr Penelas Alvarez:
Do you have experience in the marketing of fishing vessels like *Grand Prince* and, if so, how have you gained that experience?

Mr Alonso Perez (Interpretation from Spanish):
I have taken part in fishing vessel inspections, either trawlers, longliners or bottom liners, and also in buying and selling and insurance for P&I purposes and work carried out to European standards on fishing vessels.

Mr Penelas Alvarez:
What are the main provisos to be taken into account when evaluating a vessel?

Mr Alonso Perez (Interpretation from Spanish):
One of the main factors is the age of the vessel; then of course the state of repair and whether there have been major modifications; the design in relation to the type of fishing or purpose of the vessel; and another important factor is whether the vessel has a fishing licence and for

what waters – and that might be NAFO or other waters – and the current state of the market for the purchase and sale of such vessels.

Mr Penelas Alvarez:
In your opinion, a big influence in the value of a ship is its age?

Mr Alonso Perez (Interpretation from Spanish):
Yes, that has a great deal of influence because of the wear and tear that is caused by fishing. There might be damage to the hull; there might be problems with the steering or the engines. There is wear and tear on all these things. Then there is the type of steel, whether it is high in carbon, which is tougher for the purposes of using in very cold waters or in ice.

Mr Penelas Alvarez:
In your opinion, what would the market price for *Grand Prince* be at the present moment?

Mr Alonso Perez (Interpretation from Spanish):
According to my calculations, it would be somewhere between 58 million and 62 million pesetas. In francs, that is just over one million.

Mr Penelas Alvarez:
How did you arrive at the description in your report?

Mr Alonso Perez (Interpretation from Spanish):
Well, there are a number of ways of carrying out an evaluation. Age and condition are important factors. The evaluation has to be based on the residual value of the boat and that is, of course, after 36 years of use in this case, but there was a recent sale at 45 million pesetas and that is a factor to be taken into account. There is more modern equipment for steering that has been incorporated into this boat and that is why the figure is a bit higher than that.

Mr Penelas Alvarez:
In your opinion, what is the value in a short-term period based on the characteristics of the *Grand Prince*?

Mr Alonso Perez (Interpretation from Spanish):
Given the age of the vessel and the type of converted fishing vessel that it is, I think it is just scrap value only.

Mr Penelas Alvarez:
Finally, I inform you that the maritime authorities in Réunion valued the *Grand Prince* at 3 million French francs. Do you find that an accurate value?

Mr Alonso Perez (Interpretation from Spanish):
Could you repeat thc amount?

Mr Penelas Alvarez:
Three million French francs, 1,730 euro.

Mr Alonso Perez (Interpretation from Spanish):
That is not correct.

Mr Penelas Alvarez:
Three million French francs, 1,737,000 euro.

Mr Alonso Perez (Interpretation from Spanish):
That is about 300 million pesetas. Well, you could buy a new vessel with that amount. As I said to you, if you took a new vessel of this design that was only to be used for bottom-line fishing, it would be about 400 million pesetas, so I think the estimate given is extremely high, it is exaggerated or they have valued the wrong type of vessel.

Mr Penelas Alvarez:
Thank you. I have no further questions for you.

The President:
Would France like to cross-examine this expert?

INTERVENTION BY JUDGE EIRIKSSON
[PV.01/3, E, p. 12]

Judge Eiriksson:
Could we have some clarification on the exchange rates here? The figures you gave do not accord with what you were saying before.

Mr Penelas Alvarez:
Yes. The maritime authorities in Réunion valued the vessel at 3 million French francs. Let me check. I am sorry, that is 13 million French francs. That is the correct figure.

The President:
Would you like to put that question to the expert?

Mr Penelas Alvarez:
I correct the evaluation by the French authorities. The price of this vessel was 13 million French francs. Do you find that an accurate value?

Mr Alonso Perez (Interpretation from Spanish):
No. Once again, I quickly calculated in my head into pesetas from the figure in euro, so I knew that it would be in the region of 300 million pesetas.

Mr Penelas Alvarez:
The figure in euro was correct and he understood the figure.
Thank you very much, Mr Alonso.

The President:
(To the Agent of France) You have the expert now for cross-examination.

CONTRE-INTERROGATOIRE DE M. ALONSO PEREZ
PAR M. QUÉNEUDEC (FRANCE)
[PV.01/3, F, p. 10, E, p. 12]

M. Quéneudec :
Capitaine Alonso, vous serait-il possible de répondre à la question que j'ai déjà posée à l'expert précédent. Lorsque vous avez procédé à l'évaluation de la valeur du *Grand Prince*, avez-vous été en mesure de connaître l'identité du propriétaire actuel de ce navire ?

Mr Alonso Perez (Interpretation from Spanish):
I am not sure I understood the question correctly.

The President:
Please repeat the question.

M. Quéneudec :
Pouvez-vous nous dire si, au moment de l'établissement du rapport de votre évaluation du *Grand Prince*, vous avez connu le nom du propriétaire actuel de ce navire ?

Mr Alonso Perez (Interpretation from Spanish):
There is a name of a company here. Paik is the name of the company that I have.

M. Quéneudec :
Merci, Monsieur le Président.

The President:
Thank you very much.

The Agent for Belize may now continue his statement.

Argument of Belize (continued)

STATEMENT OF MR PENELAS ALVAREZ
AGENT OF BELIZE
[PV.01/3, E, p. 12–14]

Mr Penelas Alvarez:
Mr President, Members of the Tribunal, you have heard the authorized testimony of two prominent persons in the fishing field. According to them, the value of *Grand Prince* is in the region of 360,000 euro in the best of cases. They have already evidenced that the price estimated by the French surveyor, Mr Chancerel, on behalf of the maritime authorities in La Réunion is totally unrealistic, reaching a figure which is close to the price of a new, modern vessel of similar characteristics of *Grand Prince* but built originally as a longliner and fitted with the most sophisticated equipment.

I am not aware of the experience of Mr Chancerel with those kinds of vessels. I know that there are not many in La Réunion. When making his appraisal, Mr Chancerel did not consider the purchase price of the ship, 45 million pesetas; its fishing possibilities, which is a very important element; the fact that it is an extremely old ship; the matter of its conversion from a trawler into a longliner, and so forth. In my opinion, with all respect to Mr Chancerel, he did not make a very extensive study of this particular vessel.

Now we have an accurate idea of the value of *Grand Prince*; that is, 360,000 euro. Other circumstances should also be taken into consideration when assessing the reasonableness of the bond: the small quantity of fish carried on board, 18 tonnes of toothfish; that the Captain had clear instructions from the shipowner not to fish in the said area; that the vessel was about to proceed to Brazil where she had good possibilities of fishing under a Brazil fishing licence; the full cooperation of the Captain, the crew and shipowner of *Grand Prince* with the French authorities; and finally the amount of the fine imposed by the [criminal] court of Saint-Denis to the Captain which, although it has been appealed, is in the amount of 200,000 French francs.

Finally, we must recall that, as stated by this Tribunal in paragraph 86 of the Judgment pronounced in the *"Monte Confurco" Case*, the value of the fish and the fishing gear seized is also to be taken into account as a relevant factor in the assessment of the reasonableness of the bond. Following the valuation made by the French authorities, the amount of these items is 153,000 euro, which should be considered as part of the guarantee.

The result is that even contemplating the worst scenario for the shipowner, the final and firm decision of a domestic court, the court of appeal or the Supreme Court in Paris, would be fully guaranteed by a bank guarantee in the amount of 206,000 euro.

For all those reasons, Mr President, I reproduce in full the submissions stated in our Application. I thank you for your kind and patient attention.

The President:
Have you concluded your statement?

Mr Penelas Alvarez:
Yes.

The President:
Would France be able to present its statement at 11.30 or 12 o'clock?

M. Alabrune :
Monsieur le Président, si vous permettez, nous souhaiterions intervenir à l'heure prévue initialement, c'est-à-dire 14 heures.

The President:
Thank you very much.
The hearing is adjourned until two o’clock.

Adjournment at 11 a.m.

PUBLIC SITTING HELD ON 6 APRIL 2001, 2.40 P.M.

Tribunal

Present: *President* CHANDRASEKHARA RAO; *Vice-President* NELSON; *Judges* CAMINOS, MAROTTA RANGEL, YANKOV, YAMAMOTO, KOLODKIN, PARK, MENSAH, BAMELA ENGO, AKL, ANDERSON, VUKAS, WOLFRUM, LAING, TREVES, MARSIT, EIRIKSSON, NDIAYE, JESUS; *Judge* ad hoc COT; *Registrar* CHITTY.

For Belize: [See sitting of 5 April 2001, 3.00 p.m.]

For France: [See sitting of 5 April 2001, 3.00 p.m.]

AUDIENCE PUBLIQUE DU 6 AVRIL 2001, 14 H 40

Tribunal

Présents : M. CHANDRASEKHARA RAO, *Président*; M. NELSON, *Vice-Président*; MM. CAMINOS, MAROTTA RANGEL, YANKOV, YAMAMOTO, KOLODKIN, PARK, MENSAH, BAMELA ENGO, AKL, ANDERSON, VUKAS, WOLFRUM, LAING, TREVES, MARSIT, EIRIKSSON, NDIAYE, JESUS, *juges*; M. COT, *juge* ad hoc; M. CHITTY, *Greffier*.

Pour Belize : [Voir l'audience du 5 avril 2001, 15 h 00]

Pour la France : [Voir l'audience du 5 avril 2001, 15 h 00]

The President:
I now invite the Agent of France to make his statement.

« GRAND PRINCE »

Plaidoirie de la France (suite)

EXPOSÉ DE M. ALABRUNE
AGENT DE BELIZE
[PV.01/4, F, p. 1]

M. Alabrune :
Monsieur le Président, Messieurs les Juges, avant de commencer cette déclaration, je souhaiterais appeler votre attention sur des documents que la partie française a transmis au Tribunal. Il s'agit d'une note verbale du Ministère des affaires étrangères du Belize datée du 4 janvier, il s'agit deuxièmement d'une lettre venant de l'organisme IMMARBE, datée du 26 mars dernier. Il s'agit enfin d'un procès-verbal d'audition de personnes gardées à vue qui vous a été transmis et qui date du 10 janvier 2001.

The President:
We do not have a copy of that.

M. Alabrune :
Je pense que ce document vous a été transmis.

The President:
Yes. But that is not a new document.

M. Alabrune :
C'est un document que nous avons transmis aujourd'hui afin que vous l'ayez et que vous disposiez d'une copie en propre.

The President:
I now give the floor to the Agent of the Applicant to indicate whether he has any objection to the submission of these documents by France.

Argument of Belize (continued)

STATEMENT OF MR PENELAS ALVAREZ
AGENT OF BELIZE
[PV.01/4, E, p. 4]

Mr Penelas Alvarez:
No, Mr President. However, I would like to make a brief comment on these documents.

The President:
You are given the opportunity to do so now. I give the floor to the Agent of the Applicant to offer his comments on these documents.

Mr Penelas Alvarez:
Mr President, Members of the Tribunal, I have no objection to these documents. However, I should like to make reference to a letter from IMMARBE of Belize, which issued the two letters that have just been handed to the court. I refer to the letter dated 30 March 2001, following the ones submitted by the French party, which [clarify] the contents of the same. Let me very briefly make reference to this letter. I must say that the objective of these documents is to create confusion regarding the current registration status of the ship.

Let me read to you a paragraph of the letter, which is already on the file. It states that

> The undersigned, Director and Senior Deputy Registrar of the International Merchant Marine Registry of Belize, duly empowered by the Merchant Ships Act, …, hereby certifies that the vessel GRAND PRINCE is registered under the flag of Belize, holding registration Number …

and the number is then quoted. This letter clarifies the documents that France has submitted today.

Thank you very much, Mr President.

The President:
Thank you.

The Agent of France may resume his statement.

« GRAND PRINCE »

Plaidoirie de la France (suite)

EXPOSÉ DE M. ALABRUNE
AGENT DE BELIZE
[PV.01/4, F, p. 2–7]

M. Alabrune :
Je vous remercie, Monsieur le Président.

Monsieur le Président, Messieurs les Juges, la requête du Belize devrait, selon nous, être écartée par le Tribunal pour les raisons que nous avons exposées à l'audience d'hier. Toutefois, le Tribunal ayant souhaité entendre les arguments de l'autre partie sur le fond de sa requête, nous entendons y répondre et démontrer, à présent, que la demande de mainlevée n'est pas fondée.

Pour pouvoir apprécier le bien-fondé de cette demande, le Tribunal doit nécessairement partir de l'analyse des principaux éléments qui sont à l'origine de cette procédure. Ces éléments principaux sont simples et sont au nombre de cinq.

Il y a d'abord le fait qu'une infraction grave a été commise par le navire *Grand Prince*.

Il y a ensuite la circonstance que la procédure mise en oeuvre pour sanctionner cette infraction a été conduite avec diligence.

Il y a en troisième lieu la question de la caution qui a été fixée pour que la saisie du navire puisse être levée.

Il y a en quatrième lieu la donnée fondamentale de la confiscation du navire prononcée à titre de peine.

Il y a enfin l'élément tenant à ce que cette peine a été déclarée d'exécution immédiate.

Je me propose de reprendre successivement chacun de ces cinq éléments.

Le premier point à considérer est le fait qu'une infraction grave a été commise. La partie adverse a été discrète sur ce point, mais n'avait pas contesté, dans sa requête, que deux délits avaient été commis, à savoir, premièrement que le *Grand Prince* a omis de signaler son entrée dans la zone économique française et de déclarer le tonnage de poissons détenus à bord au moment de l'entrée dans la zone économique. Deuxièmement, le *Grand Prince* a pratiqué la pêche dans cette zone économique sans autorisation. De plus, et c'est un élément très important, le capitaine du navire a formellement reconnu avoir commis ce double délit.

De ce fait, nous avons été très étonnés d'entendre la partie adverse affirmer ce matin que le *Grand Prince* avait traversé la zone en direction du Brésil et sans y pêcher. Comment la partie adverse peut-elle affirmer qu'il n'y a pas eu de pêche illicite dans la zone des Kerguelen alors que le capitaine lui-même avait reconnu qu'il y avait eu pêche illicite ? Comment la partie adverse peut-elle affirmer, comme elle l'a fait ce matin, que le navire était entré dans la zone le jour même de son arraisonnement, le 26 décembre, alors que le navire s'était bien gardé de signaler son entrée dans la zone au moment où il y est entré ? Comment la partie adverse peut-elle affirmer que le *Grand Prince* traversait la zone en direction du Brésil alors que le capitaine du *Grand Prince* a lui-même déclaré devant les gendarmes, dans le procès-verbal qui est entre vos mains, qu'il venait de Durban et se rendait dans la zone économique des îles Kerguelen pour y pêcher ?

Il importe également de noter que le *Grand Prince*, dont on ignore toujours à qui il appartenait réellement au moment des faits, n'était pas ce navire de pêche paisible et innocent que l'on cherche à nous présenter. Contrairement à l'affirmation de la partie adverse, ce n'est pas la première fois que le *Grand Prince* commettait une infraction. En effet, après que les autorités françaises eurent communiqué à l'Etat du pavillon l'arraisonnement de ce navire, les autorités du Belize ont fait savoir, par note verbale du Ministère des affaires étrangères du Belize du 4 janvier 2001, qui est entre vos mains, qu'elles entendaient rayer le *Grand Prince* de leur registre d'immatriculation, car c'était la deuxième fois qu'une infraction était relevée à l'encontre de ce navire.

Nous avons appris ensuite, par une lettre du 26 mars 2001 venant d'IMMARBE, l'administration qui tient le registre maritime du Belize, que la procédure de retrait du pavillon du Belize avait été momentanément suspendue pour permettre la présente action devant votre Tribunal. L'armateur a obtenu cette suspension en prétendant qu'il souhaitait pouvoir se disculper devant le Tribunal international du droit de la mer. Cela ne change rien à ce qui est indiqué par la note verbale du 4 janvier, le navire *Grand Prince* avait déjà été noté par les autorités de Belize comme ayant commis une infraction.

J'en viens maintenant au deuxième point qui concerne la brièveté de la procédure. S'il ne s'est écoulé que peu de temps entre l'établissement du procès-verbal de comparution et la tenue de l'audience, ce n'est pas, comme la partie adverse cherche à vous en convaincre, pour éluder les dispositions de la Convention sur la prompte mainlevée et la prompte libération de l'équipage, mais bien au contraire, pour y satisfaire.

Les faits de l'espèce étaient en effet simples et non contestés. Le capitaine, il convient de le rappeler, avait reconnu avoir pêché dans la zone économique des Kerguelen et de nombreux indices corroboraient cet aveu, indices suffisamment présentés dans les procès-verbaux qui figurent en particulier dans les annexes de la requête. Il convenait donc de soumettre le plus rapidement possible les faits à un tribunal afin qu'il soit rapidement décidé des sanctions, et de manière à ce qu'il soit mis fin au contrôle judiciaire qui contraignait le capitaine à demeurer à la Réunion. C'est pour cette raison que le procureur a convoqué le capitaine à l'audience correctionnelle la plus proche, conformément et dans le cadre des lois en vigueur.

Il n'y avait pas matière à ouvrir une information et plus aucun acte de procédure n'a donc été accompli avant l'audience correctionnelle. Dès lors, il n'y avait aucune raison de laisser perdurer une situation intermédiaire. Il n'y avait donc pas à proprement parler de changement de pratique de la part des juges, mais une adaptation de la procédure au fait de la cause.

Ceci a permis de laisser le moins longtemps possible le capitaine et l'armateur dans l'attente, dans l'expectative, mais tout en leur laissant un délai suffisant pour organiser leur défense. Le capitaine n'a donc été privé d'aucun droit. Il ne paraît d'ailleurs pas, à la lecture du jugement du tribunal correctionnel, que le capitaine ou son conseil se soient plaint de la célérité de la procédure, alors qu'ils auraient pu protester devant le tribunal correctionnel le 23 janvier et demander, s'ils estimaient que la procédure était trop rapide, un renvoi de l'audience à une date ultérieure pour préparer leur défense. Ils ne l'ont pas fait. Le 23 janvier, il n'y a aucune contestation de la part du capitaine quant à la date et quant aux fait que l'audience devait se tenir le jour même. Il n'y a pas contestation de cette date, tout simplement parce que le capitaine reconnaît les faits.

J'en viens maintenant au troisième point qui concerne la caution. Selon le demandeur, la rapidité du tribunal français aurait empêché le règlement de la caution permettant d'obtenir la mainlevée de la saisie et dont il conteste aujourd'hui le montant. En réalité, l'armateur, homme d'affaires avisé, comme le montre la rapidité avec laquelle le *Grand Prince* a été vendu d'une société à une autre, aurait eu largement le temps de payer une caution ou d'offrir une garantie bancaire suffisante, s'il l'avait voulu. Il ne pouvait ignorer qu'il lui serait demandé le versement d'une caution. Dès le 26 décembre 2000, date de l'arraisonnement du navire, il pouvait commencer à prendre des dispositions pour la mise en place d'une garantie dont il pouvait approximativement déterminer le montant.

S'agissant du montant de la caution, le Tribunal observera que ce montant fixé par le juge d'instance à 11 400 000 francs français se situe entre le niveau fixé par votre Tribunal pour le *Camouco* à 8 millions de francs et le montant qui avait été fixé par votre Tribunal également pour le *Monte Confurco* à 18 millions de francs.

Il est également à noter que le 19 février, c'est-à-dire après l'intervention du jugement du tribunal correctionnel, l'armateur saisit le juge d'instance – vous avez cette pièce également dans votre dossier – à propos de la caution, mais vous remarquerez qu'il ne conteste pas le montant de la caution. Ceci montre que le 19 février, il n'estimait donc pas que le montant était déraisonnable, mais que ce montant était en corrélation avec la valeur du *Grand Prince*, valeur dont on veut aujourd'hui nous faire croire qu'elle est infiniment moindre. Je dois dire, à ce propos, que nous contestons, avec la plus extrême vigueur, les estimations qui ont été avancées ce matin par les experts de l'autre partie en ce qui concerne la valeur du bateau.

J'en viens maintenant à la question de la forme de la caution. Le juge d'instance a certes ordonné le paiement de la caution à la Caisse des Dépôts et Consignations sous forme d'espèces ou de chèque, mais je dois dire qu'il est évident que, s'il avait été demandé par l'armateur au juge d'instance, à un moment utile, c'est-à-dire avant que le tribunal correctionnel ne se prononce, d'accepter que cette caution soit réglée sous la forme d'une garantie bancaire, il est évident que si cette demande avait été présentée au juge d'instance, elle aurait pu être satisfaite, comme d'ailleurs cela a été le cas pour le *Camouco* et le *Monte Confurco* où, à la suite des décisions prises par votre Tribunal, les juges ont donné la possibilité de s'acquitter de cette caution sous la forme d'une garantie bancaire. Mais il n'y a pas eu de demande de cette nature avant le 23 janvier, il n'y a pas eu d'appel de la décision du juge d'instance.

Ce qu'il faut retenir également, c'est qu'avant l'intervention du jugement sur le fond, l'armateur n'a jamais tenté de régler la caution ni fait la moindre proposition pour le faire. Il a préféré attendre l'issue du procès correctionnel, espérant qu'il échapperait à la confiscation. Il n'a d'ailleurs pas été surpris par la date du procès correctionnel puisque cette date était fixée par le procureur de la République dès le 11 janvier.

Ce n'est que presque un mois après le jugement au fond, c'est-à-dire en février, qu'il saisit le juge d'instance d'une autre demande de modification de la forme de la caution et il le fait à un moment où il savait pertinemment que le juge d'instance était incompétent, puisque le tribunal correctionnel s'était prononcé le 23 janvier. Cette demande adressée par l'armateur le 19 février semble montrer qu'elle était présentée uniquement pour créer un conflit qui permettrait d'invoquer la violation de l'article 292 de la Convention.

J'en viens au quatrième point sur lequel votre Tribunal s'était également interrogé dans les questions qu'il a adressées à la partie française et qui concerne la confiscation du navire. Vous savez en effet que le tribunal correctionnel, le 23 janvier, tenant compte de la loyauté dont avait fait preuve le capitaine qui n'avait pas nié avoir commis une infraction, a prononcé à l'encontre du capitaine une peine d'amende modérée de 200 000 francs, que le tribunal correctionnel a alloué 20 000 francs à chaque partie civile, mais qu'il a prononcé la confiscation du navire.

La confiscation de la chose qui a servi à commettre l'infraction est, comme nous l'avons rappelé dans nos observations écrites, prévue en droit français par l'article 131-6 du code pénal lorsqu'un délit est puni d'une peine d'emprisonnement. Il s'agit d'une mesure fréquemment prononcée en répression de certaines infractions. Le droit pénal français, outre les peines classiques d'amende et d'emprisonnement, prévoit toute une série de peines complémentaires ou alternatives afin de mieux adapter la répression au comportement délictueux et empêcher la répétition de l'infraction.

S'agissant du *Grand Prince*, le tribunal correctionnel a pris soin d'indiquer les raisons qui l'ont conduit à prononcer la confiscation. Je cite le jugement rendu le 23 janvier que vous avez également dans votre dossier :

> Attendu ... qu'il importe essentiellement dans ce type de délit, dont la découverte nécessite la mise en place d'importants et coûteux moyens matériels, d'en éviter la réitération et d'empêcher que les coupables puissent tirer profit de leur action délictueuse.

Il convient de signaler au Tribunal que si les infractions de pêche sont punies en droit français par des peines d'emprisonnement, cette peine d'emprisonnement n'est applicable qu'aux ressortissants français, mais n'est pas applicable à des ressortissants d'Etats Parties à la Convention des Nations Unies sur le droit de la mer. Sont ainsi parfaitement respectées la Convention des Nations Unies sur le droit de la mer et la supériorité du traité par rapport aux lois françaises, principe formulé à l'article 55 de la Constitution française, que d'ailleurs l'autre partie a eu l'amabilité de nous rappeler.

J'ajoute enfin que la France – et cela a été déjà mentionné hier par le Professeur Quéneudec – n'est pas, loin de là, le seul pays à prévoir la confiscation de navires surpris en action de pêche illicite. C'est le cas notamment d'Etats tels que Fidji, la Grenade, la Jamaïque, la Nouvelle-Zélande, la Norvège, le Portugal, la Russie, et d'autres encore et, pour ne prendre qu'un exemple, dans le cas du premier Etat que j'ai cité, Fidji, le *Marine Space Act* de 1977 prévoient dans sa section 18, je cite :

> *On conviction of the owner, master or licensee of an offence under section 16, the court may also order the forfeiture to the Crown of the fishing vessel and any fish, fishing gear, apparatus, cargo and stores found therein or thereon.*

J'en viens au cinquième point sur lequel le Tribunal s'est interrogé et qui concerne l'exécution provisoire des peines prononcées par le tribunal correctionnel. Il faut dire sur ce point qu'il est évident que le prononcé d'une peine telle que la confiscation n'a véritablement de sens que s'il est possible d'en faire une application immédiate. C'est pour cette raison que l'article 471 du code de procédure pénale dispose, dans son dernier alinéa, je cite, que « Les sanctions pénales prononcées en application des articles 131-6 à 131-11 du Code pénal peuvent être déclarées exécutoires par provision. » Nous avons vu que la confiscation fait partie des peines qui sont prévues par l'article 131-6. Il résulte de l'application de ce texte qu'il ne peut pas être sursis à l'exécution d'un jugement de confiscation, même si un appel est formé contre ce jugement de confiscation.

Contrairement à ce que soutient faussement, sur ce point, l'autre partie, la décision du juge correctionnel de rendre exécutoire immédiatement la confiscation du navire n'avait pas pour but d'empêcher l'Etat du pavillon d'intenter une action en mainlevée devant le Tribunal international du droit de la mer. La finalité poursuivie consistait, comme l'a dit le tribunal correctionnel, dans l'attendu que nous avons cité précédemment, à éviter que les coupables puissent tirer profit de leur action délictuelle et, a-t-il ajouté encore, « pour permettre l'effectivité de la peine ».

Il convient en outre de faire remarquer qu'en matière de confiscation d'une chose qui a servi à commettre l'infraction, la confiscation est, pour des raisons que vous comprendrez aisément, presque toujours assortie de l'exécution immédiate. Tel est le cas en matière de répression du blanchiment de capitaux, de faux-monnayage, de trafic de stupéfiants, de faux témoignage, de chantage ou encore de délit d'outrage à la justice. Tel est aussi le cas s'agissant de la punition du crime contre l'humanité. Ce n'est pas pour moi une manière d'assimiler l'activité de pêche illicite à une activité criminelle puisque, en droit français, elle est qualifiée de délit, et même si plusieurs organisations écologistes et les pêcheurs pratiquant la pêche légale et réglementée qualifient souvent de pirates ceux qui s'adonnent à une grande échelle à la pêche illicite. En tout cas, contrairement aux affirmations du demandeur, la décision d'exécution immédiate de la confiscation n'a rien d'extraordinaire.

Il convient, pour être complet sur cette procédure, d'ajouter que le *Grand Prince*, ayant été confisqué avec effet immédiat, la propriété du navire s'est trouvée, comme l'a très bien expliqué hier le Professeur Quéneudec, transférée à l'Etat français, mais que ce transfert de propriété à l'Etat français, du fait de l'appel, n'est pas encore définitif. Nous savons en effet que l'affaire du *Grand Prince* a été portée devant la cour d'appel de Saint-Denis de la Réunion. La cour d'appel devra à nouveau apprécier les faits de la cause, la cour d'appel pourra éventuellement confirmer le jugement et maintenir la confiscation et elle pourra aussi, si elle l'estime nécessaire, modifier ou réformer le jugement rendu par le tribunal correctionnel.

Cette modification peut être dans différentes directions, elle peut très bien augmenter ou réduire le montant de l'amende prononcée contre le capitaine. Elle pourra maintenir la confiscation ou, au contraire, elle pourra ordonner la restitution du navire à son ancien propriétaire. Ce seront les pouvoirs de la cour d'appel. Mais, quelle que soit la décision que rendra la cour d'appel, il ne pourra plus être exigé de caution ni ordonné de mainlevée qui n'ont plus de raison d'être à ce stade avancé de la procédure.

Tels sont, Monsieur le Président, Messieurs les Juges, les éléments principaux que le Tribunal serait amené à prendre en considération dans l'examen de la demande de mainlevée. Pris ensemble, ces éléments conduisent à la conclusion que l'allégation avancée de la violation de la Convention par la France n'est pas fondée, qu'elle n'est ni plausible, ni soutenable. Dans ces conditions, le Tribunal devrait saisir cette occasion pour bien préciser que la procédure de l'article 292 n'est pas la voie de recours automatiquement ouverte à tout armateur de pêche dont les navires se livrent, sur une grande échelle, à des activités de pêche illicite.

Comme nous l'avions souligné hier, votre décision sera donc très importante parce qu'il s'agira d'une question de principe. Votre décision est bien sûr très attendue par les parties, elle est attendue par la communauté juridique internationale, et j'ajoute, si vous me permettez, Monsieur le Président, que votre décision est attendue sur l'île de la Réunion par tous ceux qui travaillent dans le secteur économique de la pêche et qui sont angoissés par le pillage des ressources halieutiques situées dans les eaux sous juridiction française dans cette région. Le Tribunal doit savoir, par exemple, que le *Camouco*, dont la saisie été levée suite à votre décision, continue son activité de pêche illicite sous un autre nom, *Arvisa Primero*.

Votre décision est attendue par les gardes côtes qui veillent jour et nuit, dans des conditions extrêmement difficiles, pour surprendre et appréhender ceux qui se livrent à la pêche illicite. Votre décision est attendue par les juges de l'île de la Réunion qui ont appliqué scrupuleusement les règles du droit international et du droit français et dont l'honneur est aujourd'hui mis en cause puisqu'ils sont accusés de fraude à la loi. Votre décision est attendue par les organisations qui, à l'échelle internationale, veillent à la préservation des équilibres écologiques et alertent presque quotidiennement l'opinion mondiale contre les méfaits commis par les pirates de la mer. Votre décision enfin est attendue par de nombreux Etats, en particulier des Etats du sud, qui sont des Etats côtiers et dont les eaux sont très souvent pillées par ces pirates de la mer. Nombreux sont en effet les Etats qui n'ont pas les moyens matériels suffisants pour organiser la surveillance de leurs eaux et réprimer l'exercice de la pêche illicite.

Je vous remercie, Monsieur le Président.

The President:
Thank you very much.

Would the Agent of the Applicant like to add anything to what he said earlier?

Reply of Belize

STATEMENT OF MR PENELAS ALVAREZ
AGENT OF BELIZE
[PV.01/4, E, p. 9–13]

Mr Penelas Alvarez:
Mr President, Members of the Tribunal, we have heard again how we can avoid prompt release by invoking domestic regulations. Perhaps I may make reference to what happened with *Monte Confurco*, a previous case of this Tribunal, after the Tribunal pronounced its judgment. The Tribunal decided that *Monte Confurco* should be released by France upon a posting of a reasonable bond fixed by this Tribunal. While the shipowner was trying to pay the bond, the week after the judgment was pronounced, the [criminal] court of Saint-Denis carried out a prompt confiscation proceeding, as in this case. It decided to execute the confiscation notwithstanding appeal. In practical terms, the *Monte Confurco* is still detained in La Réunion. That is the reality. It is difficult for me to say this, but that judgment is now wet paper. The vessel is detained in La Réunion. That is how the authorities in La Réunion are acting and how they regard the Convention and the decisions of this Tribunal.

Perhaps I may briefly comment on what the French representative mentioned in the context of illegal fishing in French waters. France has many fewer fishing incidents than most of the coastal States while France, as a powerful country, has many more means to control its waters. I shall give an example. Ireland has many fishing incidents with German, French and Spanish vessels. Ireland arrests ships and carries out judicial proceedings but always permits the prompt release of the ships against a reasonable bond. In Spain we also have many problems with the French vessels in the [Bay of Biscay]. The French use illegal fishing gear. They are arrested; proceedings follow, but they are always permitted to be released upon a bond. That happens with Argentina, Angola and Ghana, and with most other countries involved. The only country which is trying to deal with these matters in a different way, disregarding article 73.2 of the Convention, is France. The other countries fight this unacceptable practice because illegal fishing cannot be justified.

The President:
We do not have the facts of those cases. You have not submitted documents in support of what you say. It would be appreciated if you would avoid reference to other matters which are not before us.

Mr Penelas Alvarez:
Yes, Mr President. The representatives of France were also making reference to other countries where confiscation was permitted.

The President:
It is not a question of facts; it is a question of law. If you want to refer to the laws of any country, you are at liberty to do so.

Mr Penelas Alvarez:
Thank you. In any event, it cannot be alleged that several fishing incidents are faced in order to avoid the means provided by the Convention for fighting such incidents. The request for prompt release cannot be avoided.

As I mentioned yesterday, these proceedings are independent of those carried out by the domestic courts. Both run in parallel. As we also indicated, if the theory sustained by

France prevails, a State could avoid prompt release of vessels and crews just by carrying out speedy proceedings for prompt confiscation or prompt imprisonment, as the case may be, and deciding the execution of the decision notwithstanding appeal. By invoking domestic laws the requirement stated under article 73.2 of the Convention would be evaded. That would affect not only vessels but crews.

It is obvious that the court of appeal in La Réunion or the Supreme Court in Paris could overturn the decision of the court of first instance. There are arguments in defence of confiscation not being a proportional sanction to the offence committed. Evidence of that is the low amount of the fine imposed upon the Captain: 200,000 French francs.

However, the most important factor is that even if the said decision is overturned by the court of appeal or the Supreme Court, that court will not pronounce anything regarding release upon a bond or other security as it is not the subject matter of the appeal. We would still have to wait until the Supreme Court pronounced a final and firm decision.

As the French delegation explained yesterday, it is obvious that confiscation supposes in principle the attachment of the goods by the confiscating State. If article 73.2 of the Convention did not exist, the immediate effect would be the detention of the vessel and its expropriation by the detaining State. However, as far as article 73.2 is applicable, which is not under discussion, the vessel must be promptly released against a reasonable bond. That requirement, as held by the Tribunal, cannot be subjected to any domestic laws or regulations, only to the posting of a reasonable bond.

I shall now comment on the ownership of *Grand Prince*. It seems that some confusion has been created concerning the certificates of class of the ship. The current shipowner bought the vessel on 27 March 2000, as is shown by the contract of sale, which was duly notarized and is enclosed as exhibit 2 of our Application. Document number 3 of the Application is evidence of the fact that on 16 October 2000 the shipowner of *Grand Prince* was Paik Commercial Corp. That ownership has also been confirmed by the International Merchant Marine Registry of Belize in its letter dated 30 March 2001, which was ordered following indications by the Registrar, and which forms part of the file.

The certificate further states that, despite the expiration of the provisional patent of navigation, the vessel is still registered in Belize. Documents relating to the status of the vessel, such as the final patent of navigation and the ship station licence of the vessel, await processing by the Registry. The certificate of class seems to create confusion. As you can see, it was issued on 23 June 1999. As stated in the same document, it expires after a term of five years. Therefore, it is evident that the document was issued when the ownership corresponded to a former owner, NOYCAN, prior to the purchase of the vessel by the current owner, Paik Commercial.

It should also be noted that the only survey, which was due in January 2000, was carried out in November 1999 by the previous owner of the vessel. That is the simple reason why Paik Commercial does not appear in the classification certificate. It has not had the necessity to make any arrangement for the time being regarding the classification certificates. If the Tribunal wishes our party to provide further evidence as regards ownership, we should be happy to do so.

In conclusion, France has breached the Convention by first fixing a totally unreasonable bond and, moreover, only one week thereafter, by a prompt confiscation proceeding combined with an execution notwithstanding appeal, impeding any possibility of release.

For all those reasons, I maintain all our submissions, which I shall now repeat:

STATEMENT OF MR PENELAS ALVAREZ – 6 April 2001, p.m.

1. To declare that the Tribunal has jurisdiction under article 292 of the United Nations Convention on the Law of the Sea to hear the present application.

2. To declare the present application admissible.

3. To declare that France failed to comply with article 73, paragraph 2, of the Convention, as the guarantee fixed for release of Grand Prince is not reasonable as to its amount, nature or form.

4. To declare that France failed to comply with article 73, paragraph 2, of the Convention by having evaded the requirement of prompt release under this article by not allowing the release of the vessel upon the posting of a reasonable, or any kind of, guarantee alleging that the vessel is confiscated and that the decision of confiscation has been provisionally executed.

5. To decide that France shall promptly release the Grand Prince upon the posting of a bond or other security to be determined by the Tribunal.

6. To determine that the bond or other security shall consist of an amount of two hundred and six thousand one hundred forty nine (206,149) Euros, or its equivalent in French Francs.

7. To determine that the monetary equivalent to (a) 18 tonnes of fish on board the Grand Prince held by the French authorities, and valued on 123,848 Euros (b) the fishing gear, valued on 24,393 Euros (c) the fishing materials valued on 5,610 Euros, totalling 153,851 Euros, shall be considered as security to be held or, as the case may be, returned by France to this party.

8. To determine that the bond shall be in the form of a bank guarantee.

9. To determine that the wording of the bank guarantee shall, among other things, state the following:

A. In case France returns to the shipowner the items referred to under point 7 (of the present submissions):

> "The bank guarantee it is issued in consideration of France releasing the Grand Prince, in relation to the incidents dealt with in the Order of 12 January 2001 of the Court of First Instance of Saint-Paul and that the issuer undertakes and guarantees to pay to France such sums, up to 206,149 Euros, as may be determined by a final and firm judgement or decision of the appropriate domestic forum in France or by agreement of the parties. Payment under the guarantee would be due promptly after receipt by the issuer

of a written demand by the competent authority of France accompanied by a certified copy of the final and firm judgement or decision or agreement."

B. In case France does not return to the shipowner the items referred to under point 7 (of the present submissions):

"The bank guarantee it is issued in consideration of France releasing the Grand Prince, in relation to the incidents dealt with in the Order of 12 January 2001 of the Court of First Instance of Saint-Paul and that the issuer undertakes and guarantees to pay to France such sums, up to 52,298 Euros, as may be determined by a final and firm [judgement or] decision of the appropriate domestic forum in France or by agreement of the parties. Payment under the guarantee would be due promptly after receipt by the issuer of a written demand by the competent authority of France accompanied by a certified copy of the final and firm judgement or decision or agreement."

10. To determine that the bank guarantee shall be invoked only if the monetary equivalent of the security held by France is not sufficient to pay the sums as may be determined by a final and firm judgement or decision of the appropriate domestic forum in France.

Mr President, Members of the Tribunal, thank you very much for your kind attention.

The President:
I presume that those are your final submissions.

Mr Penelas Alvarez:
Yes, that is right.

The President:
Will you please have them signed and handed over to the Registrar?

Mr Penelas Alvarez:
Yes.

The President:
Thank you very much.
I now give the floor to the Agent of France.

M. Alabrune :
Monsieur le Président, permettez-vous que le Professeur Quéneudec s'exprime en réponse avant que je présente les conclusions finales ?

The President:
Yes.

Duplique de la France

EXPOSÉ DE M. QUÉNEUDEC
CONSEIL DE BELIZE
[PV.01/4, F, p. 11–12]

M. Quéneudec :
Monsieur le Président, Messieurs les Juges, brièvement, une remarque, et une seule, pour constater que nous sommes d'accord avec la partie adverse pour dire que la procédure de l'article 292 de la Convention est indépendante des procédures judiciaires nationales. Nous n'avons pas dit autre chose hier. Mais ces procédures judiciaires nationales, et leurs résultats, sont des éléments que le Tribunal ne peut ignorer parce qu'il est saisi d'une demande de mainlevée dans le cadre de l'article 292, car la procédure organisée par l'article 292 de la Convention ne peut pas être envisagée comme s'exerçant dans l'abstrait. Cette procédure prend racine dans une série de faits concrets, à savoir : un arraisonnement d'un navire surpris en infraction de pêche, la saisie de ce navire, la confirmation de cette saisie par un juge, lequel précise que la saisie peut être levée moyennant le versement d'une caution suffisante, et une poursuite intentée contre le capitaine en tant qu'auteur présumé d'une série d'infractions débouchant sur une condamnation dudit capitaine. Au regard du Tribunal, ce sont là les éléments de fait qui sont à la base de la mise en oeuvre de la procédure de prompte mainlevée. La prompte mainlevée suppose, bien entendu, la fixation d'une caution, mais elle suppose aussi le versement de la caution ou la présentation d'une garantie pour que la mainlevée de saisie puisse intervenir. Si ceci n'est pas fait, il ne peut pas y avoir mainlevée.

La question qui se pose est simplement de savoir si, dans le cadre d'une action en prompte mainlevée, sur la base de l'article 292, il est possible de demander au Tribunal de se prononcer sur la légalité au regard de la Convention sur le droit de la mer du prononcé par un juge répressif d'une confiscation à titre de sanction pour un délit de pêche illicite.

Il ne faut pas en effet que le Tribunal perde de vue que, dans cette affaire en particulier, le point de départ, la base de l'affaire, c'est une violation de la Convention, une violation des dispositions de la Convention, commise par un navire de pêche ne respectant pas les droits souverains d'un Etat côtier dans sa zone économique exclusive.

C'est la seule remarque que je souhaitais faire, Monsieur le Président. Je vous demanderais maintenant de bien vouloir donner la parole à l'agent du Gouvernement français pour qu'il présente les conclusions finales du Gouvernement français dans cette affaire.

Merci, Monsieur le Président.

« GRAND PRINCE »

EXPOSÉ DE M. ALABRUNE
AGENT DE BELIZE
[PV.01/4, F, p. 12]

M. Alabrune :
Monsieur le Président, avec votre permission, je lirai les conclusions finales du Gouvernement de la République française.

> Le Gouvernement de la République française prie le Tribunal, rejetant toutes conclusions contraires présentées au nom de l'Etat du Belize,
>
> 1. A titre principal, de constater que la demande de mainlevée déposée le 21 mars 2001 au nom du Belize est irrecevable, qu'en tout état de cause le Tribunal n'a pas compétence pour en connaître et que cette demande doit, dès lors, être écartée.
>
> 2. A titre subsidiaire, de dire et juger que les conditions auxquelles est normalement soumise l'adoption par le Tribunal d'une décision de prompte mainlevée dès le dépôt d'une caution raisonnable, ne sont pas remplies dans les circonstances de l'espèce et qu'il y a donc lieu de débouter le requérant de sa demande.

Ceci conclut mon intervention, Monsieur le Président. Nous vous remettrons le texte de nos conclusions. Je vous remercie, Monsieur le Président.

CLOSURE OF THE ORAL PROCEEDINGS – 6 April 2001, p.m.

Closure of the Oral Proceedings
[PV.01/4, E, p. 14–15]

The President:
Thank you. Will you please give a signed copy to the Registrar? I thank the Agent of France.

That brings us to the end of the oral proceedings in the "Grand Prince" Case. I would like to take this opportunity to thank the Agents and Counsel of both parties for the presentations that they have made before the Tribunal over the past two days. The Tribunal appreciates the personal courtesies shown by Agents and Counsel on both sides.

The Registrar will now address questions relating to documentation.

The Registrar:
Thank you, Mr President.

In conformity with article 86, paragraph 4, of the Rules of the Tribunal, the parties have the right to correct the transcripts of their presentations and statements made by them in the oral proceedings. Any such corrections should be submitted as soon as possible, but in any case not later than the end of Tuesday, 10 April 2001.

In addition, the parties are requested to submit the originals of documents submitted by facsimile or as copies. The parties are also requested to certify that all the documents that have been submitted and which are not originals are true and accurate copies of the originals of those documents. For those purposes, they will be provided with a list of the documents concerned.

In accordance with the Guidelines concerning the preparation and presentation of cases before the Tribunal, they are also requested to furnish the Registry with additional copies of documents that have not been supplied in sufficient numbers.

Thank you, Mr President.

The President:
The Tribunal will now withdraw to deliberate on the case. The Judgment will be read on a date to be notified to the Agents. The Tribunal has tentatively set a date for the delivery of the Judgment. That date is 20 April 2001. The Agents will be informed reasonably in advance if there is any change in this schedule.

In accordance with the usual practice, I request the Agents to remain at the disposal of the Tribunal in order to provide any further assistance and information that it may need in its deliberations prior to the delivery of the Judgment.

The sitting is now closed.

The sitting closes at 3.45 p.m.

"GRAND PRINCE"

PUBLIC SITTING HELD ON 20 APRIL 2001, 3.00 P.M.

Tribunal

Present: *President* CHANDRASEKHARA RAO; *Vice-President* NELSON; *Judges* CAMINOS, MAROTTA RANGEL, YANKOV, YAMAMOTO, KOLODKIN, PARK, BAMELA ENGO, AKL, ANDERSON, VUKAS, WOLFRUM, LAING, TREVES, MARSIT, EIRIKSSON, NDIAYE, JESUS; *Judge* ad hoc COT; *Registrar* CHITTY.

For Belize: [See sitting of 5 April 2001, 10.00 a.m.]

For France: Mr Michel Trinquier,
Deputy Director for the Law of the Sea, Fisheries and the Antarctic, Office of Legal Affairs of the Ministry of Foreign Affairs,
as Counsel.

AUDIENCE PUBLIQUE DU 20 AVRIL 2001, 15 H 00

Tribunal

Présents : M. CHANDRASEKHARA RAO, *Président*; M. NELSON, *Vice-Président*; MM. CAMINOS, MAROTTA RANGEL, YANKOV, YAMAMOTO, KOLODKIN, PARK, BAMELA ENGO, AKL, ANDERSON, VUKAS, WOLFRUM, LAING, TREVES, MARSIT, EIRIKSSON, NDIAYE, JESUS, *juges*; M. COT, *juge* ad hoc; M. CHITTY, *Greffier*.

Pour Belize : [Voir l'audience du 5 avril 2001, 10 h 00]

Pour la France : M. Michel Trinquier,
sous-directeur du droit de la mer, des pêches et de l'Antarctique à la direction des affaires juridiques du Ministère des affaires étrangères,
comme conseil.

Reading of the Judgment
[PV.01/5, E, p. 4–7, F, p. 1–4]

The Registrar:
The Tribunal will today deliver its Judgment in the *"Grand Prince" Case*, Application for Prompt Release, Case No. 8 on the List of cases, Belize, Applicant and France, Respondent. The Tribunal heard oral arguments from the parties at three public sittings on 5 and 6 April 2001.

The hearings concluded with the final submissions of both parties which read as follows:

READING OF THE JUDGMENT – 20 April 2001, p.m.

On behalf of Belize:

1. To declare that the Tribunal has jurisdiction under article 292 of the United Nations Convention on the Law of the Sea to hear the present application.

2. To declare the present application admissible.

3. To declare that France failed to comply with article 73, paragraph 2, of the Convention, as the guarantee fixed for release of Grand Prince is not reasonable as to its amount, nature or form.

4. To declare that France failed to comply with article 73, paragraph 2, of the Convention by having evaded the requirement of prompt release under this article by not allowing the release of the vessel upon the posting of a reasonable, or any kind of, guarantee alleging that the vessel is confiscated and that the decision of confiscation has been provisionally executed.

5. To decide that France shall promptly release the Grand Prince upon the posting of a bond or other security to be determined by the Tribunal.

6. To determine that the bond or other security shall consist of an amount of two hundred and six thousand one hundred and forty nine (206,149) Euros or its equivalent in French Francs.

7. To determine that the monetary equivalent to (a) 18 tonnes of fish on board the Grand Prince held by the French authorities, and valued on 123,848 Euros (b) the fishing gear, valued on 24,393 Euros (c) the fishing materials valued on 5,610 Euros, totalling 153,851 Euros, shall be considered as security to be held or, as the case may be, returned by France to this party.

8. To determine that the bond shall be in the form of a bank guarantee.

9. To determine that the wording of the bank guarantee shall, among other things, state the following:

   A. In case France returns to the shipowner the items referred to under point 7 (of the present submissions):

   > "The bank guarantee it is issued in consideration of France releasing the Grand Prince, in relation to the incidents dealt with in the Order of 12 January 2001 of the Court of First Instance of Saint-Paul and that the issuer undertakes and guarantees to pay to France such sums, up to 206,149 Euros, as may be determined by a final and firm judgement or decision of the appropriate domestic forum in

France or by agreement of the parties. Payment under the guarantee would be due promptly after receipt by the issuer of a written demand by the competent authority of France accompanied by a certified copy of the final and firm judgement or decision or agreement."

B. In case France does not return to the shipowner the items referred to under point 7 (of the present submissions):

"The bank guarantee is issued in consideration of France releasing the Grand Prince, in relation to the incidents dealt with in the Order of 12 January 2001 of the Court of First Instance of Saint-Paul and that the issuer undertakes and guarantees to pay to France such sums, up to 52,298 Euros, as may be determined by a final and firm judgement or decision of the appropriate domestic forum in France or by agreement of the parties. Payment under the guarantee would be due promptly after receipt by the issuer of a written demand by the competent authority of France accompanied by a certified copy of the final and firm judgement or decision or agreement."

10. To determine that the bank guarantee shall be invoked only if the monetary equivalent of the security held by France is not sufficient to pay the sums as may be determined by a final and firm judgement or decision of the appropriate domestic forum in France.

On behalf of France:

The Government of the French Republic requests the Tribunal, rejecting all submissions to the contrary made on behalf of the State of Belize,

1. First, to note that the Application for prompt release filed on 21 March 2001 on behalf of Belize is not admissible, that, in any case, the Tribunal has no jurisdiction to entertain the Application and that it must, therefore, be rejected.

2. Alternatively, to adjudge and declare that the conditions normally governing the adoption by the Tribunal of a decision concerning prompt release upon the posting of a reasonable bond have not been fulfilled under the circumstances of this case, and that, therefore, the Application by the Applicant should be denied.

Mr President.

The President:
Judge Thomas Mensah is not able to attend today's reading of the judgment, but asked that he be allowed to record his final vote from Iran. I will ask the Registrar to read the decision of the Tribunal on this matter.

READING OF THE JUDGMENT – 20 April 2001, p.m.

Mr Registrar.

The Registrar:
The decision of the Tribunal adopted on 12 April 2001 reads as follows:

> Judge Thomas A. Mensah has informed the Tribunal that he will be absent from Hamburg with effect from 14 April 2001, since he is required to visit Iran as Chairman of the 'F4' Panel of the United Nations Compensation Commission (UNCC) to inspect certain archeological sites in respect of which the Government of Iran has submitted claims for compensation to the 'F4' Panel pursuant to Security Council resolution 687/1991. He has informed the Tribunal that the Government of Iran has made the necessary arrangements for the visit.
>
> Judge Mensah has sought the permission of the Tribunal to record his vote in writing in the *"Grand Prince" Case* although he will be absent when the formal vote is taken.
>
> Judge Mensah was present at the public sittings held in this case on 5 and 6 April 2001. He also participated in the deliberations of the Tribunal up to a point at which it had reached the substance of its decision.
>
> The Tribunal decides that, in the special circumstances mentioned by Judge Mensah, he should be allowed to record his final vote from Iran by facsimile.

Judge Mensah recorded his final vote in accordance with the decision of the Tribunal.
Mr President.

The President:
I now call on the Agent of the Applicant to note the representation of Belize.

Mr Penelas Alvarez:
[*Belize is represented by Mr Penelas Alvarez, Agent, and Ms Goicoechea Fábregas, Counsel.*]

The President:
Thank you. I now call on the Agent of the Respondent to note the representation of France.

M. Trinquier :
[*La France est représentée par M. Trinquier, conseil.*]

The President:
Thank you. I will now read relevant extracts from the Judgment in the *"Grand Prince" Case*.
[The President reads the extracts.] The sitting is now closed.

These texts are drawn up pursuant to article 86 of the Rules of the International Tribunal for the Law of the Sea and constitute the minutes of the public sittings held in *The "Grand Prince" Case (Belize* v. *France), Prompt Release*.

Ces textes sont rédigés en vertu d'article 86 du Règlement du Tribunal international du droit de la mer et constituent le procès-verbal des audiences publiques de l'*Affaire du « Grand Prince » (Belize c. France), prompte mainlevée*.

Le 2 mars 2007
2 March 2007

Le Président
Rüdiger Wolfrum
President

Le Greffier
Philippe Gautier
Registrar

Documents – Documents

Authorization – Autorisation

a) Authorization issued to Mr Penelas Alvarez by the Attorney General of Belize dated 15 March 2001, with Apostille

ATTORNEY GENERAL'S MINISTRY

Tel: 011-501-8-22504/20519 Fax: 011-501-8-23390

Belmopan, Belize, Central America

33/173/Pt.XV/01(12)

March 15,2001.

TO THE INTERNATIONAL TRIBUNAL
FOR THE LAW OF THE SEA
Registry fax number 49 40 3507 245
To the attention of the Registrar

Dear Sir,

The undersigned Attorney General of Belize and Minister responsible for International Merchant Marine Registry of Belize (IMMARBE), hereby authorizes D. Alberto Penelas Alvarez with address at Pintor Laxeiro 11, 20, Vigo, Pontevedra, Spain (phone 34 - 986 - 21301 and fax 34 986 294162) and holder of passport number 36058322A, TO FILE an application to the Tribunal for the Law of the Sea, on behalf of Belize, under article 292 of the United Nations Convention on the Law of the Sea, with respect to the detention by the French authorities of the fishing vessel GRAND PRINCE, of Belize flag, which holds registration number 07972047 and call letters V3UJ7.

For the avoidance of any doubt, this authority supersedes and is given in place of the authority dated 8th March, 2001 and signed by the Solicitor General, Mr. Edwin L. Flowers.

Issued in Belize City, on the 15th day of March, 2001.

(GODFREY P. SMITH)
ATTORNEY GENERAL

APOSTILLE

(Convention de La Haye du 5 Octobre 1961)

Country Belize

1. Public Document Letter

2. Has been signed by Godfrey P. Smith

3. Acting as Attorney General

4. Bearing the seal/stamp of Attorney General

CERTIFIED

5. At Belize City **6. On** 21st March 2001

7. By P. [illegible]

8. Under No. 619/2001

9. Seal **10. Signature**

Deputy **REGISTRAR GENERAL**

REGISTRAR GENERAL BELIZE

b) Notification of the appointment of Mr Penelas Alvarez by the Attorney General of Belize dated 26 March 2001

ATTORNEY GENERAL'S MINISTRY
Tel: 011-501-8-22504/20519 Fax: 011-501-8-23390
Belmopan, Belize, Central America

SGF 15/01(01)

March 26th, 2001

TO: The International Tribunal for the Law of the Sea

ATTN: The Registrar (Fax: 49-40 - 35607 245)

Dear Sir:

Further to our letter dated 15 March, 2001 (Our Ref. 33/173/Pt.XV/01(12) regarding the application for prompt release of the fishing vessel 'GRAND PRINCE", we hereby confirm the appointment of Mr. Alberto Penelas Alvarez as agent to act in this matter on behalf of Belize.

The address of the agent in Hamburg is:

FIDE TREUHANDGESELLISCHAFT
KATTREPELSBUCKE
20095 HAMBURG

Yours truly,

(GODFREY P. SMITH)
ATTORNEY GENERAL

c) Désignation de M. Alabrune en qualité d'agent du Gouvernement français par le directeur des affaires juridiques du Ministère des affaires étrangères de la France en date du 3 avril 2001

MINISTERE
DES
AFFAIRES ETRANGERES

DIRECTION DES AFFAIRES JURIDIQUES

Le Directeur

République Française

Paris, le 3 avril 2001

RECEIVED
04 APR 2001

Téléphone : 01.43.17.53.00
Télécopie : 01.43.17.43.59
Référence : N° DJ/BB/CT

Monsieur le Greffier,

J'ai l'honneur de vous faire savoir que, dans le cadre de l'affaire concernant l'arraisonnement du navire "GRAND PRINCE", objet de votre correspondance en date du 22 mars, Monsieur François ALABRUNE , Directeur adjoint des Affaires juridiques au Ministère des Affaires étrangères, est désigné en qualité d'agent du Gouvernement français. Il sera accompagné de Messieurs Jean-Pierre QENEUDEC, professeur émérite de droit international à l'Université de Paris I et Michel TRINQUIER, Sous-Directeur du droit de la Mer, des Pêches et de l'Antarctique au Ministère des Affaires étrangères ainsi que de Maître Jacques BELOT, Avocat à Saint Denis de la Réunion.
Pour les besoins de cette affaire, Monsieur ALABRUNE a élu domicile au Consulat Général de France à Hambourg.

Je vous prie de bien vouloir agréer, Monsieur le Greffier, l'expression de ma considération distinguée.

Ronny ABRAHAM

Monsieur Gritakumar E. CHITTY
Greffier
TRIBUNAL INTERNATIONAL DU DROIT DE LA MER
Am Internationalen Seegerichtshof 1
22609 HAMBOURG
REPUBLIQUE FEDERALE D'ALLEMAGNE

Designation of Judge *ad hoc* – Désignation d'un juge *ad hoc*

a) Lettre de M. Alabrune au Greffier en date du 3 avril 2001, avec en annexe :
- curriculum vitae de M. Cot (non reproduit)

MINISTERE
DES
AFFAIRES ETRANGERES

DIRECTION
DES
AFFAIRES JURIDIQUES

Téléphone : 01.43.17.53.03
Référence : /DJ/BB

REPUBLIQUE FRANCAISE

Paris, le 3 avril 2001

Monsieur le Greffier,

Je souhaiterais me référer à l'article 17, paragraphe 2, du Statut du Tribunal international du droit de la mer, qui dispose que, "si le Tribunal, lorsqu'il connaît d'un différend, comprend un membre de la nationalité d'une des parties, toute autre partie peut désigner une personne de son choix pour siéger en qualité de membre du Tribunal".

Le Tribunal comprenant un juge ressortissant du Belize, le Gouvernement français souhaite désigner Monsieur Jean-Pierre COT, Professeur émérite des Facultés de droit, dont le curriculum vitae est joint à la présente, en qualité de juge "ad hoc" pour siéger comme membre du Tribunal.

Je vous serais reconnaissant de bien vouloir porter la présente lettre à la connaissance du Président du Tribunal.

Les coordonnées de M. COT sont les suivantes: 5, rue Félix Delhasse, B-1060 Bruxelles, téléphone: 00 32 2 539 43 50, Fax: 00 32 2 539 42 83, e-mail: jean.pierre.cot@euronet.be; jeanpierrecot@aol.com

Je vous prie d'agréer, Monsieur le Greffier, l'expression de ma considération distinguée.

Agent du Gouvernement français

Monsieur Gritakumar E. CHITTY
Greffier
TRIBUNAL INTERNATIONAL DU DROIT DE LA MER
Am Internationalen Seegerichtshof 1
22609 HAMBOURG
REPUBLIQUE FEDERALE D'ALLEMAGNE

b) Statement of Mr Penelas Alvarez dated 4 April 2001 concerning the nomination of a judge *ad hoc* by France

RECEIVED 04 APR 2001

INTERNATIONAL TRIBUNAL FOR THE LAW OF THE SEA
TO THE ATTENTION OF THE REGISTRAR

The "Grand Prince" case

Dear Sir.:

I acknowledge receipt of the letter of France appointing a judge ad hoc.

Article 19 paragraph 1 of the Rules, with the aim of avoiding that the appointment of a judge ad hoc is used in a wrong way or as an obstacle to the normal course of proceedings or the normal organisation of the Tribunal, requires, very clearly, that the party who intends to choose a judge ad hoc "shall notify the Tribunal of it´s intention as soon as possible and in any event "not later that two months before the time limit fixed for the filing of a counter memorial.

In the present case, France is informing about the appointment of the judge ad hoc only two days prior to the hearings fixed by the Tribunal, and when the time limit for filing a counter memorial has already expired . This party was only notified of such a decision today, that is, the day before the hearings, which prevents us, and we can imagen that also the Tribunal, from analysing the competence of the proposed judge to act as member of the Tribunal , and in it´s case to make the correspondent opposition.

It must be noted that France was notified of the Order of the Tribunal fixing the dates for the hearings on the 22nd March , 2001. It is unacceptable that since then France have not informed the Tribunal about it´s decision until yesterday. Further, on the 2nd April , 2001 the representatives of the parties met with the President of the Tribunal and neither in that occasion France mentioned nothing about his pretension of appointing a Judge ad hoc.

It is quite evident that France is once more (in the present case) trying to put obstacle to the proceeding.

Notwithstanding, and in order not to obstacle the work of the Tribunal, avoiding further incidents , will respect the any decision the Tribunal takes in respect of this matter.

Hamburg, 4 April , 2001.

Alberto Penelas
As agent for Belize.

c) Letter from the Registrar to Mr Penelas Alvarez dated 4 April 2001

INTERNATIONAL TRIBUNAL FOR THE LAW OF THE SEA
TRIBUNAL INTERNATIONAL DU DROIT DE LA MER

Am Internationalen Seegerichtshof 1, 22609 Hamburg, Germany
Tel: 49 (40) 3560-7270 Fax: 49 (40) 3560-7275

United Nations DC-1, Suite 1140, New York, NY 10017
Tel: 1 (212) 963 6480 Fax: 1 (212) 963 0908

4 April 2001
BY FACSIMILE

Sir,

THE "GRAND PRINCE" CASE

I have the honour to inform you that the Tribunal met today to consider the observations made by the Agent of Belize in his letter of today in the matter of Mr. Cot being chosen as Judge *ad hoc* by the Government of France.

The Tribunal considers that Mr. Cot fulfils the conditions required by the Statute of the Tribunal.

Accordingly, the Tribunal sees no objection to the choice of Mr. Cot as Judge *ad hoc* in the present case.

Accept, Sir, the assurances of my highest consideration.

Gritakumar E. Chitty
Registrar

Mr. Alberto Penelas
Agent of Belize
c/o Fides Treuhandgesellschaft

Fax: 3010 060

Present contact address: Hotel Louis C. Jacob, Hamburg, Fax: 822 55 444

Completion of Documentation – Complément d'information

a) Letter from the Registrar to Mr Penelas Alvarez dated 22 March 2001

INTERNATIONAL TRIBUNAL FOR THE LAW OF THE SEA
TRIBUNAL INTERNATIONAL DU DROIT DE LA MER

Am Internationalen Seegerichtshof 1, 22609 Hamburg, Germany
Tel: 49 (40) 3560-7270 Fax: 49 (40) 3560-7275

United Nations DC-1, Suite 1140, New York, NY 10017
Tel: 1 (212) 963 6480 Fax: 1 (212) 963 0908

22 March 2001

BY FACSIMILE

Dear Mr. Penelas,

Application for prompt release under article 292 of the United Nations Convention for the Law of the Sea

I am in receipt of a copy of the Application submitted by facsimile on 21 March 2001 on behalf of Belize, under article 292 of the Convention.

I have gone trough the Application and I wish to communicate the following for appropriate action.

1. The Application does not expressly state that an agent has been appointed by Belize and does not communicate the address of the agent in Hamburg or Berlin, as required under article 56, paragraph 1, of the Rules.
2. The Application does not contain a certification that a copy of the Application and all supporting documentation has been delivered to the flag State, as required under article 110, paragraph 8, of the Rules.
3. The signature of the agent is not authenticated by the diplomatic representative of Belize in Germany or by a competent governmental authority, as required under article 54, paragraph 3, of the Rules.
4. The translation into English of Annex 13 to the Application is not certified as accurate, as required under article 64, paragraph 2, of the Rules.
5. Extracts of documents annexed to the Application are not legible. The following pages (with reference to the page numbers indicated on the copy sent by facsimile) should be communicated in a legible form: 44, 47, 48, 49, 50, 51, 52 and 53.

Yours sincerely

~~Grita~~kumar E. Chitty
Registrar

Mr. Alberto Penelas Alvarez
Abogados Maritimos y Asociados

Fax 0034 986 29 41 62

b) Letter from the Registrar to Mr Penelas Alvarez dated 30 March 2001, attached:
- list of documents for completion of documentation

INTERNATIONAL TRIBUNAL FOR THE LAW OF THE SEA
TRIBUNAL INTERNATIONAL DU DROIT DE LA MER

Am Internationalen Seegerichtshof 1, 22609 Hamburg, Germany
Tel: 49 (40) 3560-7270 Fax: 49 (40) 3560-7275

United Nations DC-1, Suite 1140, New York, NY 10017
Tel: 1 (212) 963 6480 Fax: 1 (212) 963 0908

30 March 2001

BY FACSIMILE

Sir,

The "Grand Prince" Case

You will find attached a note concerning documents we would like to receive in connection to the Application for prompt release filed with the Tribunal on 21 March 2001.

Accept, Sir, the assurances of my highest consideration.

Gritakumar E. Chitty
Registrar

Mr. Alberto Penelas Alvarez
Agent of Belize

Fax 0034 986 29 41 62

THE "GRAND PRINCE" CASE

Completion of documentation

The Registry has gone through the documentation submitted and would appreciate receiving the following:

1. A copy of the procès-verbal of violation no. 4/00 of 26 December 2000 (referred to in the Order of the Court of First Instance of Saint Paul of 12 January 2001, Annex 13 to the Application);

2. A copy of "Procès-verbaux no. 09/2001 P.C.G. 'La Jonquille'" of the Maritime Police (referred to in the Record of Arraignment from the office of the Prosecutor, Annex 8 to the Application).

c) Letter from the Registrar to Mr Védrine dated 30 March 2001, attached:
- list of documents for completion of documentation

INTERNATIONAL TRIBUNAL FOR THE LAW OF THE SEA
TRIBUNAL INTERNATIONAL DU DROIT DE LA MER

Am Internationalen Seegerichtshof 1, 22609 Hamburg, Germany
Tel: 49 (40) 3560-7270 Fax: 49 (40) 3560-7275

United Nations DC-1, Suite 1140, New York, NY 10017
Tel: 1 (212) 963 6480 Fax: 1 (212) 963 0908

30 March 2001

BY FACSIMILE

Excellency,

The "Grand Prince" Case

You will find attached a note concerning documents we would like to receive in connection to the Application for prompt release filed with the Tribunal on 21 March 2001.

Accept, Excellency, the assurances of my highest consideration.

Gritakumar E. Chitty
Registrar

His Excellency
Mr. H. Védrine
Minister for Foreign Affaires
of the Republic of France

Fax 0033-1-45 51 60 12

CC: Mr. Ronny Abraham, Director, Direction des Affaires juridiques
Fax 0033-1-43 17 55 05

THE "GRAND PRINCE" CASE

Completion of documentation

The Registry has gone through the documentation submitted and would appreciate receiving the following:

1. A copy of the procès-verbal of violation no. 4/00 of 26 December 2000 (referred to in the Order of the Court of First Instance of Saint Paul of 12 January 2001, Annex 13 to the Application);

2. A copy of "Procès-verbaux no. 09/2001 P.C.G. 'La Jonquille'" of the Maritime Police (referred to in the Record of Arraignment from the office of the Prosecutor, Annex 8 to the Application).

d) Lettre de M. Alabrune au Greffier en date du 30 mars 2001, avec en annexe :
- procès-verbal d'infraction n° 04/00

Date : 30 mars 2001

MINISTERE
DES
AFFAIRES ETRANGERES

DIRECTION
DES
AFFAIRES JURIDIQUES

Le Directeur-Adjoint

TELECOPIE

RECEIVED
30 MAR 2001
17.35 BA.

Nombre total ~~de pages : 10 (+ 1 page~~ de garde)

Téléphone : 01 43 17 53 00
Télécopie : 01 43 17 55 05

EXPEDITEUR :	DESTINATAIRE :
Monsieur François ALABRUNE	**Monsieur Gritakumar E. CHITTY** **Greffier** **TRIBUNAL INTERNATIONAL DU DROIT DE LA MER** **HAMBOURG** **Fax : 00 49 40 35 60 72 75**

OBJET : COMPLEMENT AUX OBSERVATIONS DU GOUVERNEMENT FRANCAIS.

MESSAGE :

Monsieur le Greffier,

Comme suite à votre fax de ce jour, je vous prie de bien vouloir trouver ci-joint des documents dont la communication est souhaitée par le Tribunal.

Veuillez agréer, Monsieur le Greffier, l'expression de ma considération distinguée.

François ALABRUNE

MARINE NATIONALE

FORCE D'ACTION NAVALE

COMMANDEMENT MARITIME
DE NOUVELE CALEDONIE

FREGATE NIVOSE

PROCES VERBAL D'INFRACTION
N°04/00 NIVOSE

- L'an deux mille, le mardi 26 décembre,

- Nous, soussignés Marc LANNE, capitaine de frégate, commandant la frégate de surveillance NIVOSE, Gilles DEPELLEY, capitaine de corvette, commandant en second de la frégate de surveillance NIVOSE, Stéphane BAYON de NOYER, lieutenant de vaisseau, commandant de l'aéronef AS 565 SA PANTHER N°6436,

Vu
- La loi du 1er mars 1888 modifiée, relative à l'exercice de la pêche dans les eaux sous souveraineté ou juridiction française, s'étendant au large des côtes des territoires d'outre-mer;
- La loi N° 66-400 du 18 juin 1966 modifiée, sur l'exercice de la pêche maritime et l'exploitation des produits de la mer dans les terres australes et antarctiques françaises et son décret d'application N° 69-408 du 25 avril 1969;
- La loi N° 76-655 du 16 juillet 1976 relative à la zone économique au large des territoires de la République;
- La loi N° 83-582 du 5 juillet 1983 modifiée relative au régime de la saisie et complétant la liste des agents habilités à constater les infractions dans le domaine des pêches maritimes;
- Le décret N°84-846 du 12 septembre 1984 fixant les modalités d'application de la loi 83-582 du 5 juillet 1983.
- Le décret N° 78-144 du 3 février 1978 portant création d'une zone économique au large des côtes des terres australes françaises;

étant en patrouille de police des pêches dans la zone économique des côtes du territoire de la République, en l'espèce au large des îles Kerguélen, dans les Terres Australes et Antarctiques Françaises, arborant le pavillon de police des pêches, à la position GPS: LAT. 47°44,3' SUD - LONG. 073°22' EST, le mardi 26 décembre 2000 à 08 heures 58 E, constatons que Monsieur Ramon Francisco PEREZ NOVO, né à RIBEIRA, le 05 octobre 1957, de nationalité espagnole, capitaine du navire de pêche palangrier "GRAND PRINCE", d'une longueur de 39,67m, d'une largeur de 10m, d'un tirant d'eau de 4,8m, d'une jauge brute de 669 tonneaux, propulsé par un moteur diesel de 4000 chevaux, battant pavillon de BELIZE, portant l'indicatif international "V3UJ7", enregistré sous le numéro 07972047, déclaré appartenir à la compagnie "PAIK commercial corporation" est en infraction pour :

1. -Avoir sans autorisation pêché dans la zone économique exclusive des îles Kerguelen, sous juridiction française.
2. -Ne pas avoir signalé son entrée dans la zone économique exclusive des îles Kerguelen et n'avoir pas déclaré détenir une vingtaine de tonnes de poisson à son bord.

Avons constaté chronologiquement, en heures du fuseau ECHO ce qui suit:

- Le 26 décembre 2000, à 08H53, l'hélicoptère du NIVOSE au cours de sa patrouille de surveillance maritime détecte un écho radar à une position proche de LAT:47°47'SUD - LONG:73°44'EST et l'identifie comme navire de pêche.

- A 08H58, le NIVOSE étant en position LAT: 47°44,3'SUD - LONG: 73°22'EST, le commandant constate à son tour, en passerelle, sur le radar de navigation, un écho à 16,3 milles marins, en position LAT:47°49'SUD - LONG 73°45'EST.
Au même moment, l'hélicoptère ayant reçu l'ordre de rejoindre cette position, identifie le navire de pêche du nom de "GRAND PRINCE". Ses radars de navigation sont stoppés. Le commandant d'aéronef constate très clairement qu'un pêcheur en tenue de travail (ciré de couleur orange, gants de manutention) sur le poste de pêche tribord sectionne un cable de palangre de couleur verte.

- A 09H00, le NIVOSE prend contact sur VHF 16 et donne l'ordre de stopper au GRAND PRINCE, l'hélicoptère brandit simultanément devant sa passerelle un panneau sur lequel le mot STOP est inscrit en très grosses lettres. Le GRAND PRINCE réduit immédiatement sa vitesse. Les interrogations de l'enquête de pavillon commencent en anglais depuis le NIVOSE sur VHF canal 16 puis canal 12.

- A 09H03, le commandant d'aéronef constate que le personnel sur l'arrière du GRAND PRINCE remonte une ligne.

- A 09H09, l'interlocuteur sur le GRAND PRINCE ne comprend pas tout et demande que l'on parle espagnol ou plus lentement en anglais. Lorsqu'on lui demande de nous passer le capitaine il répond "momento, por favor" puis nous dit que le capitaine ne parle pas anglais.

- A 09H13, il déclare avoir cinq tonnes de poisson à bord, l'équipage est composé de 35 personnes, 10 espagnols et 25 chiliens.

- A 09H17, le GRAND PRINCE dit ne pas avoir déclaré son entrée dans la zone économique exclusive des îles Kerguelen.

- A 09H19, le commandant d'aéronef aperçoit une rangée de six bouées sur le travers bâbord du GRAND PRINCE pour 500 yards.

- A 09H21, le GRAND PRINCE est visible depuis le NIVOSE, il lui est annoncé sur VHF 12 l'intention de le visiter, il lui est demandé de rassembler son personnel sur l'avant.

- A 09H30, le GRAND PRINCE dit avoir quitté Durban le 26/11/00, sa destination probable est Walwis Bay (Namibie). On lui redemande de faire rallier les 33 personnes sur l'avant, le capitaine et le patron des pêches restant en passerelle.

- A 09H35, tout le personnel n'est pas encore rassemblé, 21 personnes sont sur le pont principal à l'arrière de la passerelle et en ont profité pour récupérer le cordage sectionné à l'arrivée de l'hélicoptère et le lover dans un caisson sur l'arrière du bâtiment.

- A 09H42, le GRAND PRINCE est à 1,3 milles marins du NIVOSE, le groupe de six bouées est visible à 1000 yards sur l'avant du NIVOSE.

3/6

- A 09H45, le commandant d'aéronef note quelques mouvements de personnel sur l'arrière du bateau, en particulier, une personne cagoulée avec des vêtements chauds qui entre dans le bateau par le poste de pêche tribord.

- A 09H53, 28 personnes sont rassemblées sur l'avant.

- A 10H07, les 33 membres d'équipage sont rassemblés sur l'avant, l'hélicoptère posé sur le NIVOSE à 10H04 décolle avec deux commandos et le chef de l'équipe de visite à son bord. Ils seront hélitreuillés à 10H10 sur le GRAND PRINCE.

- A 10H24, les premiers comptes rendus du chef de l'équipe de visite confirment la présence de 33 personnes à l'avant et deux en passerelle. Sur le pont principal et la plage avant, il repère des ancres de fond, des filets, des casiers des lignes de palangre neuves. Il confirme la présence d'une ligne de palangre fraîchement coupée lovée derrière la passerelle. Sur l'arrière, il note des hameçons et des têtes d'appâts. Il y a des légines fraîches entières dans le bac attenant à l'atelier de remontée de la palangre. Sur le toit de la passerelle il aperçoit un grand nombre de bouées. L'équipage est docile.

- De 10H30 à 10H39, 4 membres de l'équipe de visite embarquent dans l'hélicoptère et sont treuillés sur le GRAND PRINCE.

- A 10H45, le chef de l'équipe de visite pénètre en passerelle. Les cartes sont rangées, les appareils de navigation sont stoppés, le capitaine et le patron de pêche se soumettent à la palpation de sécurité sans difficulté. Il n'y a pas d'arme en passerelle.

- De 10H50 à 11H04, 4 personnes dont le commandant en second du NIVOSE embarquent dans l'hélicoptère puis sont treuillées sur le GRAND PRINCE.

- A 11H00, le capitaine du GRAND PRINCE reconnaît sa position à l'intérieur de la ZEE des îles Kerguelen à LAT.: 47°46' SUD - LONG: 73°44' EST. Il signe le point sur la carte 4711 "Iles d'Amsterdam aux îles Kerguelen".

- A 11H10, commence l'investigation des documents de la passerelle.
Le commandant en second du NIVOSE constate la présence du point de 11H00 ECHO signé par le capitaine du GRAND PRINCE.
D'après la patente de navigation qui expire le 29 décembre 2000, le GRAND PRINCE appartient à la PAIK commercial corporation / 35 A Regent street / PO BOX 1777 / BELIZE city / BELIZE.
Le journal de navigation s'arrête le 23 décembre 2000 à la position: LAT:47°40' SUD LONG: 75°30' EST.
Sur la liste d'équipage, il y a 37 noms. Le capitaine en a rayé deux. Il dit qu'ils sont partis en vacances depuis DURBAN.
Le capitaine est domicilié à Ribeira, 10 rue da Carballeira. Sa carte professionnelle porte le N°484011672/6.101.
Le patron de pêche est Antonio SEVILLA LUSTRES, de nationalité espagnole, né à Ribeira le 25/07/60, domicilié Avenida Ferrol, 107 Ribeira. Sa licence de pêche porte le N° 484004676/1.037.

- A 11H37, le patron des pêches reconnaît que le poisson pêché est du "Robalo", ce qu'il traduit en anglais par "Patagonian tooth fish", c'est à dire en français "légine".

P.04

4/6

- De 12H15 à 14H50, le NIVOSE part remonter les bouées repérées à 09H19 et à 09H42. Il est alors à la position 47°48,4' SUD - 073° 44,4' EST. La manoeuvre est rendue difficile par les conditions météorologiques (vent de 30 noeuds). La ligne est remontée péniblement et casse alors que quatre bouées seulement sont à bord. L'une d'elles de couleur orange, marquée "75 DYNOPLAST AS ALESUND MADE IN NORWAY", et portant le chiffre 5, est traversée par un mat métallique sur lequel sont attachées deux lampes flashs cylindriques oranges de marque "CAVILA ELECTRONICA MODEL PULSAR REF 27.005". Au sommet de ce mat, il y a une antenne fouet noire montée sur un socle en plastique gris sur lequel le chiffre 3 est inscrit en jaune. Les trois autres bouées sont roses avec un anneau bleu et portent l'inscription "A4 THE ORIGINAL POLYFORM MADE IN NORWAY". Une deuxième tentative permet de remonter outre les deux dernières bouées, la ligne de plus d'un kilomètre, puis une ancre de fond et enfin une palangre qui est halée à bord jusqu'au premiers hameçons avant d'être volontairement coupée. Les deux dernières bouées sont oranges et portent l'inscription "A5 POLYFORM M6001 ALESUND MADE IN NORWAY".

- A 12H39, commence l'investigation de sécurité en passerelle. Depuis l'un des deux ordinateurs de la passerelle, on imprime une liste de numéros de téléphone de bâtiments et de stations à terre dont Crozet et Kerguelen. Parmi le matériel de radio et de navigation, on note un émetteur récepteur MF/HF, et un fax-téléphone INMARSAT qui sonnera à plusieurs reprises au cours de la visite. Il y a un poste de repos pour douze flash dont trois inoccupés.

- A 13H02, le commandant en second du NIVOSE accompagné du capitaine se rendent dans l'usine. Une forte odeur de poisson s'en dégage. Sur bâbord du local sont disposées, en deux blocs, environ 200 cagettes d'appâts préparés, accrochés sur des hameçons à une ligne.
Le plan de travail pour la mise à l'eau des palangres n'a pas été rincé, il est encore jonché d'écailles.
Sur la partie tribord de l'usine, de l'avant vers l'arrière, on trouve:
A proximité immédiate du poste de remontée de la palangre, un bac contenant 16 légines fraîches entières. Les joues de certaines ont été retirées. Le capitaine reconnaît la fraîcheur de ce poisson en le touchant devant la caméra.
Sur le plan de travail de découpe, les outils sont encore plein de viscères, la table n'est pas rincée, on y trouve des bouts de nageoires, le sol est jonché de sang frais et de viscères. En contrebas du plan de travail, un bac contient une eau brunâtre.
Sur le côté, un autre bac contient des filets de poisson frais.
Un bac de rinçage alimenté par un tuyau d'où coule de l'eau en continu contient une dizaine de poissons frais sans queue ni tête en cours de lavage. Sur le bord du bac, il y a trois pièces de poisson frais. Le capitaine nous dit que tout ce poisson a été pêché aujourd'hui.
Contre la paroi tribord de l'usine, sur un tapis roulant on compte une douzaine de poissons frais sans queue ni tête emballés dans des sacs plastiques, prêts à descendre dans les tunnels de congélation.
L'investigation se poursuit vers le local des tunnels de congélation. Au passage on remarque quatre ancres de fond.

- A 13H20, devant les trois tunnels de congélation, le commandant en second du NIVOSE compte une vingtaine de cartons marrons sur des étagères. A l'intérieur, dans des plastiques il y a des pièces de poisson ou des filets, frais d'apparence, dont la température varie entre +1.6°C pour les pièces et –0.3°C pour les filets.
Le tunnel de congélation du milieu est vide, la porte en est ouverte. Les deux tunnels qui l'encadrent contiennent environ 54 cartons de poisson en pièces ou en filets; certaines grosses pièces sont dans des sacs de toile blancs. Les températures relevées à cœur sur les pièces du tunnel au fond du local (bâbord du bâtiment) varient entre –1°C et –12°C selon les pièces.

5/6

Celles prises dans le tunnel situé à l'entrée du local indiquent des valeurs de -0,1°C. Le capitaine nous dit que la température ambiante normale de ces tunnels est de –40°C. Toutefois la température prise par nos soins enregistre -9°C.

- A 13H45, le capitaine nous dit que ce poisson a été pêché cette nuit. Il précise que chaque tunnel contient environ une tonne trois de poisson. Dans ce local on retrouve un petit cahier à spirale de couleur rose sur lequel sont enregistrées les quantités de poisson chargées dans les soutes congelées et leur répartition.

- A 13H50, débute l'investigation dans les soutes congelées. Des cartons vides dépliés occupent environ les deux tiers de la première soute. On y trouve des cartons de langoustes et l'alimentation de l'équipage. Sur le tapis roulant qui, depuis la porte de la soute descend dans la deuxième soute en contrebas, le commandant en second du NIVOSE constate la présence de 20 sacs de toile blancs contenant des légines dont la température enregistrée est de –1.3°C. Le thermomètre de la soute indique une température ambiante de -22°C.
De part et d'autre de ce tapis roulant, dans la deuxième soute, plus vaste, un important volume de cartons d'appâts congelés est entassé sous des filets. Au fond de la soute, contre la paroi qui fait toute la largeur du bâtiment (soit environ dix mètres), des cartons et des sacs de légines sont entreposés sur une hauteur de deux mètres et une largeur d'un mètre. Ce volume correspond environ à 1/8ème de cette soute dont la capacité, selon le patron de pêche, est de 120 tonnes. Le commandant en second du NIVOSE évalue donc à quinze tonnes le poisson congelé dont la température relevée à cœur est de –18°C. La température ambiante de la soute est mesurée à -22°C. A ce moment la quantité totale de poisson détenu à bord peut être estimée à une vingtaine de tonnes.
En remontant de la soute, on constate un emplacement pour dix batteries de bouée dont sept sont en place.

- Vers 14H10, l'investigation de sécurité dans les chambres du capitaine et du patron de pêche permettra de mettre à jour la position de deux balises inscrite à la main sur un papier ainsi que les modes d'emploi de quelques appareils en passerelle, dont l'ordinateur de navigation, un stock de Tee-shirt "BLICE ENTREPOTS SA" et une fiche sur le cours de la légine. Il n'y a pas d'armes.

- A 14H55, on édite depuis l'ordinateur de la passerelle un cahier de pêche daté du 08/09/00 au 07/10/00.

- A 15H20, sur le pont principal, le commandant en second du NIVOSE remarque une bouée orange numérotée 4 avec un mât et un dispositif pour recevoir deux flash. A proximité, il y a cinq bouées roses non gréées; deux d'entre elles portent la marque "POLYFORM N6001 ALESUND MADE IN NORWAY"et A5 sur la partie bleue supérieure. Sur bâbord, il y a six ancres de fond.

- A 15H49, sur le toit de la passerelle, le commandant en second du NIVOSE compte huit bouées oranges sur bâbord. Quatre d'entre elles sont équipées d'un dispositif pour recevoir une batterie (bouées numérotées 5, 4, 3, 2). Les quatre autres bouées sont équipées d'un dispositif pour recevoir des flashs lumineux (numéros 3, 2, et 6 plus une sans numéro); parmi ces dernières, les bouées 2, 3, et 6 portent l'inscription "75 DYNOPLAST AS ALESUND MADE IN NORWAY. Sur tribord du toit de la passerelle, une bouée orange portant la lettre C est à moitié dégonflée et comporte un mât avec un dispositif pour recevoir batterie et flash, enfin on y compte 19 bouées roses similaires à celles trouvées sur le pont.

P.05

6/6

- A 16H30, à la demande du commandant en second du NIVOSE, le patron de pêche montre le poste de repos pour 10 antennes fouet dans l'échappée machine. Sept sont en place et portent les numéros: 1, 2, 4, 6, 8, 11, 12. Ces antennes ont des caractéristiques similaires à celles de l'antenne présente sur la bouées repêchée.

Compte tenu des divers éléments ci-dessus rapportés, constatons qu'il y a bien infraction à la réglementation française sur la pêche maritime dans la zone économique exclusive des îles Kerguelen.

Le 26 décembre 2000 à 20heures, pour faire suite aux constatations rapportées ci-dessus, à la demande du directeur départemental des affaires maritimes de La Réunion, et agissant selon les ordres du commandant de la marine à La Réunion, le navire de pêche palangrier "GRAND PRINCE" est dérouté vers le Port des Galets (La Réunion). Notification de ce déroutement a été portée sur le nouveau journal de navigation ouvert rétroactivement à cet effet à la date du 24 décembre par le capitaine.

Un procès-verbal d'appréhension est dressé le 26 décembre 2000. Notification a été faite à 20heures E au capitaine du "GRAND PRINCE", qui a signé après traduction par le patron de pêche. Copie en est remise au capitaine du "GRAND PRINCE". Les scellés ont été apposés en la présence constante du capitaine du "GRAND PRINCE".

Le capitaine de frégate Marc LANNE,
commandant la frégate NIVOSE

Le capitaine de corvette Gilles DEPELLEY,
commandant en second de la frégate NIVOSE

Le lieutenant de vaisseau Stéphane BAYON de NOYER
commandant de bord de l'hélicoptère AS 565 SA PANTHER N°6436

- procès-verbal de synthèse de la Gendarmerie maritime

GENDARMERIE NATIONALE Commandement de la Gendarmerie Maritime Patrouilleur Côtier de Gendarmerie JONQUILLE C.U.: 11530 - PV N° 9 / 2001	PROCEDURE D'ENQUETE PRELIMINAIRE PROCES-VERBAL DE SYNTHESE	

Analyse et références (éventuellement)

« DELITS DE PECHE Analyses et références in fine »

L'an deux mil un,
Nous soussigné, **LANCOU**, Jean Luc, adjudant, officier de police judiciaire,
Vu les articles 16 à 19 et 75 à 78 du code de procédure pénale.
rapportons les opérations suivantes que nous avons effectuées, agissant en uniforme et conformément aux ordres de nos chefs

Le 26 décembre 2000, nous sommes avisés par le PC opérations de la marine nationale à la Réunion qu'un navire de pêche battant pavillon de Bélize nommé "Grand Prince" a été surpris dans la zone économique des îles de Kerguélen dans les terres australes et antarctiques Françaises par la frégate de surveillance "Nivose" de la marine nationale en mission de surveillance des pêches dans cette zone.

Ce palangrier est en action de pêche, sans autorisation, à environ 55 nautiques dans la zone économique. D'autres part, il n'a pas signalé son entrée dans la zone économique ni le tonnage de poisson détenu à bord (17,5 tonnes de légines) au centre de transmissions des l'îles de Kerguélen.

L'ordre de déroutement est notifié 26 décembre 2000 à 20 heures 00 (E) au capitaine du "Grand Prince".

Le 3 janvier 2001, monsieur LAUQUE, substitut près le procureur de la République près le tribunal de grande instance de Saint - Denis est informé des faits. Nous l'avisons qu'il existe à l'encontre de Ramon Francisco PEREZ NOVO, capitaine du navire, des indices faisant présumer qu'il a commis des délits de pêche. Il nous demande de lui signaler l'arrivée à quai du palangrier et de procéder à l'enquête. Le 9 janvier 2001, à 8 heures 00, monsieur le substitut est avisé de l'arrivée du navire. Il se rend à bord lors du début des investigations et nous laisse saisi de l'enquête.

La police de l'air et des frontières, les services sanitaires et l'administration des douanes sont avisés le 8 janvier 2001.

La navire accoste à Port Réunion le mardi 9 janvier 2001 à 10 heures 15 (Delta).

Les militaires de notre unité qui nous ont secondé dans nos opérations sont cités nominativement dans la procédure pour chacun des actes qu'ils ont accomplis. Nous avons reçu le concours d'un gendarme de la brigade nautique de la gendarmerie nationale de Port. Des interprètes en langue espagnole, un informaticien et un laboratoire photo ont été requis sur autorisation du parquet.

Le 26 décembre 2000 à 8 heures 53 (E), l'hélicoptère de la frégate de surveillance "Nivose" au cours de sa patrouille maritime détecte un écho radar à la position L 47° 47' (Sud) et G 073° 44' (Est) et l'identifie comme un navire de pêche. A 8 heures 58 (E) cet écho est identifié à vue, il s'agit du palangrier Grand Prince, en action de pêche. Le commandant de l'aéronef constate que le navire est en action de pêche. A 9 heures 19 (E), il constate la présence de six bouées à la mer, sur le travers bâbord à 500 yards, soit 450 mètres environ.

L'O.P.J.

PCG JONQUILLE

Une visite est effectuée à bord à partir de 10 heures 30 (E). Au cours de celle-ci le capitaine PEREZ NOVO Ramon Francisco reconnaît être dans la zone économique Française à la position 47° 46' Sud et 073° 44' Est. Dans ses cales, il est trouvé 15 tonnes de légine congelée et dans les tunnels de congélation 2,5 tonnes de légine fraîche. Dans l'usine il est constaté des légines fraîches ainsi que des appâts accrochés sur des hameçons. Le "Nivose" remonte entre 12 heures 15 (E) et 14 heures 50 (E) les bouées repérées précédemment par l'hélicoptère.

Les procès-verbaux d'appréhension 05/2000, 06/2000 et 07/2000 "Nivose" sont notifiés au capitaine du Grand Prince à 20 heures 00 (E). Une copie lui est remise.

Le procès verbal d'infraction 04/2000 "Nivose" est établi par le commandant, le commandant en second et le commandant d'aéronef du "Nivose".

Un exemplaire de ces procès-verbaux est remis à monsieur le directeur départemental et régional des affaires maritimes de la Réunion.

Le 5 janvier 2001, à notre demande, le chef du district nous certifie que le "Grand Prince" n'a pas signalé son entrée dans zone économique des Kerguélen ni la quantité de poissons détenue à son bord (Pièce n° 25).

Le 8 janvier 2001, un militaire de notre unité, est hélitreuillé à bord du "Nivose" à la mer. Il procède aux auditions de :

Capitaine de frégate LANNE Marc, commandant (Pièce n° 11). Il nous remet les procès verbaux d'infraction 04/2000 (Pièce n° 2) et d'appréhensions 05, 06 et 07/2000 (Pièce n° 3, 4 et 5), cinq cassettes vidéo, cinq pellicules photos, huit disquettes photos numériques, une marque de pêche, un grappin et ligne de palangre avec hameçons (PV de saisie pièce n° 12, scellés n° 1 à 9).

Capitaine de corvette DEPELLEY Gilles, commandant en second (Pièce n° 13). Il a procédé aux constatations sur le "Grand prince" le 26 décembre 2000.

Lieutenant de vaisseau BAYON DE NOYER Stéphane, commandant l'aéronef embarqué (Pièce n° 14). Il a constaté l'action de pêche du "Grand prince" le 26 décembre 2000 ainsi que la présence de bouées à proximité du navire.

De leurs auditions et du procès verbal d'infraction 04/2000 "Nivose" il ressort les éléments probants suivants :

- Le 26 décembre 2000, 08 heures 53 (E), le navire "Grand Prince" se trouve à la position 47° 47' Sud et 073° 44' Est, soit 55 nautiques à l'intérieur de la Z.E.E. de Kerguélen. Ce navire n'a pas signalé son entrée dans la zone ni le tonnage de poissons détenus à bord. Il est en action de pêche en mettant à l'eau une palangre. Le commandant de l'hélicoptère constate qu'un pêcheur sectionne une palangre de couleur verte sur le poste de pêche tribord et que le personnel sur l'arrière du "Grand Prince" remonte une ligne. A 9 heures 19 (E), il constate la présence de six bouées à la mer, sur le travers bâbord à 500 yards, soit 450 mètres environ.

- Le navire obtempère rapidement à l'injonction de stopper et l'équipe de visite monte à bord à partir de 10 heures 30 (E). Le capitaine reconnaît se trouver dans la zone économique des îles de Kerguélen en portant sa position sur la carte 4711 du bord. Le journal de navigation n'est plus rempli depuis le 23 décembre 2000. Il est constaté la présence d'appâts décongelés préparés sur hameçons, de légines fraîches entières, en cours de préparation et en cours de congélation dans les tunnels.

L'O.P.J.

GENDARMERIE MARITIME
PCG JONQUILLE *Pièce N° 1 - Feuillet N° 3*

- Le "Nivose" récupère à la mer le matériel de pêche repéré par l'hélicoptère à proximité du "Grand prince". Il s'agit d'une marque de pêche portant l'inscription "5" avec lampe et gonio, bout, ancre de fond et palangre avec hameçons. Ce matériel est similaire à celui trouvé à bord du "Grand Prince".

Le 9 janvier 2001, nous procédons à une étude comparative entre la marque de pêche (Scellés n° 7) portant l'inscription "5" relevée par le "Nivose" et la marque de pêche portant l'inscription "4" trouvée à bord du "Grand Prince". Nous constatons ainsi TRENTE ET UN points de similitudes qui établissent sans aucun doute possible que la marque de pêche "5" appartient bien au "Grand Prince". L'ancre de fond (Scellés n° 8) et la ligne de palangre (Scellés n° 9) sont également similaires au matériel détenu à bord du "Grand prince" (Pièce n° 17 procès-verbal de comparaisons) et (Pièce n° 16 procès-verbal d'investigation).

A 10 heures 15, dès l'arrivée à quai du "Grand prince", PEREZ NOVO Ramon Francisco, capitaine du navire, est placé en garde à vue (Pièces n° 6, 7, 8, 9 et 10). Il est le capitaine du navire depuis le 27 octobre 2000. De ses déclarations, il ressort qu'il reconnaît être en action de pêche, à l'arrivée de l'hélicoptère, il pense que le capitaine de pêche posait une palangre. Il reconnaît se trouver dans la ZEE des Kerguélen et ne pas avoir signalé sa présence ni le tonnage détenu à bord au district. A bord, c'est le capitaine de pêche qui est responsable de la pêche. La décision d'aller pêcher dans la ZEE a été prise d'un commun accord entre-eux. Il déclare que toute la légine se trouvant à bord a été pêchée à l'extérieur de la ZEE.

A 15 heures 00, nous procédons à l'audition de SEVILLA LUSTRES Antonio, capitaine de pêche. Il déclare que le "Grand Prince" est rentré pour pêcher dans la ZEE dans le courant de la nuit du 25 au 26 décembre 2000. Vers 7 heures 15, le 26 décembre 2000 il a donné l'ordre de filer une palangre. Au moment où l'hélicoptère est arrivé, il a donné l'ordre à un marin de couper sur le poste tribord le bout de retenue de la palangre. Il reconnaît que le matériel de pêche remonté par le "Nivose" appartient bien au "Grand Prince" (Pièce n° 15).

Le 10 janvier 2001, l'informaticien requis nous informe que les fichiers des carnets de pêche des ordinateurs ont été supprimés. Cependant il trouve un fichier du 6 avril 2000 mentionnant des positions dans la zone économique des îles de Kerguélen. Il trouve également un fichier sur le télex relatant des faits du 30 août au 25 octobre 2000, notamment un fax concernant l'assistance dans le sauvetage de "l'Amur" ainsi que divers documents (Pièce n° 22).

A 19 heures 00, nous procédons à la saisie des documents officiels du "Grand Prince" (Pièce n° 28, scellés n° 10 à 25).

En conclusion, il ressort des constatations effectuées par le "Nivose" et de notre enquête que le "Grand Prince" était en action de pêche à l'intérieur de la zone économique des îles de Kerguélen dans le nord-est à 55 nautiques de la limite extérieure. Il n'a pas signalé son entrée en zone économique ni le tonnage de poisson détenu à son bord.

De l'enquête effectuée, il ressort que les faits commis par PEREZ NOVO Ramon Francisco constituent des délits pour avoir :

- Dans la zone économique exclusive des côtes du territoire de la République en l'espèce au large des îles de Kerguélen dans les terres australes et antarctiques Françaises, étant capitaine du "Grand Prince", navire battant pavillon de Bélize, omis de déclarer sa présence et sa quantité de pêche au chef du district de Kerguélen.

Délits prévus et réprimés par l'article 2 et 4 de la Loi 66-400 du 18.06.1966 modifié par la loi 97-1051 du 18.11.97 et l'article 2 et 4 de la loi 83-582 du 05.07.1983.

L'O.P.J.

GENDARMERIE MARITIME
PCG JONQUILLE

P.V 9/2001
Pièce N° 1 - Feuillet N° 4

- Dans la zone économique exclusive des côtes du territoire de la République en l'espèce au large des îles de Kerguélen dans les terres australes et antarctiques Françaises, étant capitaine du "Grand Prince", navire battant pavillon de Bélize, avoir pratiqué la pêche sans avoir obtenu au préalable l'autorisation prévue par la loi.
Délit prévu et réprimé par les articles 1 et 2 du 1er mars 1988 modifiée par la Loi 96-609 du 05 juillet 1996, Article 2, 4, 10 de la Loi 66-400 du 18.06.1966 modifiée par la loi 97-1051 du 18.11.97. Article 2 et 4 de la loi 83-582 du 05.07.1983.

Le 11 janvier 2000, PEREZ NOVO Ramon Francisco est présenté devant le procureur de la République à Saint Denis.

Nous faisons parvenir directement la présente procédure constituée en double exemplaire tel que le détail figure au bordereau d'envoi, accompagnée des pièces à convictions.

Fait et clos à le Port, le 11 janvier 2001.

L' officier de police judiciaire

Responses to questions from the Tribunal – Réponses aux questions du Tribunal

a) List of questions of 5 April 2001

LIST OF QUESTIONS

To both parties

1. What effect would the French position with regard to jurisdiction and admissibility have on the object and purpose of article 292 of the Convention?

2. Could the confiscation of the *Grand Prince* be overturned by the Court of Appeal ? If this would be so, could the Court of Appeal decide the release of the vessels upon payment of a bond?

3. With reference to the Annexes to the Application, the Certificate of Class, dated 23 June 1999, gives the name of the owner as "NOYCAN B. L.-MONANA-VIGO." The Provisional Patent of navigation, dated 16 October 2000, names the owner as the PAIK COMMERCIAL CORP. Belize. The Certificate of Class, still bearing the name of the owner as NOYCAN B. L.-MONANA- VIGO, was endorsed in Vigo on 2 November 1999 by the Classification Society. There is no further endorsement showing that the ordinary (annual) survey had been performed in 2000 by the Classification Society. In these circumstances the ownership of the vessel is unclear. Who is the beneficial owner of the vessel?

4. What are the legal meaning and effects of the word "confiscation" in French law?

To Belize

5. Did Belize in the period between 12 and 23 January 2001 mention to the French authorities the possibility of submitting the question of prompt release to an international court or tribunal?

6. "Grand Prince" was arrested on 26 December 2000, its seizure was confirmed on 12 January 2001; it was confiscated on January 23rd. What were the reasons for indicating the intention to submit the question of release to the Tribunal only on 6 March 2001?

7. Which were the "several arrangements with the authorities in Réunion ... done in order to be able to avoid the detention of the vessel" (para. 19 of the Application.

2

<u>To France</u>

8. Is it possible for the Government of France to throw some more light on the notion of "provisional execution" of the confiscation?

9. The decision to confiscate *Grand Prince* was adopted 9 days after the confirmation of its seizure and the determination of a bond for its release. What was the reason for the French authorities in the Réunion for changing their previous practice concerning the treatment of foreign vessels violating French rules on the exclusive economic zone?

b) Réponses de la France aux questions posées par le Tribunal en date du 6 avril 2001

Réponses aux questions posées par le Tribunal

RECEIVED 06/04/2001

Réponse à la question n°1

La position adoptée par la France en ce qui concerne la compétence et la recevabilité, si elle était retenue par le Tribunal, aurait pour effet de préciser davantage les conditions de recours à la procédure de l'article 292 de la Convention. L'objet et le but de cette disposition n'en seraient nullement affectés. En effet, si le but et l'objet de l'article 292 sont bien de permettre une prompte mainlevée d'immobilisation , la suite que le Tribunal peut donner à une demande de mainlevée est toujours subordonnée à :

a) l'appréciation du bien-fondé de l'allégation de violation de la Convention ;
b) l'appréciation du caractère raisonnable de la caution, lorsque cette allégation paraît bien fondée.

Réponse à la question n°2

En aucun cas la Cour d'appel ne peut décider de la mainlevée de l'immobilisation du navire dès le dépôt d'une caution. L'immobilisation a en effet un caractère provisoire et cesse de produire effet dès qu'une décision a été rendue sur le fond.

En revanche, la Cour d'appel qui examine à nouveau la cause comme l'a fait le Tribunal correctionnel, pourrait décider qu'il n'y a pas lieu de prononcer la confiscation du navire et le restituer à son propriétaire.

Réponse à la question n°3

La France, en ce qui la concerne, ignore quel était le propriétaire effectif du navire "Grand Prince"au moment où il a été arraisonné.

Elle ne peut que regretter que les Experts cités par le requérant n'aient pas donnés de renseignements à ce sujet.

Elle peut seulement faire état des constatations suivantes :

La "Paik Commercial Corp.", présentée comme étant propriétaire du navire, a été fondée le 1er janvier 2000 à Bélize. Le 21 mars 2000, cette société a acheté le navire à la "Reardon Commercial Corp.". Cette dernière société a elle-même été fondée à Bélize le 14 mai 1999. Ces sociétés ont toutes deux leur siège social à la même adresse : 35 A Regent Street, Belize-City.

Réponse à la question n°4

La confiscation est la main-mise de l'Etat sur un objet.

L'article 131.21 du Code Pénal dispose que "la chose confisquée est, sauf disposition particulière prévoyant sa destruction ou son attribution, dévolue à l'Etat."

Réponse à la question n°8

L'exécution provisoire a pour objet de rendre exécutoire une décision de justice en dépit de l'exercice d'une voie de recours.

En matière pénale, le principe est que l'appel suspend l'exécution de la peine prononcée par le Tribunal correctionnel.

Il n'en est différemment que lorsque la loi prévoit que le juge peut assortir sa décision de l'exécution provisoire. Tel est le cas de la confiscation du bien qui a servi à commettre l'infraction qui peut, selon l'article 471 du Code de procédure pénale être déclarée exécutoire par provision.

Réponse à la question n°9

Les autorités françaises n'ont pas changé leur pratique. Elles ont simplement pris en considération les particularités de l'espèce. Lorsque le Capitaine du Grand Prince a été interrogé le 9 janvier par la gendarmerie, il a déclaré qu'il avait appareillé de Durban le 2 ou 3 décembre 2000 et qu'il était dans la zone économique française "en commun accord avec le capitaine de pêche pour la raison suivante : c'est un endroit où il y a du poisson..." (Procès verbal d'interrogation, pièce jointe).

Il n'y avait donc aucune raison d'attendre davantage avant de soumettre les faits reconnus par le Capitaine au Tribunal correctionnel.

Il est vraisemblable que si des investigations supplémentaires avaient dû être menées, il aurait été décidé d'ouvrir une information. Tel n'a pas été le cas en l'espèce.

Fait à Hambourg le 6 avril 2001

F. ALABRUNE
Agent du Gouvernement
de la République française

c) Reply of Belize to questions posed by the Tribunal dated 6 April 2001

INTERNATIONAL TRIBUNAL FOR THE LAW OF THE SEA

Reply to questions posed by the Tribunal

6 April 2001

To question n. 1

What effect would the French position with regard to jurisdiction and admissibility have on the object and purpose of article 292 of the Convention ?

As mentioned yesterday , this an independent proceeding of those carried out by the domestic courts. Both run in paralell .

As we also indicated , if the theory sustained by France prevails, then every State could avoid prompt release of vessels and crews just by carrying out a speedy proceeding for prompt confiscation or prompt imprisonment , and deciding provisional execution of the decision.

Through this way , invoking domestic Laws, would be evaded the requirement stated under article 73.2 of the Convention. This would affect not only vessels but also crews, which could be promptly imprisoned .

Which is the purpose and objective of art. 292 of the Convention ?

To deal with matters were it is alleged that in whatever way a vessel is detained by a State without the possibility of being released upon the posting of a reasonable bond

To end with, I will recall that as was held by this Tribunal in the Monte Confurco case , paragraph 70 of the Judgement, the release of prompt detention can be subject only to a reasonable bond.

To question n. 2

Could the confiscation of Grand Prince be overturned by the Court of Appeal ?

If this would be so, could the Court of Appeal decide release of the vessels upon payment of the bond.

It is obvious that the Court of Appeal, or the Supreme Court in Paris, could perfectly overturn the said decision. There are arguments to defend that confiscation is not a proportional sanction in relation with the offence comitted. Evidence thereof if the amount of the fine impossed to the Captain of 200,000 FF , which is in a low level in comparison with other cases before the local courts.

But the most important thing is that even In case the said decision is overturned the Court of Appeal , this Court will not pronounce nothing regarding release upon a bond or other security, as it is not the subject matter of the appeal. We would still have to await until the Supreme Court pronounced a final and firm decision.

To questlon n. 3

Regarding ownership of Grand Prince.

It seems that some confusion as to the ownership of the vessel has arised from a reference in the Certificates of Class , enclosed as exhibit 17 of the application, to Noycan as shipowning company.

The current shipowner bought the vessel on the 27th March 2.000, as it is shown by the contract of sale , duly notarized and apostilled enclosed as exhibit 2 of our application.

Document number 3 of the application evidences that on the 16 October 2.000 the shipowner of Grand Prince was Paik Commercial Corp.

This ownership has also been confirmed by the Intenational Merchant Marine Registry of Belize in its letter dated 30 march 2001, which was ordered following indications of the Registrar and which is part of the file.

The certificate further states that despite the expiration of the provisional patent of navigation is still registered in Belize, being documents related to Status of the vessel , such as the final patent of navigation and ship station licence of the vessel, pending of being processed by the Registry .

The certificate of class which seems to create the confusion , as you can see, was issued on the 23 June 1.999, and as it is stated in the same document it expires in a term of five years.

Therefore it is evident that the document was issued when the ownership corresponded to Noycan, **previously** to the purchase of the vessel by the current owner, Paik Commercial.

Note also that thc only survey due on January 2000 were carried out in November 1999 by the previous owner of the vessel .

That's the simple reason why Paik Commercial does not yet appear in the classification society documents, as they have not had the necessity to make any arrangement for the time being regarding the classification certificates.

Notwithstanding, Mr. President, whether the Tribunal wishes us to provide any further evidence as regards to ownership , we will be more than happy to do that.

To question n. 4

What are the legal meaning and effects of the word confiscation in french Law.

It is obvious that confiscation supposes, in principle, the attachment of the goods by the confiscating State. As to its effects, if article 73.2 of the Convention did not exist them the inmediate effect would be the detention of the vessel and its expropiation by the detaining State. However, as far as article 73.2 is applicable, which I feel is not under discussion, then the vessel must be promptly released against a reasonable bond, and this requirement, as held by the Tribunal cannot be sujected to any domestic laws or regulations, but only to the posting of a reasonable bond.

Despite what we have expossed, following the request of the Tribunal, we must insist that we are not questioning in this proceeding the legality of those measures, but only that related to prompt release, which cannot be avoided by alleging domestic Laws or procedings.

As conclusion, France breached the convention by first fixing a totally unreasonable bond, and moreover, by, only one week thereafter, impeding by a prompt confiscation proceeding combined with provisional execution, any possibility of release.

Questions 5, 6 and 7 have been answered with the occasion of Belize statements during the morining of the 6th April 2001

Alberto Penelas Alvarez
As Agent for Belize

Additional documents submitted before the closure of the written proceedings
Documents additionnels soumis avant la clôture de la procédure écrite

Submitted by Belize

a) Article 55 de la Constitution française

RECEIVED 02/04/2001

article 55

"Les traités ou accords régulièrement ratifiés ou approuvés ont, dés leur publication, une autorité supérieure à celle des lois, sous réserve, pour chaque accord ou traité de son application par l'autre partie."

b) Reply to the Observations of the French Government, attached:
- ***acte d'appel*** **of 31 January 2001 (in French) (not reproduced)**

INTERNATIONAL TRIBUNAL FOR THE LAW OF THE SEA

REPLY TO THE "OBSERVATIONS OF THE FRENCH GOVERMENT", STATED IN LETTER DATED 28 MARCH , 2.001, REGARDING THE APPLICATION FOR PROMPT RELEASE OF "GRAND PRINCE"

1.- We are arranging for translation of the said letter into english language.

2.- Notwithstanding, we whish to advance to the Tribunal the following comments:

a) Firstly, we consider that France should comply with the rules of the Tribunal and appear in this proceeding (as this party has done) through an agent duly authorizased , and to present any arguments through a "statement in response" , according to article 111.4º f the Rules of the Tribunal.

b) Without prejudice of the above, it seems that France is forgetting, or trying to forget, that article 73.2º sanctions that the coastal States can arrest and carry out judicial proceedings to ensure compliance with the laws and regulations adopted by it, but always **<<in conformity with the convention>>**.

c) What is at stake is solely the question whether France has or not respected in this case the provisions of article 73.2º of the Convention. That , and only that, is the subject matter of the case before this Tribunal.

d) As we will explain with more detail during the hearings , and we are sure that the Tribunal has it clear, a State cannot allegue a domestic precept or Law to justify a breach of the Convention, as the provisions of the latest prevail over domestic Laws.

e) Without prejudice of the above, we must point out that under paragraph 24 of the application we indicated that , in fact, and irrespectively of the question related to the reasonableness of the guarantee fixed by France

j) We advanced in our application that France was trying to convert articles 73 and 292 of the Convention in "dead letters". Now is trying to avoid even the control by the Tribunal of the correct application of the said precepts.

k) Therefore, it is evident that the present case has substance and a very important content.

I call your attention, Mr president , that the argument which France is using to try to evade the requirement stated under article 73.2° supposes that a State could avoid prompt release , not only of vessels, but also crews, by just carrying a quick or a summary process (upon arrival of the detained vessel to Port) .

French legislation (article 4 of Law n° 66-400 of 18 June 1966) provides for <<Imprisonment>> of the persons fishing without permission withing the Exclusive Economic Zone.

In this particular case it has been confiscated the vessel, but it could well happen that the Judgement of the Correctionnel Tribunal of Saint Denis decided the imprisonment of the crew. If that were the case, and if we followed the tesis of France, the crew would have to remain in prision , irrespectively of the appeal of the decision, and of what article 73.2 requires ; "arrested vessels and their crews shall be promptly released upon the posting of a reasonable bond or other security"

And this, Mtr. President is unacceptable, extremely grave, and constitutes a flagrant breach of the Convention.

l) To some extent I can understand the interest of France in avoiding the present proceeding , as , if we bear in mind the content of the Convention and the case-law of the this high Tribunal, it is very difficult to defend the actuation of France in this particular matter.

I recall in this reagard the words of the Tribunal :

"The release from detention can de subject **only** to a reasonable bond."

It obviously that prompt release of vessels and crews cannot be sujected to any domestic precepts which are not in conformity with the provisions of the Convention.

(payment in cash of 11,400,00.00 FF) , 8 days after the notification to the Captain of Grand Prince of the "ordennance" where the said guarantee was fixed, the Tribunal Correctionnel of Saint Denis decided to confiscate the vessel, and to execute provisionally the confiscation.

We also explained under paragraphs 25, 26, 27 and 28 of the same application that the mentioned decision was never notified neither to the Captain nor to the shipowner or to the State of Belize, reason why we could not hand it over to this International Tribunal .

However, we informed very clear to the Tribunal about the existence and content of said decision, and we argued that such actuation was a way of evading the relevant exigencies for the States parties to the Convention under article 73.2° , which have been remarked and construed by this International Court.

We are now this Tribunal to decide whether such actuation is "in conformity" with article 73 of the Convention. This should not concern so much France.

f) In our application it was very clearly stated that there are four different and independent violations by France of article 73 of the Convention.

Three related to the nature, form and amount of the bond (paragraphs 38, 39 and 40) , and one related to the way through which France impeded to release the vessel against any kind of guarantee (we refer in this respect to paragraph 37)

g) And Mr. president, if you look at the guarantee fixed by France you will note that it is exactly what this Tribunal considered as an unreasonable in all the previous cases for prompt release.

h) Only yesterday, curiously after having received France our application, the Lawyer appointed by the Captain of the vessel in Reunion received copy of the decision of confiscation. We celebrate to have in the proceeding copy of said decision.

i) We must recall that the said decision has been appealed. We hereby enclose copy of the Acte D´Appeal filed in the name of the Captain of the vessel against the decision of confiscation, which France has forgotten to enclose to his Letter. The date for the appeal is still pendent.

For all the above, we consider that ; 1º) the "observations" stated in the letter of France should be done by an agent duly appointed by France and through a "statement in response" , according to article 111.4º f the Rules of the Tribunal ; 2º) the arguments stated in the same letter are inadmissible.

29 march , 2.001

Alberto Penelas Alvarez
(Agent for Belize)

c) Certification of the registration of the *Grand Prince* from the Director of INMARBE dated 30 March 2001, with Apostille

INTERNATIONAL MERCHANT MARINE REGISTRY OF BELIZE
"IMMARBE"

TO WHOM IT MAY CONCERN

The undersigned, Director and Senior Deputy Registrar of the International Merchant Marine Registry of Belize, duly empowered by the Merchant Ships Act, 1989/1996, hereby certifies that the vessel GRAND PRINCE is registered under the flag of Belize, holding registration Number 07972047 and call letters V3UJ7.

It is also certified that there are documents relating to the status of the vessel that are pending to be processed, -including the cancellation of status which execution was suspended-, based on particular circumstances involving the situation of the vessel and relating to the detention instructed by the French authorities.

It is further certified that, despite the expiration of the Patent of navigation and Ship station license the vessel, is still considered as registered in Belize until final decision of this Administration pending to the result of the court proceeding in which the vessel is engaged at the present time.

Issued in Belize City on the 30th March, 2001.

INTERNATIONAL MERCHANT MARINE REGISTRY OF BELIZE • IMMARBE •

SABINA GONZALEZ S.
Director and Senior Deputy Registrar

MARINA TOWERS, SUITE 204, NEWTOWN BARRACKS, BELIZE CITY, BELIZE, CENTRAL AMERICA
Telephones: 501-2-35026, 35031, 35047 - Telefax: 501-2-35048, 35070

APOSTILLE

(Convention de La Haye du 5 Octobre 1961)

Country Belize

1. Public Document Letter

2. Has been signed at Sabina Gonzalez S

3. Acting as Director & Senior Deputy Registrar

4. Bearing the seal/stamp of IMMARBE

CERTIFIED

5. At Belize City **6. On** 2nd April, 2001

7. By C. C. Pennil

8. Under No. 718/2001

9. Seal **10. Signature**

REGISTRAR GENERAL

REGISTRAR GENERAL BELIZE

d) Request regarding possible application of article 28 of the Statute of the Tribunal dated 2 April 2001

RECEIVED
0 3 APR 2001

INTERNATIONAL TRIBUNAL FOR THE LAW OF THE SEA

The "Grand Prince" case.

Appears: Alberto Penelas Alvarez, as agent for Belize

States:

That in view of the position of the French State in the present proceeding, and for the case it does not appear in the case by a duly legalised agent or otherwise fails to defend the case, this party hereby requests the Tribunal to continue the proceedings and pronounce the correspondent Judgement , basing the present petition on Article 28 of the Statute of the Tribunal.

It is Justice, which I respectfully pray in Hamburg, on the 2nd April 2.001

Alberto Penelas Alvarez
As agent for Belize

Additional documents submitted after the closure of the written proceedings (article 71 of the Rules of the Tribunal)
Documents additionnels soumis après la clôture de la procédure écrite (article 71 du Règlement du Tribunal)

Submitted by Belize

Note from Mr Penelas Alvarez transmitting:
- notification of the *Cour d'appel* of Saint-Denis concerning the date for a hearing (in French)

RECEIVED 10 APR 2001

INTERNATIONAL TRIBUNAL FOR THE LAW OF THE SEA

10 April, 2.001

REF.: GRAND PRINCE CASE

We hereby enclose copy of the document insued by the court of Appeal in Saint Denis, which has just been Notified to us, where it is fixed date for the appeal on the merits of this case for the Next 13 September 2.001.

We seem it convenient to put this fact in the knowledge of the Tribunal as it can constitute an element more to take into account when pronouncing a decision.

Alberto Penelas
As agente for Belize

REPUBLIQUE FRANÇAISE

COUR D'APPEL DE SAINT-DENIS

PARQUET GENERAL

SAINT-DENIS, le 29 Mars 2001

LE PROCUREUR GENERAL PRES LA COUR D'APPEL DE SAINT-DENIS

à

Maître ANTOINE
266 rue Maréchal leclerc

97400 ST DENIS

REÇU LE : 09 AVR. 2001
Réf. :

Nos références :
RG n° 01/00090
aff :
PEREZ NOVO Ramon Francisco

C/

STE ARMEMENT SAPMER
ARMEMENT DES MASCAREIGNES
ARMEMENT LE CARREC
COMATA LA COMPAGNIE MARITIME DES TERRES AUSTRALES "COMATA"
COMITE REGIONAL DE PECHE MARITIME ET ELEVAGES MARINS DE LA REUNION

aud du 13 Septembre 2001
à 08:30

J'ai l'honneur de vous faire connaître que l'affaire citée en références est fixée à l'audience du 13 Septembre 2001 à 08:30

P. LE PROCUREUR GENERAL

Michel BAUD
Substitut Général

Soumis par la France

a) Letter of the Director of INMARBE to the Honorary Consul of France in Belize dated 26 March 2001

INTERNATIONAL MERCHANT MARINE REGISTRY OF BELIZE
"IMMARBE"

March 26, 2001

RECEIVED 06/04/2001

Mr. Ernesto Vasquez
Honorary Consul of France
Belize City

Dear Mr. Vasquez:

This is in reply to your request for an update on the latest developments relating to the vessel GRAND PRINCE, which was detained by the French Authorities due to alleged infringement of the fishing regulation in the exclusive economic zone of Kerguelen.

We would like to inform you that while we were in the process of canceling ex-officio the vessel's status, the owners requested an opportunity to defend themselves of the accusations by submitting an appeal to the Tribunal for the Law of the Sea.

Under this context and being Belize a member of the Convention on the Law of the Sea we considered fair to allow the affected party to file its petition for which purposes we requested our competent authorities to grant the authorization for them to represent themselves at the mentioned Tribunal.

Depending on the result of this court proceeding we will decide whether or not to enforce our decision to delete the vessel from our records.

Regards,

SABINA GONZALEZ S.
Director

Cc: Carmen Silva, Ministry of Foreign Affairs

b) Note verbale from the Ministry of Foregin Affairs of Belize to the Embassy of France in El Salvador dated 4 January 2001

MINISTRY OF FOREIGN AFFAIRS

P.O. Box 174
New Administrative Building
Belmopan, BELIZE, C.A.
Tel: (501) 8-22322 / 22167
Fax: (501) 8-22854 E-mail: belizemfa@belize.gov.bz

Our Reference: FA/FRSA/10/01 (78)

NOTE NO. 07

The Ministry of Foreign Affairs of Belize presents its compliments to the Embassy of France in El Salvador and has the honour to refer to the Note of 3 January 2001 with reference to the detention of Belize flagged vessel "**Gran Prince**".

The Ministry of Foreign Affairs wishes to inform that Belize's shipping registry has confirmed that the vessel was registered with the Belize registry. However, as this is the second reported violation committed by the vessel, the punitive measures being imposed by the Belizean authority is its de-registration effective today 4 January 2001.

The Ministry Foreign Affairs of Belize avails itself of this opportunity to renew to the Embassy of France the assurances of its highest consideration.

Embassy of France
El Salvador

4 January, 2001

c) Procès-verbal d'audience de personne gardée à vue du capitaine du *Grand Prince* dressé par la Gendarmerie maritime

GENDARMERIE NATIONALE Commandement de la Gendarmerie Maritime **Patrouilleur Côtier de Gendarmerie JONQUILLE** C.U.: 11530 - PV n° 09 / 2001	**PROCEDURE D'ENQUETE PRELIMINAIRE** PROCES - VERBAL D'AUDITION DE PERSONNE GARDEE A VUE	Pièce n° 7 Feuillet n° 1/ 5

Analyse et références (éventuellement)

Voir P.V de synthèse

L'an deux mil un, le neuf janvier,
Nous soussigné, adjudant LANCOU Jean-Luc, officier de police judiciaire, ---------
Vu les articles 16 à 19 et 75 à 78 du code de procédure pénale.---------------------------
Rapportons les opérations suivantes que nous avons effectuées, agissant en uniforme et conformément aux ordres de nos chefs. ---------------------------------------
Assisté de Melle VAR Sophie, interprète en langue espagnole,

PERSONNE CONCERNEE

NOM : PEREZ NOVO Prénom: Ramon Francisco
Capitaine du navire de pêche GRAND PRINCE
né(e) le: 5 OCTOBRE 1957 à RIBIERA (Espagne)
fils de José et de NOVO MARTINEZ Joséfa, situation de famille marié deux enfants
demeurant à : Rua da carballeira 10, RIBIERA (Espagne), de nationalité espagnole ,
passeport n° 33225501 - T valable jusqu'au 15/03/2010 , délivré par l'Espagne.

Le 9 janvier 2001, de 10 heures 15 minutes à 11heures 30, PEREZ NOVO Ramon Francisco a bénéficié d'un temps de repos, dans le véhicule de dotation lors du transport du navire à notre unité ainsi qu'au bureau de notre unité, lors de la notification des droits.

La personne entendue. *L'interprète.* *L'OPJ.*

Au bureau de la brigade, entendons en présence de Melle VAR Sophie, interprète, la personne dénommée ci-dessus qui nous déclare 11 heures 30 minutes.

""""""Je suis le capitaine du navire de pêche "GRAND PRINCE" depuis la fin du mois d'octobre 2000. Je suis arrivé à l'île Maurice par avion le 24 octobre 2000. J'ai appareillé de Port -Louis le 10 novembre 2000, avec le GRAND PRINCE . J'ai accosté à BEIRA AU MOZANBIQUE environ 12 à 15 jours plus tard. Je suis resté deux jours pour appareiller pour DURBAN EN AFRIQUE DU SUD où j'ai accosté à la fin du mois de novembre 2000. J'ai appareillé de DURBAN le 2 ou le 3 décembre 2000 et depuis cette date le GRAND PRINCE est à la mer.---
--- Le 26 décembre 2000, il est exact que je me trouvais dans la zone économique des îles de Kerguélen lors du contrôle par le frégate "Nivose". J'ai été réveillé par le capitaine de pêche lors de l'arrivée de l'hélicoptère au dessus du GRAND PRINCE. Le capitaine de pêche est responsable de la pêche. Au moment où l'hélicoptère est arrivé la navire remontait une palangre qui s'était cassée pour une raison que je ne connais pas. ----
--- Je suis rentré dans le zone économique vers une heure le 26 décembre 2000. J'ai pris contact par radio avec le district des îles de Kerguélen, à deux ou trois reprises avec la radio MF/HF ICOM du bord. Je n'ai pas eu de réponse et je suis parti me coucher. Je sais qu'il faut signaler son entrée et le tonnage détenu à bord avant de rentrer dans la zone économique Française.""""""

Le 9 janvier 2001, à 12 heures 30 minutes.
L'intéressé déclarant ne pas savoir lire, ni écrire, ni comprendre ni parler le français, lecture des renseignements d'état civil et de la déclaration ci-dessus lui a été faite par l'interprète, dans une langue qu'il comprend en laquelle il persiste n'ayant rien à y changer, à y ajouter ou à y retrancher. » --

La personne entendue. *L'interprète.* *L'OPJ.*

GENDARMERIE MARITIME
P.C. JONQUILLE

P.V n° 09/2001
Pièce n° 7
Feuillet n° 2 / 5

Du 12 heures 30 à 14 heures 00, PEREZ NOVO Ramon Francisco bénéficie d'un temps de repos à bord du PCG "Jonquille", un repas lui est servi. (Entretien avec Maître ANTOINE Alain de 13 heures 00 à 13 heures 30).-----------------

La personne entendue. *L'interprète.* *L'OPJ.*

Le 9 janvier 2001, à 14 heures 00, en présence de Melle VAR Sophie, nous procédons à une deuxième audition de PEREZ NOVO Ramon Francisco, qui déclare :

""" La palangre qui était à la mer appartient au GRAND PRINCE. Il n'y a pas eu d'incident particulier lors de la visite du bord ni lors du déroutement vers la Réunion. C'est le capitaine de pêche qui a donné l'ordre très rapidement lors de l'intervention de l'hélicoptère. J'ai demandé au capitaine de pêche s'il y avait beaucoup d'appareils à l'eau (palangre), il m'a déclaré qu'il y en avait quinze. Un appareil dispose de 80 à 90 hameçons distancés d'une longueur de 1,5 mètres à 2 mètres entre chaque hameçons. Le journal de navigation du Grand prince s'arrête le 23 décembre 2000 et la position indiquée (47° 40' Sud et 075° 30' Est) est celle de 12 heures (horloge du bateau qui correspond à l'heure du fuseau de l'île Maurice). C'est la dernière position qui a été portée au journal de navigation. C'est moi qui ai rempli le nouveau journal de navigation du 24 au 26 décembre 2000 à la demande de l'équipe de visite pendant le contrôle. Je n'ai rein pêché dans la zone économique, il s'agissait de mon premier jour de pêche, dans cette zone. Le poisson qui se trouvait dans les tunnels de congélation a été pêché le 25 décembre 2000 en dehors de la zone économique. je pense que ce poisson a été placé en tunnel de congélation au cours de la matinée du 26 décembre 2000. Pendant cette visite du 26 décembre 2000, j'ai porté en présence de l'officier du Nivose, ma position sur la carte du Grand prince, carte 4711 Iles d'Amsterdam aux îles Kerguélen qui était 47° 45,80' sud et 073° 43,96' Est, j'ai signé la carte, il s'agissait de la position GPS du bord. Pour moi je me situais à 40 nautiques à l'intérieur de la zone économique. Je suis rentré dans la zone économique Française en commun accord avec le capitaine de pêche pour la raison suivante: c'est un endroit où il y a du poisson et notre pêche depuis le début de la marée n'est pas formidable. Nous avons pêché en début de marée entre 12 et 15 tonnes de légines. - - -
- - - Le Grand Prince est la propriété de READON COMMERCIAL CORP. International Business Compagny à VIGO en Espagne. Je pense qu'il y a plusieurs armateurs, je ne connais qu'un seul (José NOGUEIRA demeurant en Espagne). J'ai un salaire fixe payé en Espagne par READOM COMMERCIAL CORP. - - -
- - - Je reconnais les infractions relevées à mon encontre à savoir: être en action de pêche dans la zone économique française du fait que le navire posait une palangre, ne pas avoir déclaré mon entrée en zone économique ni le tonnage de poisson détenu à bord."""""

Le 9 janvier 2001, à 16 heures 00.
L'intéressé déclarant ne pas savoir lire, ni écrire, ni comprendre ni parler le français, lecture des renseignements d'état civil et de la déclaration ci-dessus lui a été faite par l'interprète, dans une langue qu'il comprend en laquelle il persiste n'ayant rien à y changer, à y ajouter ou à y retrancher. » --

La personne entendue. *L'interprète.* *L'OPJ.*

GENDARMERIE MARITIME
P.C. JONQUILLE

P.V n° 09/2001
Pièce n° 7
Feuillet n° 3 / 5

Assisté de Melle VAR Sophie, interprète en langue espagnole.

Du 9 janvier 2001à 16 heures 00 au 10 janvier 2001,à 14 heures 00, PEREZ NOVO Ramon Francisco, bénéficie d'un temps de repos , partie au bureau de notre brigade, partie dans le véhicule de dotation et dans la chambre de sûreté de la brigade de gendarmerie de Saint Gilles les Bains (Entrée le 9 janvier 2001 à 20 heures 00, sortie le 10 janvier 2001 à 07 heures 30). Un dîner lui a été servi le 9 janvier et un petit déjeuner le 10 Janvier 2001. Présentation devant monsieur le Substitut, à bord de la "Jonquille" le 10 janvier 2001 entre 08 heures 45 et 09 heures 00. Notification de la prolongation de 09 heures 00 à 09 heures 30. Un déjeuner servi le 10 janvier 2001.

La personne entendue. *L'interprète.* *L'OPJ.*

Le 10 janvier 2001, à 14 heures 00, en présence de Melle VAR Sophie, nous procédons à une audition de PEREZ NOVO Ramon Francisco, qui déclare :

""" Je confirme mes déclaration du 9 janvier 2001. Je n'ai aucune observation à formuler sur les conditions de ma garde à vue.

Question: Connaissez-vous le nom de précédant capitaine du navire ?
Réponse: Je ne le connais pas personnellement mais je l'ai rencontré lors de la relève à Port - Louis. Son nom est inscrit sur le journal de navigation du bord à la date de la relève soit le 25 octobre 2000. Il s'agit de Manuel SAMPEDRO GARCIA.

Question: Sur la photo du "Grand Prince", prise par l'hélicoptère au début du contrôle reconnaissez-vous la ligne de palangre derrière et sur le tribord du navire ?
Réponse: Je reconnais une palangre sur l'arrière du navire et une corde de retenue sur tribord.

Question: Que déduisez-vous de cette photo, en sachant que vous dormiez ?
Réponse: C'est un appareil sans hameçon.

Question: Savez - vous quelles étaient les intentions du capitaine de pêche au vue de cette photo prise par l'hélicoptère dans la ZEE de Kerguélen ?
Réponse: Je pense qu'il s'agit d'une palangre qui s'est cassée lors de la mise à l'eau.

Le 10 janvier 2001 à 15 heures 00.
L'intéressé déclarant ne pas savoir lire, ni écrire, ni comprendre ni parler le français, lecture des renseignements d'état civil et de la déclaration ci-dessus lui a été faite par l'interprète, dans une langue qu'il comprend en laquelle il persiste n'ayant rien à y changer, à y ajouter ou à y retrancher. » ---

La personne entendue. *L'interprète.* *L'OPJ.*

GENDARMERIE MARITIME
P.C. JONQUILLE

P.V n° 09/2001
Pièce n° 7
Feuillet n° 4 / 5

De 15 heures 00 à 19 heures 00, PEREZ NOVO Ramon Francisco, bénéficie d'un temps de repos au bureau de notre brigade. (Audition de 15 heures 15 à 16 heures 00 par les service du poste de sûreté du territoire de la Réunion, dans le cadre du commission rogatoire n° .1/00/56 délivrée par madame ATZORI, vice président, chargé de l'instruction).

La personne entendue *L'interprète* *L'OPJ*

De 19 heures 00 à 21 heures 00, PEREZ NOVO Ramon Francisco, nous assiste lors de la remise des documents officiels du navire Grand Prince. (PV de saisie pièce n° 28).

La personne entendue *L'interprète* *L'OPJ*

A 21 heures 00 , en présence de Melle VAR Sophie, nous procédons à une audition de PEREZ NOVO Ramon Francisco qui nous déclare :

""" A votre demande je vous ai remis tous les documents officiels du navire. Sur le scellés n° 10, l'armateur du navire est "PAIK COMMERCIAL CORP. - 35 A Regent street P.O. BOX 1777 - BELIZE City, BELIZE" certificat provisoire délivré le 16 octobre 2000 et valable jusqu'au 29 décembre 2000. Sur le scellés n° 12, le navire est la propriété de HASKELL SHIPPING ET PROPERTIES LTD 49 south Mall, Cork, Ireland. Le représentant est Joseph Anthony O'Connor Attorney-in-fact.- - -
- - - A bord c'est le capitaine de pêche qui a des contact avec l'armateur. A la mer ces contact sont établi avec l'inmarsat du bord. J'ai eu un seul contact lord de mon engagement, à VIGO, avec un des armateur NOGUEIRA José. Je n'ai eu aucun contact avec les représentant de l'état du pavillon de BELIZE. A ma connaissance, le capitaine de pêche n'a pas d'autre contact qu'avec l'armateur. A ma connaissance le Grand Prince est le seul navire de la société. - - -
- - - C'est l'armateur qui décide du lieu de débarquement du produit de la pêche. Chaque marée dure entre cinquante et soixante jour. """"""

Le 10 janvier 2001, à 21 heures 30.
L'intéressé déclarant ne pas savoir lire, ni écrire, ni comprendre ni parler le français, lecture des renseignements d'état civil et de la déclaration ci-dessus lui a été faite par l'interprète, dans une langue qu'il comprend en laquelle il persiste n'ayant rien à y changer, à y ajouter ou à y retrancher. » --

La personne entendue. *L'interprète.* *L'OPJ.*

GENDARMERIE MARITIME
P.C. JONQUILLE

P.V n° 09/2001
Pièce n° 7
Feuillet n° 5 / 5

Du 10 janvier 2001à 21 heures 30 au 11 janvier 2001à 09 heures 15, PEREZ NOVO Ramon Francisco, bénéficie d'un temps de repos , partie au bureau de notre brigade, partie dans le véhicule de dotation et dans la chambre de sûreté de la brigade de gendarmerie de Saint Gilles les Bains (Entrée le 10 janvier 2001 à 22 heures 30, sortie le 11 janvier 2001 à 07 heures 30). Un dîner lui a été servi le 10 janvier et un petit déjeuner le 11 Janvier 2001.

La personne entendue *L'interprète* *L'OPJ.*

Suivant les instructions de monsieur le procureur de la République à Saint-Denis, PEREZ NOVO Ramon Francisco est mis en route le 11 janvier 2001 à 09 heures 15, pour être conduit devant ce magistrat.

La personne entendue. *L'interprète.* *L'OPJ.*

www.ingramcontent.com/pod-product-compliance
Lightning Source LLC
LaVergne TN
LVHW081515300926
849161LV00006B/1193